THE BA

BERLIN

1945

C000052244

THE BATTLE OF
BERLIN
1945

TONY LE TISSIER

The
History
Press

First published 1987
This edition published 2022

The History Press
97 St George's Place, Cheltenham,
Gloucestershire, GL50 3QB
www.thehistorypress.co.uk

© Tony Le Tissier, 1987, 2008, 2022

British Library Cataloguing in Publication Data.
A catalogue record for this book is available from the British Library.

ISBN 978 0 7509 9891 8

Typesetting and origination by The History Press
Printed and bound in Great Britain by TJ Books Limited, Padstow, Cornwall.

Trees for Life

Contents

Preface

This book is an attempt at a definitive account of the last battle to have been fought on the grand scale in Europe, involving as it did some three and a half million combatants.

Although it has been only sixty years since the events related here took place, the task of putting the story together has been rather like the reconstruction of an ancient vase from an incomplete set of fragments, for the vanquished lost virtually all their records, and the victors, for reasons which became clearer during the course of reconstruction, have always been evasive about much of the pertinent detail.

Fortunately, more and more missing pieces appeared during the course of the task, sufficient – I hope – to produce a reasonably comprehensive and rewarding pattern of events.

To assist the reader through the complexities of this operation, I have endeavoured to illustrate the various parts and phases with a series of maps and drawings, incorporating as many of the place-names mentioned in the text as were feasible. Reference to the maps on which these names appear has been included in the index.

A.H. Le T

1

The Plan

At about 0200 hours on 16 April 1945, Marshal Georgi Konstantinovitch Zhukov, organiser of the heroic defence of Leningrad and Moscow, victor of the historic battles of Stalingrad and Kursk-Orel, Deputy Supreme Commander of the Soviet Armed Forces and, since January 1945, Commander of the 1st Byelorussian Front, arrived at his forward command post on a spur of the Seelow Heights above the village of Reitwein. The man who had won the first victory of the Great Patriotic War over the Wehrmacht at Jelnya in the defence of Moscow was about to bring the same war to a triumphant conclusion with the seizure of the Nazi capital in time to celebrate the most glorious May Day in the history of the Soviet Union.[1]

With daylight his command post should give him a grandstand view of the troops in action on the main axis of advance, the highway from Küstrin (now Polish *Kostryn*) on the River Oder directly to Berlin barely forty miles away, where the sky glowed a dull red from the effects of incessant bombardment being inflicted on the city by the Anglo-American air fleets.[2]

Below him in the darkness, the misty, dank valley-bed of the Oderbruch seethed with activity as several hundred thousand men prepared themselves for battle. They had received their final briefings on their immediate objectives, and the regimental banners had been brought into the line for the oath-taking ceremonies that bound each soldier to do his duty to the utmost in the forthcoming conflict. Victory was certain, and with it the annihilation of the Fascist beast that had brought so much suffering and destruction to their country. For this 'Operation Berlin' over two and a half million Soviet troops had been allocated to the three Army Groups ranged along the Oder–Neisse river line, together with half of all the armour and one-third of all the artillery available for operational use out of the nation's vast resources.[3]

Although the detailed planning and preparation for this operation had been completed in record time and he was confident of the outcome of his mission, Marshal Zhukov still had cause for unease. Firstly, he had not been given overall command of 'Operation Berlin' as had generally been expected, and secondly, his hitherto close relationship with Stalin appeared to have deteriorated alarmingly.[4]

Zhukov had been one of the few survivors of the pre-war purges of the Soviet military leadership, possibly because he was serving in the Far East at the time. He had begun his career as a cavalry conscript in 1914, and by 1937 commanded the short-lived Cossack Cavalry Corps, but it was with modern arms that he had won his first battle at Kharkin Kol in 1939 during the Japanese incursion into Outer Mongolia. Following the dismal defeats of 1941, he had come into prominence when sent to organise the defence of Leningrad as a Stavka (General Staff) trouble-shooter, and since then his career had progressed rapidly. He had a reputation for utter determination and ruthlessness in achieving his objectives, regardless of the cost in human lives, and for demanding instant and absolute obedience to orders. He had a fierce temper and rode roughshod over his subordinates, who both feared and respected him. Stalin trusted him and respected his military ability, and their relationship had become quite close. Zhukov had always unquestioningly accepted Stalin's complete authority, whether he thought him right or wrong, in the same spirit that he demanded total obedience from his own subordinates.[5] His appointment as Deputy Supreme Commander had been a popular move, but in fact had little meaning, for Stalin had no intention of delegating any of his centrally held authority, as had become palpably evident at the planning conference held in Moscow at the beginning of the month.

Zhukov had originally intended to attack Berlin two months previously. At the beginning of February, Colonel-General Chuikov's 8th Guards Army had arrived at the Oder, and on the 2nd had crossed the dangerously thin ice from the area of Göritz (now Polish *Górzyca*). By dint of some very hard fighting it had established a substantial bridgehead on the line Klessin–Podelzig–Hathenow–Rathstock–Manschnow–Kietz (the west bank suburb of the fortress town of Küstrin at the junction of the Warthe and Oder Rivers). Meanwhile Colonel-General Berzarin's 5th Shock Army had gained a small bridgehead of its own at Kienitz and had taken the remainder of the town of Küstrin from the north, but had failed to capture the citadel on the island in the centre, and was thus deprived of the use of the only bridges across the Oder in this area.[6] Further south the 33rd Army had also succeeded in reaching the west bank between Frankfurt-an-der-Oder and Fürstenberg (now *Eisenhüttenstadt*). From these footholds Zhukov had been prepared to chance his operation on only two tankfuls of fuel per vehicle and two front-line issues of ammunition per weapon, but the rapid advance from the Vistula had overextended his lines of communication and the necessary supplies were not getting through to his forward troops. Then on 6 February, Stalin had abruptly ordered Zhukov's attention away from Berlin to the task of clearing Pomerania, leaving only part of his Army Group behind on the Oder.[7]

Both Zhukov and Marshal Ivan S. Koniev of the 1st Ukrainian Front had been summoned to Moscow at the end of March with their principal staff officers in order to consolidate the plans for 'Operation Berlin'.[8] Marshal Rokossovsky, whose 2nd Byelorussian Front was also to take part, did not join them as his troops were still actively engaged mopping up along the Baltic coast. Rokossovsky was an old friend, but, as a straightforward soldier, Zhukov was openly hostile to the inclusion of political commissars in the military command structure, the source from which

Koniev came. And the latter, who had endured several experiences under Zhukov's command, disliked him intensely, and now hoped to steal the big prize from him by getting into Berlin first. This bitter rivalry between the two commanders was not accidental: Boris Nicolaevsky, in his book *Power and the Soviet Elite*, wrote that Stalin, with his great talent for exploiting human weaknesses, had:

Quickly sized up Koniev and cleverly used his feelings towards Zhukov. If we trace the history of Stalin's treatment of the two soldiers, the chronology of their promotions and awards, we shall see that as early as the end of 1941 Stalin was grooming Koniev, the politician, as a rival whom he could play off against the real soldier, Zhukov. This was typical of Stalin's foresight and bears all the marks of his style. He confers honours on Zhukov only when he has no choice, but on Koniev he bestowed them even when there was no particular reason for doing so. This was necessary in order to maintain the balance between the 'indispensable organiser of victory' and the even more indispensable political counterweight to him.[9]

In contrast to this situation, Rokossovsky presented no real problem to Stalin, for he had been a victim of the purges and most cruelly tortured before Stalin had him released from prison to command a mechanised corps in 1941. Despite all the honours and awards subsequently heaped upon him, Rokossovsky remained under a sentence of death that could be invoked at any time, and thus remained a willing and obedient servant of his master.[10]

On 29 March Zhukov and Koniev had gone over their plans with the Stavka and agreed various details, but, as Stalin had previously decreed that Marshal Zhukov's 1st Byelorussian Front alone would take Berlin, the Stavka's planned boundary lines excluded the 1st Ukrainian Front from the city itself, much to Koniev's annoyance.[11] Then on the afternoon of Easter Sunday, 1 April, Zhukov and Koniev had come before Stalin and the other members of the State Defence Committee, with General A.I. Antonov, Chief of the General Staff, and Major-General S.M. Shtemenko, Head of the Operations Planning Directorate, in attendance. The meeting began with Shtemenko reading out a signal to the effect that the Anglo-American armies were proposing to take Berlin ahead of the Soviet forces.[12] Under the circumstances, the plan appeared feasible but was clearly unacceptable to Soviet pride and ambition.[13]

Stalin had given Zhukov and Koniev two days in which to complete their plans in the Stavka before submitting them for his approval. Both operations were to begin on 16 April and were to be completed in time for the May Day celebrations. He stipulated that Zhukov would have the primary task of taking Berlin and pushing on to the Elbe, for which he would receive further reinforcements from the Stavka reserves, while Koniev would support the Berlin operation by destroying the enemy forces to the south of the city, and would have the secondary task of taking Dresden and Leipzig, both important industrial cities in the future

Soviet Zone of Occupation. The 2nd Byelorussian Front would engage the enemy forces north of the capital, beginning its offensive on 20 April. In the meantime the other fronts to the south would maintain pressure on the Germans to prevent the redeployment of strategic reserves to the 'Operation Berlin' theatre.[14]

The two marshals then reported to Stalin again on 3 April to expound their plans. A necessary preliminary for Zhukov would be the clearing of the enemy from the Seelow Heights, and he proposed doing this with a simultaneous attack from his bridgehead in the Oderbruch by four reinforced combined-arms formations – the 8th Guards, 3rd and 5th Shock and 47th Armies – clearing breaches in the German defences. This would enable the 1st and 2nd Guards Tank Armies to pass through and converge on Berlin from the southeast and northeast respectively in a classic pincer movement. To cover his northern flank, the 1st Polish and 61st Armies, supported by the 7th Guards Cavalry Corps, would cross the Oder just south of the Finow Canal and continue westwards along the line of the waterways via Eberswalde and Fehrbellin to Sandau at the junction of the Havel and Elbe Rivers. The 69th Army would cover the 8th Guards Army's southern flank and contain the Frankfurt-an-der-Oder garrison in conjunction with the 33rd Army. The latter, with the 2nd Guards Cavalry Corps, would break out of its own bridgehead, and together these two armies would push westwards along the line of the autobahn with the objectives of Fürstenwalde and eventually Brandenburg. The 3rd Army would constitute the front's reserve.[15]

Koniev needed reserves to reinforce his thrusts if it became necessary, so Stalin had him allocated the 28th and 31st Armies from the 2nd Byelorussian Front. It was appreciated that they might not be redeployed and ready in time for 16 April, but it was thought that nevertheless Koniev could afford to take the risk of starting without them. In order to ensure an artillery density of 400 guns of 76mm calibre or larger per mile along his attack line, Koniev had already been allocated an additional seven artillery divisions from the Stavka reserves.[16]

Both Fronts had an integral air army to provide fighter cover and ground strike support, but Zhukov had also been assigned the 18th Air Army with a heavy bombing capacity and several independent air corps and divisions from the Stavka reserves to support his operation. In addition he was given the support of the 2nd Byelorussian Front's 4th Air Army and some of the Baltic Fleet Air Arm for the first three days. These formations, together with the 1st Polish Composite Air Corps, gave an overall total of 7,500 combat aircraft, including 2,267 bombers, 1,709 ground-attack planes and 3,279 fighters.[17]

It was decided that Air Chief Marshal A.A. Novikov should coordinate all air activity over the Oder–Neisse theatre from a central headquarters based on the 16th Air Army. These arrangements would enable the Russians to maintain large forces in the air permanently, with the bombers of the 18th Air Army relieving the 16th Air Army at night. A basic principle of operation was that the tank forces would get priority in air support, amounting to as much as 75 percent of the daily effort. To accommodate these massive air forces some 290 base and field aerodromes had to be constructed, the bombers of the 18th Air Army being located east of Poznan.[18]

Zhukov had also been allocated the Dnieper Flotilla of the Red Navy to assist him with the numerous water-crossings involved in his sector, both in the initial phase of the operation and later within the city boundaries.[19]

The Stavka had drawn the operational boundary between Zhukov and Koniev from Guben on the Neisse via Michendorf to Schönebeck on the Elbe, but, in response to Koniev's plea, with which the Stavka were in accord, Stalin had silently erased the boundary beyond Lübben, thereby implying that whatever happened beyond that point would be up to them. 'Operation Berlin' was to be a race for glory between the two of them.[20]

Later, in his orders to the 3rd Guards Tank Army, Koniev wrote:

> On the fifth day of the operation to seize the area of Trebbin, Zauchwitz, Treuenbrietzen, Luckenwalde… To bear in mind the possibility of attacking Berlin from the south with a reinforced tank corps and an infantry division from the 3rd Guards Army.[21]

Surprisingly the Yalta Conference had not provided for proper liaison and co-ordination of effort between the Western Allies and the Soviet Command, and Stalin had been able to take advantage of this to deceive both the Allies and his own front commanders. On 28 March he had received a signal from General Eisenhower, Supreme Allied Commander in the West, who, unilaterally and against the wishes of the British leadership, had decided to disregard Berlin and direct his main thrusts on the Erfurt/Leipzig/Dresden area and the mythical 'Alpine Redoubt'.[22] Stalin had promptly replied approving these proposals and announcing his own intentions of a main thrust on Dresden with only subsidiary forces directed on Berlin. From German signal traffic the Allies had been alerted to the imminence of the Soviet offensive and had pressed Stalin for details, but it was not until the eve of the attack that he had divulged the date to them, again emphasising that his main thrust would be to the south.[23]

Here we see the beginnings of the so-called Cold War which was to follow. Yet Stalin owed much to his Western Allies, a factor that the Soviet Union never fully acknowledged. For instance, at this stage of the war about two-thirds of all Soviet military vehicles were of American origin, many of the troops wore boots and uniforms of either British or American manufacture, and the Soviet forces existed almost entirely on American-supplied concentrated foodstuffs. Their devastated heartland was quite incapable of sustaining such vast numbers of men in the field unaided, and these vehicles provided their armies with the necessary mobility to defeat the Axis forces ranged against them.[24]

The operational plans having been agreed in Moscow, there then followed two weeks of intense preparation on the Oder–Neisse Front, with prodigious feats being accomplished in the bringing forward of the required manpower, equipment, ammunition and supplies.[25]

The Soviet lines of communication were based on their railway system, linking the fronts with the war industries, ports and sundry centres of production. The distances involved were enormous, with 2,000 miles separating the war industries grouped in the Ural Mountains from the Oder, and half the lend-lease supplies coming all the way across Siberia from the Pacific ports. The Russian gauge being wider than the European, the railway tracks had to be adapted and repaired as they advanced. For this operation special railheads had been established close to the river banks, from where local distribution could be made by horse and motor transport.[26]

Units depleted in the winter fighting had to be brought up to strength, and their equipment overhauled and replenished. The Soviets were scraping the bottom of their manpower barrel by 1945, and released prisoners-of-war were being promptly rearmed, fed and thrust back into the line. For the first time the Russians had even used air transport to bring forward reinforcements.[27]

The newly allocated formations from the Stavka reserves had also been brought forward and deployed into position. A more complicated manoeuvre had been the lateral transfer of the two armies allocated to Marshal Koniev from the 2nd Byelorussian Front.[28]

The artillery concentration required vast stocks of ammunition. It was later calculated that the 1st Byelorussian Front used 1,235,000 shells (2,450 wagon loads, or 98,000 tons) on the first day of the operation alone, out of an accumulated stockpile of 7,147,000.[29]

Troops and equipment had become so thick on the ground that camouflage was difficult, but with air superiority the Soviets could afford to flaunt their build-up at the Germans. Additional bridges had been erected across the Oder to the bridgehead, some with their surfaces just below water level as a result of flooding, making them extremely difficult targets, and numerous ferry points prepared. On Zhukov's northern flank and in Koniev's sector preparations had been made for opposed river crossings, with the engineers stockpiling bridging and ferry equipment.[30]

According to Zhukov, the problem of tackling the city itself had been studied in some detail by war-gaming. First, eight aerial surveys of the city area had been made, and then detailed assault plans prepared with the aid of captured documents and prisoner-of-war interrogations. The engineers had made a large model of the city and its suburbs, which was used from 5 to 7 April for command games down to corps commander level.[31] The more detailed games, including the problems of supply, had been conducted at various formation headquarters from the 8th to the 14th of the month.[32]

Chuikov says that his 8th Guards Army had published manuals on street-fighting and had begun training cadres in these skills in February, but to what extent this had spread and was being practised within the 1st Byelorussian Front is a matter for conjecture. From Chuikov's own comments at a later stage of the operation, it is obvious that the preparation of the troops for fighting under the very different circumstances they could expect to encounter in the city was not as thorough as has been claimed. Indeed, with time so desperately short and the prospects of first having to storm the Seelow Heights and clear all the defensive positions between the Oder and the city, it would have been surprising if it had been.[33]

Despite all the factors in their favour, the Soviet leadership still found themselves with a serious problem on their hands. The end of the war was so obviously in sight that native caution dictated a widespread reluctance to risk one's life. The desire to end the war was suddenly confounded by a pernicious wariness. It was as if the steam was about to run out of this mighty engine of war; it was threatening to become unmanageable as inertia began setting in.

The Political Department, being responsible for morale, decided to tackle this problem by stepping up the recruiting campaign for Party and Komsomol members, thus enlarging the reliable nucleus already established in every unit. In this they were remarkably successful, according to the published figures. On this occasion, by cross-posting where necessary, they ensured a nucleus of eight to twenty full or probationary Party members in every unit of company size, and also established a reserve of political instructors and Party organisers to replace casualties. With over 2,000 applications received for Party membership on 15 April in the 1st Byelorussian Front alone, it seems that many soldiers were anxious to ensure their future under the Soviet regime now that the Great Patriotic War had confirmed its supremacy.[34]

Another measure they had decided to adopt was the introduction of regimental colours to be carried into battle, before which oath-taking ceremonies would be held at which the soldiers would be sworn to their duty. The standard bearers were naturally appointed from the Party faithful, who as usual were expected to set an example to the others. The carrying of banners in action thus became an unique feature of this battle. However, although the banners provided good propaganda material, they also tended to draw enemy fire, and the initial effect on the fighting troops was soon nullified by the heavy casualties exacted in the first phase of the operation. The reluctance to take risks, later camouflaged by somewhat bombastic accounts of minor episodes, was to have a strong influence on the conduct of operations, despite all these measures.

Another complication had arisen for the Political Department. Ever since leaving Soviet soil the Russian soldiers had behaved abominably towards the civilian populations they had encountered, committing endless atrocities of murder, rape, looting, arson and wilful damage, urged on by an official campaign of revenge put out by the Soviet press and radio. In the forefront of this campaign had been the writer, Ilya Ehrenburg, and the soldiers – primitive peasants as most of them were – had responded with enthusiasm. The reason for this policy is uncertain, but it may have been designed to instil sufficient fear into the German population to cause them to abandon voluntarily the territory east of the Oder, and thus facilitate resettlement by the Poles in accordance with predetermined post-war boundaries; or simply to provide motivation for the Red Army once the sacred task of clearing the enemy out of Russia had been completed.[35]

The unparalleled extent of the devastation and the human suffering arising out of the German invasion of their country, quite apart from the atrocities of Reichsführer-SS Heinrich Himmler's extermination squads, had given the individual Soviet soldier ample grounds for seeking revenge. Official Soviet sources quoted twenty million dead, but this figure has been contested by historians, whose analyses show that the Germans could not possibly have been responsible for more than about half that number, the remainder being in fact victims of Stalin's own relentless efforts to impose his regime on the people.[36]

Then, on 14 April 1945, an officially inspired article in the national press had criticised Ehrenburg's views, thereby signalling a complete change of policy. From then on revenge against the Nazis and Fascists would be pursued remorselessly, but the German people themselves were to be wooed into the Soviet fold.[37] However, it was too late to stop the established trend, the Red Army was unable to accept such a volte-face overnight, and the atrocities were to continue unabated until the fighting was all over and the behaviour of the troops could be constrained.

The fear that the Red Army inspired, involuntarily assisted by the German's own propaganda fomenting hatred of the enemy, was fully justified. In some places overrun by them, every town official and everyone in any kind of uniform, whether policeman, postman, railway employee or forester, was summarily executed. In some cases people were dragged to death behind horses, and there were incidents of the nobility being hunted down with great savagery, some being blinded, mutilated or hacked to death. Rape was widespread, and often accompanied by murder, and in some instances women were rounded up wholesale for use by the soldiers. Even card-carrying members of the Communist Party were not exempt as victims of these outrages.[38]

Discipline in the Red Army varied greatly from unit to unit, but throughout bouts of heavy drinking would lead to serious breakdowns of discipline and acts of violence. Generally the Soviet soldier had a good and close relationship with his officers, which was not so readily extended to his commissars, for whom he had a natural distrust, despite his gullibility. His basic characteristics were those of the Russian peasant, and the qualities of patriotism, obstinacy, endurance and cunning stood him in good stead as a soldier. He tended to be unpredictable in his moods and could easily become apathetic, morose or unruly in his behaviour. Although he was slow-witted and cautious in his approach, he was by no means lacking in courage.[39]

Recruits were allocated in accordance with their intelligence rating to the air arm, artillery, engineers, armour, and finally infantry, and formations within or combining those arms were again divided into various categories. Of these the elite were those with the Guards appellation, which was awarded to those regiments and higher formations that had distinguished themselves in battle, such as Chuikov's 64th Army, which had been renamed the 8th Guards Army after Stalingrad. This title brought increased rations, but also demanded the highest standards in discipline, training and combat. Guards regiments and formations could be found throughout the first echelon formations, but when grouped into Guards Armies they normally carried more firepower than the others, and their establishments tended to be larger. Their armoured units were usually equipped with the latest Stalin tanks and T-34/85s.[40]

Breakdowns of the composition of the various types of Red Army formations are given in the Appendices to this book. In brief, the Guards armies were organised as combined-arms armies, that is with three infantry and one armoured corps, and the shock armies, having stronger artillery resources, were designed to be used against well-established fortifications at the beginning of an offensive, after which they would normally be withdrawn into second echelon.[41]

The remaining infantry armies were generally of a much lower calibre. Although well equipped with light arms, their artillery and all their transport was horse-drawn. Having the lowest priority for clothing and rations, their uniforms were often in rags and they were expected to virtually live off the land. Consequently, on the move they presented an extraordinary spectacle, reminiscent of previous Asiatic invasions, with livestock being driven alongside ungainly caravans of commandeered wagons piled high with loot. Their training was minimal and their discipline poor, authority often being exercised by their officers at pistol point.[42]

Human life was of little value in Soviet considerations, and least of all in the dozen or so penal battalions available to each of the fronts for swamping enemy positions by sheer weight of numbers, or for advancing first over minefields to clear the way for others. Not only did they cater for the disciplinary cases, but they were also a convenient means of purging real or potential opponents of the regime from the ranks.[43]

Cavalry was still used in considerable numbers, Zhukov having a cavalry corps with both of his flank guards and one in reserve. However, the most impressive arm was the artillery, which specialised in massive concentrations, many formations being held for this purpose in the Stavka Reserve, from where they were carefully assigned to the various fronts for specifically approved tasks.[44]

The Air Force remained subordinate to the Army, and was divided into Strategic, Tactical and Transport Commands. The Strategic Command of long-range bombers was the least used and least effective, but the Tactical Command had a wide range of combat aircraft and was used extensively as another form of artillery support in the front line. In concept it was thus primarily another battlefield arm with little strategic value.[45]

The Soviet armour was very good indeed. By concentrating production on just a few simplified designs, the Russians had produced some of the most outstanding fighting vehicles of the war. The new 60-ton IS-1 and IS-2 (Joseph Stalin) main battle tanks with 122mm guns, and the ubiquitous 36-ton T-34 medium tank updated to carry a 85mm gun, were formidable fighting machines and available in quantity. The T-70 light tank with its 45mm gun was used mainly for the protection of tactical headquarters in battle. However, radios were scarce and generally limited to commanders' vehicles, so that communication between tanks in action was difficult in the extreme. The SU self-propelled guns mounted on tank chassis, like their German counterparts, were primarily intended for use in the assault role, not as supporting artillery, and were particularly effective as tank-destroyers.[46]

The 1st Byelorussian Front had a chemical warfare battalion equipped with poison gas with it in the field, but this was not used. Other chemical warfare units specialised in laying smokescreens when required.[47]

Also fighting under Soviet command were the recently raised 1st and 2nd Polish Armies, the 1st Polish Composite Air Corps with 390 combat aircraft, and various other Polish units, including a tank brigade and a cavalry brigade. These had originally been founded from those prisoners taken when Poland was overrun in 1939 that had not voluntarily transferred to the British Army in 1942. Their numbers had later been augmented by drafting in partisans and recruits called to the colours after the 'liberation' of their country. However, the Soviet culling of any Poles capable of leadership had left considerable gaps in the rank structure that had to be filled with Russians, and although the senior figures wore Polish uniforms they were in fact Red Army officers of Polish descent.[48]

The Russians also used converted German prisoners of war for propaganda, spying, infiltration and subversion purposes, and even in some instances at this late stage in the war as combat units. These so-called 'Seydlitz-Troops' wore German Army uniforms from which the Nazi insignia had been removed, with armbands in the old national colours of black, white and red.[49]

Each Soviet army had from one to three NKVD (Ministry of the Interior) regiments attached, depending upon the situation. These units were not intended for use as fighting troops, but for providing a rear screen to the parent formation, and also for controlling the civilian population in the rear areas.[50]

These then were the mighty forces preparing to launch this final massive offensive of the war in Europe. The Soviets quoted the combined strengths of their three fronts in Operation 'Berlin' as being over 2.5 million troops, over 4,200 guns and mortars, 6,200 tanks and self-propelled guns, 7,500 aircraft and more than 1,000 rocket-launchers. In the actual assault areas the artillery were packed in at a density of 400 guns of 75mm calibre and over to the mile. Although we have no reason to doubt these figures, those that they quoted for the German forces opposing them were certainly exaggerated, and appear to be on the assumption that all the units listed in the German Order-of-Battle were fully manned and equipped. We know this not to have been so, but the figures served to enhance the achievements of the Soviet forces engaged.[51]

On 14 April 1945, the Russians began probing the German forward defences with forces up to regimental strength, thereby gaining some ground and enabling them to clear some of the minefields, but also alerting the enemy as to their intentions.[52] The curtain was about to go up on the final act of the war in this theatre, and stage and cast were all set.

2

The Objective

The primary soviet objective was Berlin. Between the Red Army and their objective lay the main German lines of defence, and beyond that the city's own defence system, all believed to be formidable. Within the city itself the ultimate goal was the Reichstag building.[1]

It is curious that the Russians should have chosen the Reichstag as their goal in preference to other prominent structures in the city centre, such as the Royal Palace (*Schloss*), Reich Chancellery or the Brandenburg Gate. If anything, the Reichstag represented the old Imperial or pre-Nazi Germany. The burning of the building had served as the first step in the destruction of the normal democratic process under the Nazis, and it had remained a burnt-out ruin since 1933. However, having been set the Reichstag as their goal, this building took on all the significance of a German Kremlin to the Red Army.[2]

Much of the surrounding city was now in little better condition than the Reichstag. Nevertheless, Berlin's blackened ruins still housed the organs of government of what remained of the Third Reich. Here too remained Adolf Hitler, whose haphazard, bankrupt dictatorship was clearly reflected in the state of his capital and its motley defenders preparing to meet the Soviet offensive. As the seat of government and a leading industrial city, Berlin had been a prime bombing objective for much of the war, despite the fact that it lay at the extreme range of United Kingdom-based aircraft and was usually obscured by cloud so that only blind area-bombing was possible. Having endured a total of 450 raids, Berlin was the most heavily bombed city in Germany, the United States Army Air Forces and the Royal Air Force dropping in all some 45,517 tons of bombs and mines on it. The frequency and size of the raids had gradually increased, and from mid-February 1945 onwards Berlin suffered almost continual air bombardment for thirty days and nights. The damage was worst at the centre, where Mitte District sustained 78 per cent total destruction and Tiergarten District 48 per cent. Although three-quarters of this damage was attributable to fire, the broad streets characteristic of much of Berlin had prevented the larger conflagrations experienced in other German cities.

The pre-war population of this spacious city of 4,321,000 inhabitants had been reduced by evacuation, wartime redeployment of labour, and air raid casualties.[3]

Despite a large influx of refugees from the eastern provinces in early 1945, it was now down to between two and two and a half million. It is estimated that the bombing alone killed 50,000 Berliners, but it significantly failed to extinguish the spirit of the survivors. Indeed, the gradual build-up of the attacks seems to have conditioned the inhabitants to survival under the most appalling conditions, producing an indifference to their own suffering, and preparing them for the forthcoming battle.[4]

This build-up had also enabled the city authorities and civil defence organisations to prepare for the worst of the ordeals. Following some heavy raids in August 1943, Dr Joseph Goebbels, as Gauleiter of Berlin, had secured the evacuation of a million inhabitants and closed the schools, thereby reducing the burden of 'useless mouths'. For those that remained, air raid shelters were eventually produced with a total capacity of 300,000 persons. All suitable cellars were reinforced, their exits masked with brick walls and fitted with steel doors. Public shelters were also prepared under gasometers and other buildings with concrete foundations, and in the lateral galleries of some U-Bahn (underground railway) stations. In addition, 100 massive concrete shelters were built with roofs over three feet thick, each consisting of either 18 or 36 compartments, according to the model, and capable of accommodating several hundred people.[5]

All the principal ministries were provided with their own shelters, such as the one under Goebbels's Propaganda Ministry, which was connected by tunnel with the bunker system under Hitler's Chancellery. The special Führerbunker lay some 60 feet down under several layers of earth and concrete, connected again by tunnels with other bunkers sheltering the staff, bodyguards and a fleet of vehicles.

In addition to these shelters, three enormous towers were constructed in the parks at Friedrichshain, Humboldthain and the Zoo for the dual purpose of sheltering civilians and providing elevated platforms for the anti-aircraft artillery (Flak).[6] These massive flak-towers were veritable fortresses, being both bomb-proof and shell-proof with walls six feet thick and heavy steel shutters over all the apertures. The largest and best equipped was that at the Zoo, being 132 feet high with five storeys above ground. The top floor contained the barracks for the 100-strong garrison, the fourth a fully equipped and staffed hospital intended primarily for VIPs, the third served as a secure warehouse for some of Berlin's art treasures, while the lower floors could provide shelter for 15,000 people as well as having an especially reserved section for Deutschlandsender, the official broadcasting service. The tower was completely self-contained with its own water and power supplies, and was well stocked with food and ammunition for sustaining a siege. However, it did have its drawbacks, for when the guns were in action and the rattling ammunition hoists were conveying shells up from the basement the noise was almost unbearable, and the security it offered attracted far more people than it was designed for, so that it was permanently overcrowded.[7]

Adjacent to this tower, just across the Landwehr Canal in the Tiergarten park, was a smaller one accommodating the headquarters of the 1st 'Berlin' Flak Division, and providing the radar and gun directing equipment for the main gun tower. The other two flak towers were similarly linked to adjacent control towers.

Each of these three main flak-towers carried an 8-gun battery of twin-mounted 128mm calibre guns, and was ringed with a gallery carrying a 37mm gun at each of the four corners of the tower, and a quadruple 20mm gun centrally on each side of the tower flanked by single-barrelled 20m guns.[8]

There were a dozen other flak towers of lesser proportions situated at various points in the city, and these were to prove useful in accommodating command posts and in acting as defensive positions.

All the flak within the city came under the 1st 'Berlin' Flak Division and was independent of the normal military garrison. Originally the Berlin Flak, as it was called, numbered some 500 batteries, but the capital's aerial defences had been denuded to reinforce the Oder ground defences, and now all that remained were those guns installed on the flak towers and a few others scattered around the city. These flak batteries could be expected to provide valuable support in the land battle, both against aircraft and in an anti-tank role. Unfortunately they were not all that they appeared, for since early 1943 secondary schoolboys of the Hitlerjugend (Hitler Youth) had replaced all but a few key adult personnel on the home defence batteries, while even younger boys manned the searchlights and assisted the Luftwaffen Helferinnen (female auxiliaries) with the radar and communications systems.

The Berlin Garrison Headquarters were traditionally located opposite the Zeughaus (Arsenal, now housing the German History Museum) on the Unter den Linden, and administered a miscellany of units: military police checking for stragglers and deserters, several battalions of sub-standard troops guarding installations, bridges and other vulnerable points, as well as the thousands of prisoners-of-war and foreign slave-labourers employed in the city, some penal units, an engineer battalion, and two battalions of the 'Grossdeutschland' Guard Regiment retained for ceremonial duties. These garrison troops also assisted in clearing the streets of debris after air raids. The garrison formed part of Wehrkreis (Military Area) III, which was administered by Headquarters III Corps in peacetime, and when the III Corps went off to war by a Deputy Headquarters on the Hohenzollerndamm. Deputy Headquarters III Corps in turn came under the Reserve or Home Army, whose command had been given to Heinrich Himmler, Reichsführer-SS, in 1944 after the abortive attempt on Hitler's life.[9]

At the beginning of February 1945 Hitler had declared Berlin a 'Festung' (fortress), ordering the strengthening, supply and tactical deployment of the garrison in preparation for the defence of the city, but had omitted to designate what troops were to be used for this purpose. At the same time the Commander

Deputy Headquarters III Corps had become Commander Berlin Defence Area, a logical step now that most of Wehrkreis III was either overrun or in the combat zone. However, for various reasons, including two rapid changes of commanders and the overriding commitment to reinforce the front, it was not until Lieutenant-General Hellmuth Reymann had taken over on 8 March that any actual plans were made for the defence of the city as a separate entity. At the time of his appointment Hitler had informed him that, should the need arise, sufficient front-line troops would be made available to him to man the defences, and General Reymann understood that they would come from Army Group Weichsel (Vistula) on the Oder Front.[10]

General Reymann had found the double appointment unworkable and at his request another general had been appointed to the Wehrkreis Headquarters, which was eventually evacuated before the battle and took no part in it.[11]

General Reymann's plan was naturally conditioned by the nature of the terrain. The main threat was from Soviet armour, for which much of the ground was eminently suitable, with a good network of roads and open sandy ground, often screened by woodland providing covered approaches. Although the irrigated fields in the northeast and many ditches, canals and streams provided effective anti-tank obstacles, only the Havel Lakes in the west, the Spree River running obliquely through the city, and the Müggelsee and Dahme River in the southeast could be relied upon as effective barriers to movement. However, further out at an average distance of 25 miles from the city centre there was a belt of woods and lakes running between the Alte Oder River near Bad Freienwalde to south of Königs Wusterhausen on the Dahme, offering a readily adaptable defensive position.

The system of defence devised by General Reymann, incorporating ideas put forward by Hitler and Reichsminister Dr Joseph Goebbels, consisted basically of the following:

1   A forward defence line in the east, utilising the chain of natural obstacles between the Dahme and Alte Oder Rivers, and extending for about 50 miles.

2   An obstacle belt blocking major road junctions north and south of the city.

3   An outer defence ring based roughly on the line of the city boundary, with alternative fall-back positions whenever practicable.

4   An inner defence ring based on the S-Bahn (suburban railway) circuit.

5   An innermost keep, named 'Zitadelle' (Citadel), based on the island formed by the River Spree and the Landwehr Canal, with extended bastions 'Ost' and 'West' around Alexanderplatz and Am Knie (Ernst-Reuter-Platz) respectively, encompassing all the more important government buildings, including the Reich Chancellery.[12]

The area between the outer defence ring and 'Zitadelle' was divided clockwise into eight Defence Sectors labelled 'A' to 'H', and it was intended that the defence could be conducted in depth within these individual sectors. A commander with the powers of a Divisional Commander, usually SS from Nazi Party resources but not necessarily with combat experience, was assigned to each sector. 'Zitadelle' was entrusted to SS-Brigadeführer (Major-General) Wilhelm Mohnke, commander of the 1,200-strong detachment of Hitler's lifeguard regiment, the Waffen-SS 'Leibstandarte Adolf Hitler', whose members rotated with the front-line division of the same name.

The preparations of the defences presented a mammoth task. The Chief of Engineers, Colonel Lobeck, had only the one engineer battalion at his disposal, so General Reymann, with Goebbels's permission, had two of the city's Volkssturm (Home Guard) battalions assigned to this role. The labour force itself was organised by Party officials, who, despite tremendous difficulties, still managed to muster about 70,000 people per day during the weeks preceding the attack. In addition to the Organisation Todt (official civil engineering service) and Reichsarbeitsdienst (compulsory pre-military labour service) personnel, who were the only ones with proper tools and equipment for this work, soldiers, civilians, prisoners-of-war and slave-labour gangs were employed. Although the numbers may appear small in relation to the size of the population, it should be remembered that the city's many factories were being maintained at full production day and night until the very last minute. A major transport problem was caused by the lack of fuel; movement of the labour force depending largely on the railways, which were constantly open to disruption by air raids; and there were only horse-drawn wagons with which to move the sparse building materials available. There was a drastic shortage of tools of all kinds, barbed wire, nails and anti-tank mines, and the time factor precluded the use of ferro-concrete in the construction of defensive positions. The shortage of supervisors with expertise in these matters led to some of the results being militarily useless, or even a handicap to their own troops. The greatest and best-qualified effort appears to have been expended in the preparation of 'Zitadelle' in the city centre, gradually diminishing in effectiveness towards the periphery, and to a great extent the quality of the troops initially assigned to the defences corresponded to this pattern.[13]

The forward defence line had natural strength, but only normal field positions were constructed along it at critical points, and as these were eventually manned by Luftwaffe and Volkssturm units lacking the necessary arms or training for the task, no more than a token defence could be expected from them. Though the Oder Front troops might have put these facilities to better use, circumstances were to dictate otherwise.[14]

The obstacle belt consisted of a series of roadblocks at all road junctions on the route linking Schmöckwitz with Königs Wusterhausen and along Route 246 to Beelitz in the south, and on Route 273 from Strausberg through Bernau in the north. Each roadblock was covered by defensive positions intended to accommodate one Volkssturm platoon armed with infantry and anti-tank weapons, and all built-up areas between the obstacle belt and the outer defence ring were also designated strongpoints to be defended by the local Volkssturm. However, because of the nature of the terrain, most of these positions could be easily bypassed and overcome at leisure.[15]

The first cohesive line of defence began at the city boundary with the outer defence ring. This was some 60 miles around and obviously could not be manned effectively with the limited manpower available. In the north it followed the line of the Nordgraben, a water-filled ditch of little consequence, from Tegel harbour as far as Blankenburg, thus excluding all the northernmost suburbs. From there it curved round Hohenschönhausen, where it was bordered by a mass of irrigated fields, down to the line of the S-Bahn, which it then followed through Biesendorf and Mahlsdorf to beyond the city boundary before cutting due south to the top of the Müggelsee. On the other side of the lake it crossed the wooded isthmus to the Dahme River, resuming at the eastern entrance to the Teltow Canal, which it then followed as far as the Wrede Bridge. It then followed the line Köpenicker Strasse–S-Bahn–Wildmeisterdamm to the main lateral road connecting Buckow and Marienfelde, and on to the Teltow Canal again at the Eugen-Kleine Bridge. The line then continued westwards protected by water as far as the Glienicker Bridge leading into Potsdam, and then turned due north by way of the Sacrower See and Gross-Glienicker See lakes to beyond Staaken before turning east on the northern outskirts of Spandau to end on the Havel opposite the entrance to the Tegeler See.[16]

The alternative fall-back positions in the west allowed a withdrawal across the Havel should Gatow Airfield or Spandau have to be abandoned, and boats were placed in readiness for the evacuation of the Gatow garrison. In the east the fall-back position followed the line of the Wuhle stream running northwards from Köpenick. In the south the Teltow Canal served as a fall-back position, as did the Hohenzollern Canal in the north.

The defences along the outer defence ring consisted mainly of a single meagre fire-trench with a few covered positions built at intervals along it, but each road entering the city was strongly barricaded on this line and the barricades covered by defensive positions, including a few dug-in obsolete tanks. There was a continuous anti-tank ditch masking the southern and eastern suburbs, and 20 local artillery batteries were allocated in support of the outer defence ring, plus some mobile elements of the Berlin Flak.

The inner defence ring stretched for 30 miles and was a much stronger position, being based upon the appreciable obstacle formed by the S-Bahn ring of railway tracks linking the city's mainline stations. This ring of several parallel tracks, sometimes running through deep cuttings, sometimes elevated on pylons or running along steep-sided embankments, provided a series of ready-made ramparts, anti-tank ditches or glacis, all of considerable width and giving good fields of fire to the defenders concealed in buildings along the inner perimeter. Again all the roads crossing this obstacle were strongly barricaded. They were covered by well-dug-in anti-tank weapons or 88mm anti-aircraft guns, the latter being long-famous for their effectiveness in the anti-tank role.[17]

The extent and complexity of defence arrangements within the sectors depended largely on the skill and ingenuity of the local commanders. The general scheme, which was achieved to a great degree, was to create barricades at all major road junctions and convert all strong buildings into fortified positions. At the same time the city's 483 bridges were prepared for demolition in two categories, the first category creating a maze-like approach to the city centre when eventually blown, the second category being left to the last minute.[18]

Preparations within the inner defence ring were quite elaborate. Barricades in the side streets allowed passage only to pedestrians, and those in the main streets were closed to vehicular traffic at night by means of movable sections. Machine-gun posts were prepared in cellars and upper storeys to cover these barricades, and holes were knocked through the dividing walls to allow covered passage from cellar to cellar. The generally shallow U-Bahn tunnels were also barricaded at intervals to prevent infiltration, and preparations were made for flooding some of them.

'Zitadelle' was particularly well prepared, and the arrangement at the Brandenburg Gate was said to be a model of its kind. Guns and tanks, including some powerful 'Tigers', were dug in to support the more important positions, and trenches were dug in the Tiergarten.

Communications proved a major problem in the conduct of the defence. The Luftwaffe Flak had their own communications system, but there were no radios available for the improvised garrison, which had to rely on the normal civilian telephone network and the use of runners for the passage of orders and information. Conditions in the city rendered the field radios of the front-line units arriving later virtually worthless. This invariably led to poor co-ordination between sectors and units, lack of centralised control and consequent confusion everywhere and at all levels.[19]

The supply system was no less complicated. There was no real problem about food, as there were ample stocks within the city, although regular distribution was soon disrupted by the fighting, but there was an almost immediate shortage of ammunition due to the three large depots in the outer suburbs being overrun at an early stage. The military authorities established ration, clothing and equipment stores in several U-Bahn stations, but would not make issues to the Party-sponsored Volkssturm, presumably because the matter had not been cleared at a sufficiently high level. The SS were well provided in all respects, but tended to hoard their supplies to the detriment of the other defenders. All organisations suffered from the common shortage of motor fuel.[20]

Thus the overall results were scarcely in keeping with the appellation 'Festung'. With adequate troops of the right calibre, General Reymann had a feasible outline plan for the defence of the capital, but the proper military facilities for developing the plan in depth simply did not exist any longer. However, the Nazi leadership had a completely different philosophy; Hitler's contention was that, if the Russians succeeded in reaching Berlin, they should be forced to waste their strength in the city's ruins, much as von Paulus's 6th Army had done at Stalingrad. If this plan failed and the Soviets prevailed, the Germans would have shown themselves unworthy of their leadership and would deserve extinction, just as in nature only the strongest survive.[21]

3

The Opposition

Adolf Hitler, Führer of the Third Reich and Supreme Commander of the German Armed Forces, had been installed in his new command bunker beneath the Reich Chancellery in Wilhelmstrasse since 16 January, although this was still a well-kept secret. His days of courting popularity with the mass Party rallies and public appearances were long since over. He had not even visited a single German city to witness the effects of the Allied bombing, and when his special train necessarily had to pass through these areas the curtains were drawn to exclude such distressing sights. Nor, apart from a single visit to the CI Corps on 3 March 1945, had he made any front-line visits for a considerable time. Secluded in his various remote command posts, he had become more and more removed from the reality of the world in which his subjects lived, suffered, fought and died unheeded.[1]

During the years of Nazi rule Hitler had established himself as an absolute dictator, who expressed his will to the nation by means of Führer-Orders or Führer-Decrees, while the rest of the Nazi leaders indulged in a behind-the-scenes struggle for power among themselves. His physical and mental health had suffered considerably from the strains of office, lack of exercise and possibly the attentions of his personal physician, Professor Morell, whose prescriptions have subsequently aroused some criticism. The assassination attempt of 20 July 1944 had done nothing to alleviate this condition, and since then a baleful distrust of the General Staff, and also of Reichsmarschall Hermann Göring and his Luftwaffe, had been grafted on his megalomania and ferocious despotism.[2]

He firmly believed that his presence alone was sufficient to galvanise all energies in the right direction, and that all orders to retreat, however justified, inevitably led to disaster. He attributed the loss of East Prussia to his decision to abandon his 'Wolfschanze' headquarters in Rastenburg. He also believed that the situation was bound to change in his favour, this belief being based partly on the expected appearance of some new secret weapons (for which there were no longer any production facilities), partly on the conviction that the Allies would fall out when the Anglo-American armies met up with the Russians, and partly on an absolute faith in his own star. When he learnt of the death of President Roosevelt on 12 April, he regarded it as an excellent omen.[3]

His entourage did everything to encourage him in these beliefs, and nothing to bring a sense of reality to the Führerbunker during these last days of the war. Were the consequences not so drastic, the events in the bunker would have had all the elements of a farce. Playing a leading role in this situation and closest of all to Hitler, as he had been now for several years, was the trusted Party Secretary, Reichsleiter Martin Bormann. Virtually unknown outside the Nazi leadership, his low profile hid a position of immense power, for he alone had constant access to the Führer. The other Nazi leaders both feared him and curried his favours, never knowing whether Bormann spoke in his own name or that of his master.[4]

In an oppressive atmosphere of noisy air-conditioning and sweating concrete walls, with no distinction between night and day, Hitler's courtiers kept up their internecine struggle with malicious gossip, slandering those absent and disguising the truth from each other. Despite Hitler's obvious deterioration, his presence overwhelmed reason and sane judgement in all of them, and his military staff were as obsequious as the rest.[5]

The General Staff, once a strong contender in the power struggle, had been utterly broken by the purge following the unsuccessful assassination attempt, and its leaders were now mere sycophants in Hitler's entourage. Permanently with Hitler in the Führerbunker was Field Marshal Wilhelm Keitel, nominal Chief of the Oberkommando der Wehrmacht (OKW – Armed Forces GHQ) with his headquarters in Berlin-Dahlem, but in practice acting as Hitler's personal Chief of Staff and issuing orders in the Führer's name. The OKW Chief of Staff, Colonel-General Alfred Jodl, and the Chief of Staff of the Oberkommando des Heeres (OKH – Army GHQ), Colonel-General Hans Krebs, were obliged to spend most of their time shuttling back and forth between the Führerbunker conferences and their own secret wartime headquarters in the vast bunkers known as Maybach I and II respectively, some 20 miles south of the city at Zossen-Wunsdorf.[6]

In December 1941 Hitler had supplemented his role as Supreme Commander of the Armed Forces by taking over as Commander-in-Chief of the Army with the following announcement:

> Anyone can do the little job of directing operations in war. The task of the Commander-in-Chief is to educate the Army to be National Socialist. I do not know any Army General who can do this the way I want it done. I have therefore decided to take over command of the Army.

He then further complicated the command structure by directing the Eastern Front operations exclusively through the OKH, whose responsibilities in other theatres were then given to the OKW, thus obliging the two headquarters to compete against each other over resources for their respective spheres of responsibility.[7]

Hitler's last headquarters in the Führerbunker suffered the serious defect of not being properly equipped with the normal communications facilities of the Führer Headquarters he had set up and occupied elsewhere in Europe during the course of the war. This was in part due to scale, for accommodation was extremely cramped in the Führerbunker itself, although more space could have been made in the bomb-proof shelters beneath the New Reich Chancellery building. However, the only communications facilities installed in the Führerbunker were a one-man switchboard, one field radio transmitter and a radio-telephone. Following the disappearance of the Führer Signals Detachment on the night of 22 April, wireless communication with the outside world was left dependent upon a link to two transmitters on the Funkturm in Charlottenburg nearly five miles away and then a balloon suspended above Rheinsberg, where Keitel and Jodl had their OKW headquarters. Consequently there was no direct communication with any Wehrmacht formations and Major von Loringhoven reported:

> Any rare intelligence we received came from the OKW, with whom links were very poor and intermittent. Talking on this short-wave connection required considerable physical effort. You had to concentrate hard to make out the words. Moreover, communication was often interrupted in the middle of a sentence.[8]

The head of the Luftwaffe, the once flamboyant Reichsmarschall Hermann Göring, had been rightly blamed for its shortcomings and was now a discredited figure, but still occasionally attended conferences in order to display his loyalty to the Führer and to keep in with Bormann, whose scheming had assisted his fall from grace.[9]

It was inevitable under the Nazi system that various Party officials should intervene in the preparations for the defence of the city. The most important of these was Goebbels, who, like the other Party leaders, combined several titles and responsibilities acquired in the scramble for power. Although most commonly known for his role as Minister of Public Enlightenment and Propaganda, he remained the original Gauleiter of Berlin and was now also Reich Commissar for Defence. What effect the latter title had on the issue is difficult to determine, but as Gauleiter he had a direct responsibility for the organisation of the defence of the capital. It was to him that the Commander of the Berlin Defence Area was expected to report, not only for the approval of his plans, but also for the necessary Party support to implement them.

Every Monday Goebbels held a Council of War in his office, which was attended by the military commanders, representatives of the Luftwaffe and Labour Service, the Mayor of Berlin, the Police President, various high-ranking SS and police officials, SA Standartenführer Bock, and representatives of the main Berlin industries.[10] It appears that the efficiency he applied to his Propaganda Ministry was not so readily transferable, although the same disregard for reality pertained.

He too gave out a constant stream of orders, interfering at all levels and in all directions in imitation of the Führer's own style. He would not countenance evacuation of the civilian population, an idea which he regarded as unnecessarily alarmist, but neither did he make any provision for their needs in case of siege. However, he took a genuine interest in the military situation, frequently visiting the front and consulting with the field commanders on a far more realistic basis than Hitler did.[11]

One of Goebbels's responsibilities as Gauleiter was the raising of the Berlin quota of Volkssturm units as part of the overall concept for defence. The Volkssturm had originally been raised the previous autumn as a form of Home Guard, intended purely for local defence and fortification construction purposes, from men of 16 years upwards capable of bearing arms in an emergency but otherwise not physically fit for active service. The majority came from the upper age bracket and included many First World War veterans. They were organised into companies and battalions in their home districts, but with no set establishments, so that the Berlin battalions varied in strength from 600 to 1,500. Unit commanders were appointed by the Party, some being veterans with military experience and a strong sense of duty, others merely political warriors. The Wehrmacht had no responsibility for this party-sponsored organisation, which was meant to be armed, equipped and maintained entirely from local resources. The only common issue was an armband, uniforms being either varied (even captured British Army battledress being used) or non-existent.

There were two categories of Volkssturm, the first being those for whom there were arms, and the second intended as replacements for the first, but even then the issue of arms was varied to the extent of being farcical. It was reported in one battalion, for instance, that one company had been given only two rifles, another had received Italian rifles with only a few rounds of ammunition, and a third some machine guns and an old anti-tank gun, but only Italian rifles as personal weapons. However, there was a plentiful supply of hand grenades and the new hand-held Panzerfaust and Panzerschreck anti-tank weapons, although again distribution was most uneven. Training was conducted at weekends and in the evenings when there was no construction work to do, and some three-day courses were offered at SA camps, but no Volkssturm troops were trained up to the combat role that came to be expected of them as the enemy engulfed the homeland.[12]

The commander of the 42nd Volkssturm Battalion later recounted:

I had 400 men in my battalion, and we were ordered to go into the line in our civilian clothes. I told the local Party leader that I could not accept the responsibility of leading men into battle without uniforms. Just before commitment we were given 180 Danish rifles, but no ammunition. None of the men had received any training in firing a machine gun, and they were all afraid of handling the anti-tank weapons. Although my men were quite ready to help their country, they refused to go into battle without uniforms and without training. What can a Volkssturm man do with a rifle and no ammunition? The men went home; that was the only thing we could do.[13]

Dr Johannes Stumm, who had been dismissed from the Berlin Police in 1933 by Göring for his anti-Nazi activities, and was later to become Police President under the Western Allies, also recounted:

I was able to avoid joining the Volkssturm, into whose second levy I was later conscripted. I was to be entrusted with the command of a company of the second levy of Volkssturm, although I had only served eleven weeks as a driver with a motorised unit, was not a Party member, and had only been an NCO in 1917. I at first reported sick. On 22 April I received an order to muster the company and join in the fighting, but I simply disregarded this; the company was thus saved from the fighting.[14]

Not all the Volkssturm were as badly equipped or as ineffective as indicated by these two examples. The Siemensstadt Volkssturm Battalion 3/115, for instance, fought in the eastern suburbs as a well-organised unit from 21 April until the final surrender.[15] However, as a whole, they can be seen to represent a very uncertain factor in the defence. Nevertheless, they were not the only resources upon which the Party could draw.

Another important Party functionary was the Reichsjugendführer (State Youth Leader), Artur Axmann, who had exhorted the children of the Reich earlier in the March of that year:

There is only victory or annihilation. Know no bounds in your love of your people; equally know no bounds in your hatred of the enemy. It is your duty to watch when others tire, to stand when others weaken. Your greatest honour is your unshakeable fidelity to Adolf Hitler![16]

The Hitlerjugend, originally incorporating all youths in the 14–18 year-old bracket, had taken an active part in the war effort throughout, particularly in civil defence, in which they had assisted as messengers and with salvage and relief duties. Then in 1943 the senior schoolboys had been sent to man the home defence anti-aircraft artillery in order both to release experienced adult gunners for the front and to enable an increase in the organisation to meet the Allied air offensive. Now Axmann committed his charges as infantry, a criminal act further aggravated by the fact that the Hitlerjugend's age bracket had gradually dropped during the course of the war, and boys of 12 to 16 years of age were now expected to take up arms like men and risk dying either from enemy action or hanging from a lamppost as a deserter. Mixed with adult Waffen-SS and Wehrmacht troops they fought with a fanaticism that appalled their opponents as much as did the callousness of their leaders. Needless to say, they were to suffer tremendous losses.[17]

From his headquarters in the Kantstrasse, Axmann proceeded to organise the local Hitlerjugend units to take part in the defence of the city. The boys were issued and trained with rifles, grenades and Panzerfausts, and then allocated by their companies to either the various Defence Sectors, to a special Hitlerjugend Regiment which was assigned to guarding the Havel bridges opposite Spandau on 23 April, or to the 'Axmann' Brigade, which appeared in the Strausberg area on the 21st and included a tank-hunting team mounted on bicycles for mobility.[18]

The girls too were expected to take part in the fighting with grenades and home-made Molotov cocktails, but no attempt appears to have been made to commit them by their Bund-Deutscher-Mädel (German Girls' League) units. However, later in the battle secretaries and other female staff from the various governmental departments were encouraged to join the so-called 'Mohnke' units as combatants.[19]

The Reichsführer-SS and Chef der Deutschen Polizei (State SS and Police Chief) Heinrich Himmler, who was also Minister of the Interior, had several of his SS units in the city. As previously mentioned, the Berlin-based regiment of the 'Leibstandarte Adolf Hitler' Panzergrenadier Division, which provided Hitler's ceremonial bodyguard, was about 1,200 strong and consisted mainly of combat-experienced troops from the parent formation. Their commander, SS-Major-General Wilhelm Mohnke, was also nominally head of 'Zitadelle', but in fact primarily concerned with the defence of the Reich Chancellery.

A two battalion regiment was formed from Waffen-SS resources and named 'Anhalt' after its commander, SS-Colonel Günther Anhalt, and deployed in the eastern half of 'Zitadelle'. Mohnke was also later assigned half of Himmler's own bodyguard battalion, and was said to have been further reinforced by the 2,000-strong 'Freikorps Adolf Hitler', consisting of volunteers rallying to the defence of their Führer from all over the country. According to one source, Mohnke had all these troops organised into a nine-battalion-strong 'Leibstandarte Adolf Hitler' Brigade, which was deployed along the southern edge of 'Zitadelle'.[20]

Other SS units were used as nuclei for the defence forces of the various sectors, and some SS and Feldgendarmerie (Military Police) units were employed for rounding up stragglers and deserters. The police and fire brigade services, all coming under Himmler's extensive empire, formed combat units to assist the defence, while at the same time managing to keep their normal services operating within the city as long as circumstances allowed.

Also available to assist in local defence tasks were the Plant Protection Companies maintained by the larger industrial concerns, including the post office and railways. These were recruited from old soldiers and armed only with rifles, and consequently were of limited combat value.[21]

One unusual aspect of the political influence on the conduct of the defence was the mixing of members of different organisations within strongpoints in the various sectors, so that Waffen-SS, Wehrmacht, Volkssturm and Hitlerjugend literally fought side by side.[22]

The loyalty commanded by Hitler in his immediate entourage was most curiously displayed in the conduct of Albert Speer, Reich Minister for Armaments and War Production. Hitler's architectural interests had catalysed Speer's dazzling career during the Third Reich. After coming to Hitler's notice for his architectural work, he was entrusted with the construction of the New Reich Chancellery, which he managed to complete in detail within only twelve months. Speer soon became a close intimate, working on Hitler's ideas for the grandiose transformation of Berlin and other pet projects until the course of the war forced them to be shelved. Then, when Dr Fritz Todt, Minister of Armaments and Munitions and head of the vast construction organisation bearing his name, was killed in an air crash in February 1942, Hitler appointed Speer to succeed him, thus making Speer a leading member of the hierarchy overnight.[23]

Within a remarkably short time Speer's administrative talent and methods achieved astonishing results in the increase of war production, despite the growing intensification of the Allied air offensive. However, although still personally spellbound by Hitler, Speer alone among the hierarchy was soon to perceive the extent of the dilemma in which Germany found itself. From the time of its inception in the summer of 1944, he constantly opposed Hitler's 'scorched earth' policy, for he saw these orders for wholesale destruction would make it impossible for the countries concerned to recover from the war. By persuading local Party leaders and officials to refrain from carrying out these orders, which Hitler reiterated on 20 March and 4 April 1945, Speer achieved considerable success in both German and the occupied territories.[24]

According to his own account, in February 1945 Speer had gone so far as to plan the murder of Hitler by the introduction of poison gas into the Führerbunker's ventilation system, but was foiled by a screening chimney, which had just been built around the air intake after the accidental introduction of some smoke had revealed the flaw in the system. Although unaware of this plot, Hitler was not unaware of Speer's other activities and his lack of faith in ultimate victory, but seems to have chosen to ignore these treacherous aberrations, while at the same time taking steps to diminish Speer's influence.[25]

Then on 15 April Speer had contrived to appear at Colonel-General Heinrici's headquarters near Prenzlau during a visit by General Reymann to discuss the allocation of front-line troops for the city's defences. Heinrici was naturally concerned for the fate of the city, but had not been given any specific responsibility for it, nor was he aware that he was expected to part with any of his troops to Reymann. He was in any case fully opposed to the idea of exposing the population to the consequences of street fighting, and advised Reymann to confine his efforts to making a stand on the city boundary. If the Russians succeeded in forcing his own troops from their positions along the Oder, Heinrici proposed drawing them aside from Berlin rather than getting them involved within the city.[26]

Speer had previously conspired with Heinrici to protect the Silesian industries and was now aware of the instructions received by Reymann to prepare to destroy all the bridges in the city. He had therefore brought along with him two technical experts to help plead his case: Langer, the city superintendent of roadworks, and Beck of the Reichsbahn (State Railways). Together they explained that not only did the bridges carry pedestrian, vehicular and railway traffic, but also the vital arteries of the city's gas, electrical and water supplies, and the sewage system, whose severance would cause untold hardships to the inhabitants. Reymann was in a quandary over his duty to obey orders, but eventually agreed to accept Heinrici's recommendations to remove the explosive charges forthwith and not to blow any bridges except as required in the course of military operations. Thus, as a result of this meeting, only 127 of Berlin's 483 bridges were eventually destroyed by Reymann's engineers. Speer says that Langer and another city engineer, Kumpf, were active in preventing such demolitions, even during the fighting, and there is indeed other evidence of such activity having taken place.[27]

In the meantime the growing destruction of the city and a gradual reduction in living standards was becoming more and more apparent to the inhabitants when they emerged from their shelters in the brief intervals between air raids. With blocked streets, frequently severed electricity, water and gas mains, and other hindrances to normal life, even the basic essentials were becoming increasingly difficult to meet.

To add to these depressing factors a stream of refugees poured in from the eastern provinces, bearing tales of horror and spreading a haunting fear of the Russians, who were being urged on by Ilya Ehrenburg's manifesto to the Red Army to spare no one, including women, in their revenge. Yet the prevailing mood was nevertheless one of passive resignation, a kind of numbed acceptance of events and a refusal to believe in the imminence of catastrophe. No doubt the traditional docility of the Germans towards authority contributed something to this apathy, but other factors also played a part. For instance, the population had yet to suffer from hunger; food rationing was adequate and distribution continued more or less regularly. In addition, all the semblances of public order were still in evidence; there were 12,000 police on duty in the city, the municipal transport and other services were still functioning, and the civil defence organisations were operating as efficiently as ever.[28]

To counter depression and defeatism there was an endless stream of propaganda from Goebbels's Ministry, which continued to hold out hope until the very end, while simultaneously threatening traitors and the defeatist with the most dire penalties. Even the ruins were used to bear such slogans as: 'Our faith is in total victory' – 'Bolshevism is about to meet the most decisive defeat in history' – 'On the Oder will be decided the fate of Europe' – 'We will never surrender' – 'Berlin will stay German' – 'Break our walls but not our hearts'.

Beneath these smouldering ruins the man upon whom the entire situation hinged was making plans to meet the possibility of the Allied advances splitting the Reich in two. He issued a Führer-Order on 15 April announcing that in such an eventuality the struggle would be continued, with Grand Admiral Karl Dönitz commanding the German Forces in the north, and Field Marshal Albert Kesselring those in the south.[29] His staff were confident that Hitler was planning to move out to Berchtesgaden, where he would conduct a stand from the so-called, but non-existent, 'Southern Redoubt'. However, when his discreet and unassuming mistress, Eva Braun, suddenly moved down into the bunker from her apartment in the Chancellery on 15 April declaring that she would remain with the Führer whatever happened, they took this as a strong indication that he intended staying in Berlin after all.[30]

The same evening Hitler made out his final Order-of-the-Day, which was primarily intended for the soldiers of Army Groups 'Weichsel' and 'Mitte', but was in fact produced too late for distribution to the troops before the Soviet attack began. The text is a good reflection of the prevailing atmosphere.

Führer-Order-of-the-Day

Soldiers of the Eastern Front!

For the last time our deadly enemies, the Jewish Bolsheviks, have rallied their massive forces for an attack. They intend to destroy Germany and to exterminate our people. Many of you Eastern Front soldiers already know well the fate that awaits above all German women and children: the old men and children will be murdered, the women and girls turned into barrack-room whores, and the rest marched off to Siberia.

We have been expecting this attack, and since January this year have done everything possible to build up a strong front. The enemy will be received with massive artillery fire. Gaps in our infantry have been filled by countless new units. Our front is being strengthened with emergency units, newly raised units and Volkssturm.

This time the Bolsheviks will meet the ancient fate of Asia, which means that they will bleed to death before the capital of the German Reich.

Whoever ails in his duty now behaves as a traitor to our people. Any regiment or division that abandons its position will be acting so disgracefully that it will be shamed before the women and children braving the terror of the bombing in our cities.

Above all, be on your guard against those few treacherous officers and soldiers, who, in order to preserve their pitiful lives, fight against us in Russian pay, perhaps even wearing German uniform. Anyone ordering you to retreat, unless personally known to you, will be immediately arrested and, if necessary, shot on the spot, no matter what rank he may hold.

If every soldier on the Eastern Front does his duty in these coming days and weeks, the last assault of Asia will crumble, just as the invasion by our enemies in the west will fail in the end, despite everything.

Berlin stays German, Vienna will be German again and Europe will never be Russian.[31]

Form yourselves into sworn brotherhoods to defend, not just the empty concept of a Fatherland, but your homes, your wives, your children, and with them our future.

In these hours the whole German nation looks to you, my Eastern Front warriors, and only hopes that by your resolution, your fanaticism, your weapons, and under your leadership, the Bolshevik assault will be drowned in a bloodbath.

In this moment, in which fate has removed from the earth the greatest war criminal of all time,[32] will the turning point of the war be decided.

Adolf Hitler[33]

4

The Main German Forces

The German Armed Forces to which Hitler addressed his rhetoric clearly reflected the exhausted state of the Third Reich and the anarchistic Nazi leadership that fielded them. The Germans had gone even further in scraping the bottom of the manpower barrel than the Russians, and were arming every male from twelve years upwards capable of pulling a trigger. The end of the war was in sight on all fronts, even if Hitler and his entourage could not see it in their subterranean detachment from reality.

During the first quarter of 1945 the situation had deteriorated rapidly. On 14 January the Russians had launched their winter offensive in Poland and had quickly broken through the positions held by Army Group 'Weichsel', at that time commanded by Himmler. Part of the German forces had been pushed back and penned in East Prussia for eventual destruction, and part thrown back to the Oder River, which the first Russian troops had reached on 31 January. During February and March the Soviet armies had completed their mopping up and closed up to the line of the Oder and Neisse Rivers, although the Germans continued to hold on to bridgeheads in the eastern suburbs of Frankfurt-an-der-Oder, in Küstrin at the junction of the Oder and Warthe Rivers, and at the mouth of the Oder opposite Stettin. However, at the end of March the Russians had finally succeeded in taking Küstrin and had combined and enlarged their bridgeheads opposite. They had also secured another bridgehead south of Frankfurt. Both these bridgeheads were less than 40 miles from Berlin.

In the south the Soviets had taken Vienna between 8 and 14 April, and on 9 April the Italian Front had collapsed. In the west the French, American, British and Canadian armies had crossed the Rhine in mid-March, encircled and immobilised Field Marshal Walter Model's Army Group 'B' in the Ruhr, crossed the Weser on the 10th April and pushed on eastwards, the American 9th Army reaching the Elbe near Magdeburg on the 17th.[1]

The elimination of Model's forces had left a vast vacuum west of Berlin, and on 15 April the city found itself threatened from both east and west, with the line of the Elbe virtually undefended. Although he had known since early February of the Yalta intention to divide up Germany between the Allies, Hitler realistically still expected a race for Berlin from both directions. Aware of the political importance of this goal in the post-war context, the British leaders were in fact unsuccessfully trying to get the Americans to do just that, while Stalin was determined that the prize and credit would be his alone. The German leaders did not expect the American 1st and 9th Armies to stop on the Elbe, and consequently Hitler and his staff were concerned with the defence of both the Elbe and Oder Fronts and how to share their last remaining resources in manpower and equipment between them.

In examining the state and composition of the German Armed Forces in this area we find a most bewildering array of units and uniforms. One particularly confusing aspect was the use of Corps and Army Headquarters taken out of reserve to command new formations to which they automatically gave their old titles irrespective of their composition or function. Thus the V SS Mountain Corps commanded only one Waffen-SS formation and no mountain troops, while the XI SS Panzer Corps consisted primarily of ordinary infantry units.[2]

The effects of Allied bombing and the loss of the Upper Silesian industrial area had finally brought about the total collapse of the German war industry. Production was virtually at a standstill, and there was no new equipment available to replace losses in combat or to furbish new units. Most serious of all was the lack of motor fuel of all kinds, whose production centres had at last become a priority target in the Allied bombing offensive. Of all strategic targets this certainly proved the most effective, but its value was not fully appreciated until quite late in the war. Fuel had already been in critical short supply for some months and was now having a telling effect on operations everywhere. Later both Speer and Jodl were to blame the loss of Upper Silesia on the lack of fuel for the 1,500 tanks that had been mustered for its defence and then found to be incapable of tactical manoeuvre.

The basic framework of the German ground forces was still that of the Army, more commonly known by the overall armed forces title of the Wehrmacht. However, after the abortive coup of 20 July 1944, the Army had been seriously weakened by the great purge of officers that followed and by the Nazi leaders' distrust of the survivors. Political Officers (NS-Führungsoffiziere) had been appointed to all units and formation headquarters for the purpose of promoting the Nazi spirit and to spy on possible dissidents. Himmler had been given command of the Reserve or Home Army, an appointment of considerable influence in the Army hierarchy, covering as it did all recruitment, training, development and allocation of equipment. Since then all new recruits had been assigned to the newly constituted Volkswehr (People's Army) of Volksgrenadier (Infantry) and Volksartillerie (Artillery) units, which were intended to form the nucleus of a more politically reliable post-war Army. The latter were also given priority of equipment over the Army, which thus suffered deficiencies of the same important equipment that the Volkswehr then wasted through lack of combat experience.

Fighting with the German Army were units of General Vlassov's White Russian troops raised belatedly, and with great reluctance on the part of the Nazi leaders, from anti-Stalinist prisoners-of-war who regarded themselves primarily as Russian nationalist patriots. The German forces had long used Russian auxiliaries both with and without the consent of the political leadership, but under General Vlassov there was an attempt to organise them formally. These troops fought with great desperation, knowing that they could expect no mercy at the hands of the Soviets.[3]

Also now fighting with the Army were units of the Reichsarbeitsdienst, consisting of youngsters doing their compulsory pre-military service supposedly behind the front lines, but who had been caught up in the general withdrawals and obliged to defend themselves with their personal weapons. The Reichsarbeitsdienst units had acquitted themselves so well in the retreat from Silesia that they had been employed as infantry from then on, and soon gained a reputation for courage and daring.

Under the operational command of the Wehrmacht, although technically an entirely separate organisation, were the Waffen-SS, consisting of Panzer (Armoured), Panzergrenadier (Motorised Infantry), cavalry and mountain formations, as well as foreign volunteer elements such as the 'Nordland', 'Walloon', 'Nederland' and 'Charlemagne' Divisions, but as a result of hard usage, most of these formations were now drastically reduced in strength. They had priority of equipment over the Army and, as part of Himmler's extensive empire, they even had their own sources of supply from SS slave-labour factories. The Waffen-SS, however, like many Nazi Party organisations, was not all that they appeared to be on the surface. Their revolutionary training methods, based upon special storm-trooper tactics developed late in the First World War, had been initiated by Felix Steiner, who features later in this account as an SS General, and they were renowned for the irresistible ferocity of their attacks and indifference to casualties. The Waffen-SS had expanded considerably as the war progressed, but had also suffered tremendous casualties in their constant spearheading of attacks. Unable to compete with the conscription laws directed at the Wehrmacht, they had been obliged to recruit elsewhere and had become so diluted with foreign volunteers and non-ethnic Germans, and so indifferent to the higher command while maintaining an arrogant spirit of elitism, that they were now curiously like the French Foreign Legion in outlook, a closed community with their own rules and loyalties. By 1945 the faith of the SS generals in Hitler was wavering, and they no longer believed in final victory. Handicapped by second-rate reinforcements and wrestling with a crisis of conscience over foreign volunteers, the Waffen-SS had become prey to ideological doubts and followed leaders whose loyalty to the state was suspect.[4]

Under Himmler's aegis as Minister of the Interior, Marsch (Field) units had been raised from police, fire brigade, customs and border guards resources and sent into the line to serve under their own officers.

Then came the Party contributions of the Volkssturm and Hitlerjugend. There are no figures available for the latter, but the Volkssturm are believed to have had about 30 battalions on the Oder Front, coming from the levies raised by the Gauleiters of Stettin, Potsdam and elsewhere.

Apart from air support over the combat zone, the Luftwaffe provided three categories of troops to the land battle.[5]

First there were the parachute units. Although many of their personnel had never received parachute training, being early selections from non-flying branches of the service, they had been trained and indoctrinated in the elitist traditions of the parachutists, and these units had long been employed as shock infantry with the Army. However, at this stage replacements for casualties from further selections, including aircraftless aircrew, were being incorporated into these units without the benefit of the normal training and indoctrination.

Second, the Flak, or anti-aircraft, corps of the service, which provided 90 percent of all German anti-aircraft defence, was represented in all Army formations down to divisional level, usually under its own command and control structure. In addition to providing anti-aircraft cover for headquarter installations, supply dumps and communication centres, Flak batteries were also frequently successfully used as mobile artillery against strongpoints or in the anti-tank role, for which the 88mm gun was famous. Unlike their counterparts in most armies, the Flak corps had started life as an elite body and remained so in the field, individual batteries often fighting heroically until finally overrun or destroyed.

Lastly there were the Luftwaffe field divisions which had first been formed in 1942 and eventually attained an overall strength of 200,000 men, or one-tenth of the entire service. They had originally been formed from men skimmed from the training organisations, Flak and other ground service units, had been lightly armed and committed as infantry, only to suffer enormous casualties in consequence. By April 1945 the original units had virtually ceased to exist, but in these last desperate days more units were raised in the same manner and committed to battle. This measure was greatly facilitated by the Luftwaffe system of having all ground personnel organised into companies and battalions on their bases, but of course these units lacked all but the men's own personal weapons for this role, had no combat experience and could be expected to be of only limited value when committed as infantry.

This, then, was the miscellany of organisations available to Hitler and his generals for the defence of Berlin on the Elbe and Oder Fronts. By scraping the barrel, the numbers produced look impressive enough, and the Russians estimated that along the Oder–Neisse line they were facing about one million effectives equipped with 100,000 guns and mortars, 1,500 tanks and self-propelled guns, and 3,300 combat aircraft, but, as usual, these figures were exaggerated and continued to be so in post-war estimates.[6]

With a view to rescuing Field Marshal Model's Army Group 'B' trapped in the Ruhr pocket and to restoring the situation in the west, the OKW belatedly ordered the formation of the 12th Army towards the end of March and conferred it upon Panzer-General Walter Wenck. Four experienced corps headquarters were allocated to the new army, but two of these lacked the necessary signals equipment to operate in a tactical capacity. Manpower and equipment was found by closing military training establishments, taking tanks straight off the production lines, scouring the military depots and Reichsarbeitsdienst in the area for the last of their personnel, recruiting from the Hitlerjugend and revitalising the remains of units scattered in the Rhine battles. The officer and NCO instructors from the training establishments were of excellent value, but 90 percent of the troops were only 17- and 18-year olds. Together they provided one Panzer, one Panzergrenadier and five infantry divisions, but with the usual deficiencies of transport and signals equipment.[7]

The 12th Army, whose boundary extended from the junction of the Havel and Elbe Rivers in the north to below Leipzig in the south, at its strongest contained the following formations:

1. XXXIX Panzer Corps under Lieutenant-General Karl Arndt, which remained under command only from 21 to 26 April. Formed earlier in the month with the 'Clausewitz' Panzer, 'Schlageter' RAD, 'Potsdam' and 84th Infantry Divisions, it had been sent into the Harz Mountains to support the 11th Army and was virtually destroyed within five days, but by the time it was transferred to the newly formed 21st Army on the 26th it had been reconstituted to consist of :[8]
   'Hamburg' Reserve Division (2 regiments)
   'Meyer' Division (2 regiments)
   84th Division (3 battalions)
   'Clausewitz' Panzer Division (3 battalions).

2. XXXXI Panzer Corps under Lieutenant-General Rudolf Holste, which was based near Rathenow, and consisted of the miscellaneous units, some of which had survived the Rhine battles, including:
   'von Hake' Division (2 regiments)
   199th Division (1 regiment ex Oslo)
   'V-Weapons' Division (6,000 men)
   two anti-tank brigades.

3. XX Corps under Lieutenant-General Carl-Erik Koehler, which was initially responsible for containing the minor American bridgeheads near Zerbst, and consisted of:
   'Theodor Körner' RAD Division
   'Ulrich von Hutten' Division
   'Ferdinand von Schill' Division
   'Scharnhorst' Division.

4. XXXXVIII Panzer Corps under Lieutenant-General Maximilian Freiherr von Edelshain, which constituted the Army Reserve near

Coswig, and consisted mainly of miscellaneous units culled from the
Halle and Leipzig area, including the 14th Flak Division, most of
whose guns were static.

The 100 mile length of the Oder Front was held by Army Group 'Weichsel',
with General Hasso von Manteuffel's 3rd Panzer Army in the north and General
Theodor Busse's 9th Army opposite Berlin. Further south General Gräser's 4th
Panzer Army of Field Marshal Ferdinand Schörner's Army Group 'Mitte' held the
Neisse River line down as far as the Czechoslovakian border.

The command of Army Group 'Weichsel' had been given to Colonel-General
Gotthardt Heinrici on 20 March after two chaotic and disastrous months
under Himmler and his inept SS staff.[9] This group consisted of formations
that had survived the debacle in Poland and avoided being caught in the East
Prussian pocket. They had since been reorganised and equipped as best as the
circumstances allowed, so that on 16 April General Heinrici had at his disposal
about 850 tanks and more than 500 anti-aircraft batteries, many of which had
been taken from the Berlin defences. Heinrici had won an outstanding reputation
in the autumn of 1943 as a winner of defensive battles against great odds while
commanding the 4th Army in Russia. He had later commanded the 1st Panzer
Army and the 1st Hungarian Army in the retreat through the Carpathian
Mountains in Silesia before being given command of Army Group 'Weichsel'.
His methods of defence relied on good intelligence of enemy intentions so that
force could be concentrated in good time at the right places, and on conserving
manpower by withdrawing from the forward positions immediately before the
Soviet artillery preparation was due to begin. By this time he had become an
acknowledged German Army expert on defensive battles, a subject that had been
neglected in the pre-war training programme due to the emphasis on offensive
operations.[10]

However, Hitler too had a detailed interest in the preparations on the Oder
Front, as indicated by his visit to the CI Corps at Harnekop on 3 March, and
on 4 April he had summoned Heinrici to a meeting at which he reviewed the
defence arrangements mile by mile and issued specific instructions for their
improvement.[11]

Reinforcements had come from the meagre gleanings of Wehrmacht depots,
various odd emergency and guard units provided from OKW resources, some
Luftwaffe units, some Volkssturm battalions from Potsdam and Stettin, together
with some field units raised by the police, customs and Reichsarbeitsdienst.[12]
These had been allocated to the various formations, giving Heinrici the equivalent
of ten weak divisions in the 3rd Panzer Army and fifteen in the 9th Army, plus
his Army Group Reserve. However, the latter had been reduced through Hitler's
counterattacks on Küstrin and transfers elsewhere, and now consisted of only
the two understrength Waffen-SS Panzergrenadier Divisions 'Nordland' and

'Nederland'. These, together with the last OKW Reserve, the 18th Panzergrenadier Division, which Heinrici was also later have allocated to him, were encamped around Angermünde behind the 3rd Panzer Army. The two Waffen-SS divisions were each now down to brigade strength, but were experienced formations of battle-hardened Scandinavian, Dutch and Belgian volunteers.[13]

General Heinrici had originally counted on being allocated several armoured formations to provide him with a strong counterattack capability should the Soviet armour succeed in breaking through his lines, but at the beginning of March Hitler had ordered an offensive in Hungary to relieve the only remaining oilfields. Temporary success had only been achieved at the cost of the last of the German armoured reserves. According to Shtemenko, as early as November 1944 the Stavka had planned this attraction of the German armour to the flanks with the intention of weakening the resistance in front of Berlin.[14]

Lacking armoured reserves, Heinrici had then asked for troops of any kind to bolster his defences. This request so enraged Hitler that at a tragic-comic scene at the Führerbunker on 6 April, Göring, Himmler and Grand Admiral Dönitz hastened to appease their master by offering up all their remaining resources. They would turn out all their depots, offices and service installations, dissolve their headquarter establishments and transform into infantry and gunners all who had been rendered idle by the lack of ships and aircraft, thus producing enough manpower to form several new divisions. Göring promised 100,000 airmen, the SS would send a further 25,000 combatants, and the Kriegsmarine (Navy) would send 12,000. This grandiose gesture eventually produced only 30,000 men totally unequipped and untrained for the role expected of them, for whom in any case Army Group 'Weichsel' could only find 1,000 rifles.[15]

The 9th Army, which was expected to bear the brunt of the Soviet attack, was allocated most of the reinforcements and resources available. In addition to the 15 weak divisions, General Busse also had Colonel Ernst Biehler's 30,000-strong garrison of the Frankfurt-an-der-Oder Festung and the 23rd Flak Division within his command. After a considerable amount of adjustment, the 9th Army was finally organised as follows when the main offensive began on 16 April 1945:

1. CI Corps, consisting of the 5th Jäger (Light), 606th and 309th 'Gross-Berlin' Infantry Divisions, with the 25th Panzergrenadier Division in reserve.
2. LVI Panzer Corps, with the 9th Parachute, 20th Panzergrenadier and 'Müncheberg' Panzer Division, the latter intended as a reserve but brought forward to bolster the 20th Panzergrenadier Division at the last minute.
3. XI SS Panzer Corps, consisting of the 169th, 303rd 'Döberitz' and 712th Infantry Divisions, with the 'Kurmark' Panzergrenadier Division in reserve.

4. V SS Mountain Corps, consisting of the 286th Infantry and 391st Security Divisions, supported by the 32nd SS '30. Januar' Panzergrenadier Division.
5. Army Reserve, consisting of the 156th Infantry Division and Headquarters, 541st Volksgrenadier Division commanding the 'Dorn' and 'Pirat' Jagdpanzer (Tank-hunting) Brigades, and the equivalent of another anti-tank brigade.
6. Artillery – The 404th and 408th Volksartillerie Corps located south and north of Seelow respectively.[16]

Air support was provided by the 6th Air Fleet, commanded by Colonel-General Robert Ritter von Greim, who was based in Munich. The Germans still had about 3,000 aircraft available for service over the whole Eastern Front, of which 300 were allocated in support of Army Group 'Weichsel', but the scarcity of aviation fuel restricted sorties to the absolutely essential, and the number of serviceable airfields was also diminishing. Nevertheless, the Luftwaffe was to acquit itself well in the forthcoming battle.[17]

To make up for their deficiencies in manpower and equipment, the German generals made the best possible use of the terrain, concentrating their efforts on the vital sector between Küstrin and Berlin. Around and south of Frankfurt-an-der-Oder the high western banks of the river favoured the German defence, but the large Soviet bridgehead opposite Küstrin provided an obvious springboard for a direct drive on Berlin, which would have to start by crossing the 10-mile-wide Oder valley bottom, the Oderbruch. To improve upon this obstacle, which was already riddled with streams, canals and drainage ditches, the waters of the Bobertal Dam (in what is now Poland) were gradually released so as to substantially raise the already high water table, turning the valley bottom into a soggy mass.[18]

The second obstacle on this route was formed by the escarpment of the Seelow Heights rising 100 feet above the valley bed, and here the main line of defence was constructed in considerable depth to form a forward defensive belt and linked to a third line behind it. These defences incorporated a pattern of interlocking strongpoints and natural obstacles, utilising woods, villages and stretches of water, plus man-made abattis and anti-tank ditches.

The first line of defence was manned by the equivalent of twelve divisions, most of which it was intended would be withdrawn into the main, forward defensive belt, known as the 'Hardenberg-Stellung' at the last possible moment before the formidable artillery barrage that inevitably preceded Soviet attacks.

Next, came a prepared, but unmanned 'Stein-Stellung' upon which the survivors from the forward defensive belt could withdraw if necessary, which was based on a geographical fault forming a chain of water obstacles that ran through the villages of Diedersdorf and Lietzen. Then came the final defensive belt of anti-tank brigades along the line Neu Hardenberg–Müncheberg–Heinersdorf, where the main thrust could be expected.

For the whole of the Army Group the ammunition and fuel states were as perilously low as those in Berlin. There was even a shortage of small-arms ammunition, and the artillery had only enough shells for two and a half days of combat. These deficiencies, the weakness of the formations, the obligation not to give ground, and the absence of worthwhile reserves, all gave General Heinrici cause for concern. The sum of all the measures taken for the defence was still inadequate in the face of the impending storm, and although the Russians would have to fight hard to effect a breach in the German defences, success was only a matter of time. Once Army Group 'Weichsel' was dislodged there would be no further opportunity for regrouping or avoiding the total and final collapse of the German Armed Forces and the Reich they were seeking to protect.[19]

The indications that the Soviet attack was imminent increased. From 30 March onwards aerial reconnaissance reported numerous Russian convoys heading towards Frankfurt and Küstrin. The Russians had already constructed several bridges across the Oder to their bridgeheads, and all attempts to destroy them by aircraft, flying bombs and even frogmen had proved futile.[20] The number of Soviet guns was steadily increasing to staggering numbers with little attempt at camouflage.

Then on 14 April the Soviets launched a reconnaissance in strength from the Küstrin bridgehead, probing the German forward positions and clearing paths through the belts of mines that blocked their line of advance. That day the 9th Army claimed to have destroyed 200 Soviet tanks in this operation. Prisoner-of-war interrogation confirmed the imminence of attack.

General Busse later recorded:

On the 14th the enemy continued his attack with increased strength the whole length of the line down to Lebus. The right wing of the XI SS Panzer Corps [712th and 169th Divisions] rejected all attacks with heavy loss to the enemy. In the other sectors of the Corps the enemy penetrated as far as the second line. Near Seelow such a crisis arose that the 'Kurmark' Panzergrenadier Division had to be thrown into the fight to stop them getting too far. Unfortunately they could not be evicted that evening. In the CI Corps's sector the enemy advanced more than five kilometres towards Wriezen. The bridgehead in this sector thus achieved a depth of 15 kilometres and was fully adequate for the deployment of strong forces. Losses in men and material were high on both sides, and ours could not be replaced, a serious matter. Concerned about this, that evening Army HQ again appealed for the 18th Panzergrenadier Division and the two Panzergrenadier brigades, but without success.[21]

On the evening of 15 April Hitler agreed to General Heinrici's request to pull back all but a skeleton holding force to the main defensive position in readiness for the attack expected next morning. First light was due at 0520 hours.[22]

5

An Early Dawn

The battle commenced at 03:00 hours on 16 April 1945 with an artillery bombardment on the German forward positions.[1] The bombardment was of an intensity that defies description, the Russians using every gun, mortar and rocket-launcher they had to pulverise the defence in a 30-minute holocaust, backed by the simultaneous bombing of Letschin, Langsow, Werbig, Seelow, Friedersdorf and Dolgelin by 745 bombers of the 18th Air Army. The artillery concentration on the objectives for the initial assault was quite unprecedented and the din and psychological effect cataclysmic. The early morning mist was replaced by a cloud of smoke and debris that rose to tower over the battlefield.[2]

At 0330 hours 143 searchlights placed at 200-yard intervals along the start line were suddenly switched on, flooding the area before the Soviet forces with light and probing into the murk raised by the bombardment. This was the signal to advance and for the artillery to change to a double rolling barrage to clear the way.[3]

However, this grandiose introduction proved an utter failure. The opening barrage had fallen mainly on mainly vacated positions, the Germans having withdrawn during the night as planned. The searchlights, which were intended to give the troops two extra hours of light to work in, were not aimed at the clouds, as in the artificial moonlight technique developed by the British, but on a flat trajectory straight ahead. This bright light, contrasting vividly with the black shadows, promptly produced night blindness among the exposed troops and gave them the uneasy feeling of being silhouetted as targets for the enemy. Troops commanders passed back instructions for the lights to be extinguished, which was done but then countermanded so that an angry exchange ensued during which the operators switched their lights on and off as directed, exacerbating the situation even further. Units floundered and came to a halt, many waiting for the dawn to resolve the dilemma.[4] The rolling barrage had to be called off and the artillery changed to concentration barrages on opportunity targets. Fortunately the Germans could not see through the murk either and, not having the ammunition to use indiscriminately, withheld their fire until they had something positive to aim at. Meanwhile the area over which the Soviet troops had to advance had been reduced to a quagmire.

At first light the 16th Air Army took over the aerial battle with 455 bombers and 730 ground-attack aircraft, but the pall was so dense over the battlefield that they had to abandon their planned bombing operation. Fog closed many of the airfields, and flying conditions were such that only the EL-2 ground-attack aircraft could operate and then only in small groups, but later in the morning the PE-2 dive-bombers were able to join in.[5]

Marshal Zhukov directed the battle from a command post that had been constructed for him on the spur above Reitwein, from where he had a grandstand view of the arena over which the 8th Guards Army had to advance on the Seelow Heights, including the Küstrin–Berlin highway, his main axis of advance.

For this breakthrough battle, Zhukov had deployed the 69th Army on his northern flank alongside the 1st Polish Army, both of which had to conduct assault river crossings. Then came in succession the 47th Army, the 3rd and 5th Shock Armies, which with the 8th Guards Army formed the main thrust. The 69th Army was deployed southwards along the Reitwein Spur down to Lebus and then south of Frankfurt was the 33rd Army on the southern flank with its own bridgehead. The fortified garrison town of Frankfurt was deliberately ignored, for it would obviously crumble once it had been outflanked and isolated.

The 1st Byelorussian Front's start line in the Oderbruch was roughly the line Lebus–Podelzig–Rathstock–Tucheband–Golzow–Zechin–Alt Lewin, each army having a breakthrough frontage of between two and four miles on which to concentrate. From Podelzig onwards the area between the start line and the Seelow Heights was simply dead flat fenland crisscrossed with waterlogged ditches and incorporating the main water obstacle formed by the course of the Alte Oder, which was extended across the 8th Guards Army's front by the Haupt-Graben ditch and would require bridging when they came to it. This fenland had been turned into a swamp by deliberate inundation, as previously mentioned, and the only way across was by a meagre network of causeways carrying the few roads, tracks and railways, away from which even the infantry could move only with the greatest difficulty.[6]

Less than a mile beyond the Alte Oder/Haupt-Graben obstacle, the escarpment of the Seelow Heights closed off the arena with eroded slopes over 100 feet high. A limited number of roads and tracks provided the only ready means of access for vehicles up the front of the escarpment to the villages on the plateau above. A gap in the centre of the line opposite Alt Friedland led into the densely wooded intricacies of the Buckow ravine, a labyrinth to be avoided.

The Germans had withdrawn to their main defensive positions, leaving strongpoints to delay the Soviet advance, such as that at the village of Sachsendorf, and the last mile before the Seelow Heights was designated their main killing ground with a line of anti-tank guns along the foot of the escarpment. The German artillery and main battle tanks were deployed on the plateau above out of sight of the Soviet artillery observers, who were at a distinct disadvantage.[7]

In the 8th Guards Army's sector, elements of the 28th Guards Rifle Corps took the southern axis from Hathenow to Libbenichen, while the 29th Guards Rifle Corps advanced from Rathstock through Sachsendorf for Dolgelin, and the 4th Guards Rifle Corps advanced astride the main highway on Seelow.

Once the troops got going they made reasonable progress for the first five or six miles. The artillery blasted a way for them and the integral supporting armour was able to keep up, but soon the canals and ditches took their toll, the armour began to fall behind and coordination was lost. Isolated pockets of German resistance were encountered and had to be dealt within turn.

When they eventually reached the Haupt-Graben, they found most of the crossing points destroyed and all under heavy fire. The flooded canal being impassable for vehicles, the infantry had to cross as best they could and provide covering fire for the engineers tasked with preparing bridges for the supporting armour. In the meantime the tanks and self-propelled guns sat exposed on the narrow causeways, incapable of manoeuvre, with mined and mired fields on either side. Fortunately the air arm was able to intervene, silencing the artillery and fending off enemy aircraft.[8]

By 1000 hours the advance echelons of the 8th Guards Army had forced the Haupt-Graben and were fighting for the foot of the Seelow Heights, while its artillery moved forward for the next phase. Chuikov then gave orders for a 20-minute bombardment to precede a combined attack on Seelow, Friedersdorf and Dolgelin scheduled for 1200 hours. The problem here was to gain control of the strongly defended vehicle access routes to the escarpment by getting the infantry to work their way up the slopes and attack the anti-tank positions from the rear.[9]

However, it was at this juncture, 1100 hours, that Marshal Zhukov, exasperated and desperate with disappointment at the tardiness of overall progress and goaded by Stalin's remarks on his rival Koniev's success, decided to expedite matters by committing his two tank armies. The 1st Guards Tank Army, which was waiting on the east bank of the Oder near Göritz, was to come forward and attack in the 8th Guards Army's sector, while the 2nd Guards Tank Army, which was also on the east bank opposite Kienitz, would attack in the 3rd and 5th Shock Armies' sectors, where even less progress had been made. A second 90-minute barrage, using all available resources was ordered for 1600 hours.[10]

This change of plan proved a most extraordinary tactical blunder, totally inconsistent with Zhukov's professional record, but he was under tremendous personal pressure from Stalin and seemingly fearful of his future. The original plan was for the already committed combined-arms armies to force breaches in the German defences to enable these tank armies to pass through and converge on Berlin in a classic pincer movement. It is difficult to believe Zhukov's later contention that this eventuality had been foreseen and allowed for in the preliminary planning.[11]

For instance, in the 8th Guards Army sector there was total disruption, confusion and chaos as the causeways were cleared to allow the tanks through, isolating the troops already engaged from their reserves, supplies and support, and the situation must have been much the same within the 3rd and 5th Shock Armies. The 1st Guards Tank Army, with no time for reconnaissance or preparation of any kind, including coordination with the 8th Guards Army, then played straight into the Germans' hands, taking tremendous casualties in its attempts to force the defiles. It thus made only a limited contribution to the success of the operation, which still depended upon the infantry achieving their objectives as originally planned.

However, a penetration was made with considerable sacrifice as far as Dolgelin railway station on the crest of the escarpment, where those tanks that had got through were checked on the line of the railway and turned north to link up by chance with a penetration at Ludwigslust later in the day. The latter penetration had been effected along a narrow cobbled track through the fields from Alt Tucheband, but was again checked and held by a company of the 'Brandenburg' Panzer Regiment counterattacking from Friedersdorf.[12]

On the 8th Guards Army's extreme right flank, where the 4th Guards Rifle Corps, supported by one of the 11th Tank Corps's brigades, was in action, the 47th Guards Rifle Division had a measure of success. With the 5th Shock Army moving up on their right, the confronting 20th Panzergrenadier and 9th Parachute Divisions had been forced to yield ground and the 4th Guards Rifle Corps was able to cut the roads from Seelow to Gusow and Buschdorf, as well as the north–south railway line, gaining a foothold on, but not taking, the escarpment above Werbig. The 1st Battalion of the 'Müncheberg' Panzer Regiment, which had been holding the line of the Haupt-Graben in front of Seelow all day and inflicting heavy casualties on the Soviet armour, was obliged to pull out for replenishment that evening, enabling the 57th Guards Rifle Division on the corps's other flank to attack Seelow railway station a quarter of the way up the slope. Unlike the other formations, the 4th Guards Rifle Corps was able to maintain momentum and by midnight had started infiltrating the town of Seelow, where fierce fighting continued throughout the night.[13]

Looking elsewhere at the overall picture at the end of the day, the 61st Army on the extreme northern flank had managed to establish a toe-hold bridgehead, while the 1st Polish Army had broken across the Alte Oder from the 47th Army's sector and taken the south-eastern third of its allocated sector as far as the Zäckerick railway bridge, but at considerable cost in its supporting frontal river-crossing assault. The 47th Army had advanced about five miles and taken Alt Lewin. The 3rd Shock Army had taken Alt Trebbin and Letschin, and was facing up to the Friedland Canal obstacle, while the 5th Shock Army had pushed the 9th Parachute Division back on Platkow and Gusow. The 69th Army had been involved in some furious fighting but strong counterattacks had deprived it of nearly all its gained ground by the end of the day. South of Frankfurt, the 33rd Army had taken Lossow, Brieskow and Finkenheerd.[14]

It is evident that at least at Front and Stavka level there had been a total failure to appreciate the true nature of the ground to be fought over. The constraints imposed by the boggy fenland leading to the slopes of the Seelow Heights being factors perhaps not so readily deduced from a study of the maps. In such a situation the usual mass of Soviet tactics were of little avail, and what was required, as Chuikov says, were small groups of fast moving infantry to probe and infiltrate the weaknesses in the enemy's defences. Thus Zhukov's clumsy use of his armour, when his combined-arms armies failed to conform to his unrealistic timetable, simply served to compound the basic error.[15]

Soviet accounts make much of the unexpected strength of the German resistance, but this appears to be presented as a distraction from the failure to appreciate the situation correctly, as indeed do some comments on the role of the artillery in this operation.[16]

The failure to appreciate the nature of the ground was in a large part due to the Russians being accustomed to operating in terrain in which they could manoeuvre freely in attaining their objectives, as was the case throughout most of European Russia. In consequence, unlike in most modern armies, the appreciation of ground was not even included in the basic factors considered when drawing up a battle plan.[17]

The air side of the operation had gone better during the afternoon, when flying conditions improved, and the 16th Air Army were able to put up 647 ground-attack, dive-bomber and fighter aircraft. Its radar installations gave good support in tracking the Luftwaffe's incursions with groups of between 15 and 30 aircraft at a time, and at the end of the day it was claiming to have destroyed 131 German aircraft for a loss of 87 of its own, most of which had fallen to anti-aircraft gunfire from the ground.[18]

These figures do not tally with German claims for that day, which were 150 tanks and 132 aircraft destroyed.[19] Although hopelessly outnumbered, the Luftwaffe had acquitted itself courageously that day in support of the ground forces. Despite the encroachments at Seelow, the Germans still stood a chance of holding on to their main line of defence, and they still had some reserves at hand. The overall Russian losses in manpower had been staggering and the breakthrough battle was by no means over.

At 1645 hours, the Chief of Operations of the 9th Army, Colonel Hans-Georg Eismann, passed the following situation report to the OKH:

> The big attack on the 9th Army, involving a very stubborn and bitter struggle, has developed into an extremely tense situation at three points:
>
> 1. South of Frankfurt
> 2. Southeast of Seelow
> 3. East-northeast of Wriezen

The general situation is as follows:

Although the 9th Army has committed the whole of its reserves in immediate counterattacks everywhere to eject the enemy where he has broken through, the Main Battle Line has not held in its entirety. Of all the reserves only the 25th Panzergrenadier Division has yet to be committed, and the way that the situation has developed means that it will have to be used for a counterattack.

Army Group has requested the release of the 18th Panzergrenadier Division to the support of the 9th Army. Army Group has decided to place this division in the area east of Müncheberg tonight in order to use it to prevent the enemy breaking through at Seelow.

In detail:

The enemy forces south of Frankfurt have less armoured support. At the moment the enemy have been thrown out of Ober- and Unterlindow (northeast of Wiesenau) and of Finkenheerd. The enemy have renewed the attack north of Finkenheerd, west of Brieskow and immediately to the south of the Margarethenschacht line of strongpoints. Malchow has been retaken, as well as the Küstrin Hills (The southern end of the Seelow Heights escarpment). At the moment Lossow reports that the enemy are attacking the Küstrin Hills again, south-westerly and north-westerly over the railway. The enemy have been ejected from the training area and fighting is still in progress. The front south of Frankfurt is still holding but the enemy have resumed the attack. Of this sector one can say that, without the commitment of further reserves, the situation is not promising.

The Fortress's eastern front has only been lightly attacked but behind Frankfurt the enemy has pushed in the front a little westwards towards the main road. We have retaken Schönfliess. The Main Battle Line is unchanged. Mallnow is in our hands and a strong attack by 40 to 50 tanks was repulsed here. In this sector the Main Battle Line has been fully put to the test.

Enemy artillery is now firing from our old front line. Strong armoured forces are attacking in the area west of Sachsendorf. The enemy have taken some high ground in the area east of Friedersdorf and on both sides of Ludwigslust. A counterattack by the 'Kurmark' Division is in progress but we have no news of the outcome. The main point of the attack is here. Strong columns of motorised forces have been observed approaching from the directions of Küstrin and Göritz, possibly heralding an attack by a tank army. The Heights near Werbig are in our hands and we are attacking Werbig station. Neu Werbig and several points along the railway line are still in our hands. The Main Battle Line bulges out a little near Amt Wollop, where a regimental position is holding out. The line runs on through Vossberg and Letschin station, but Letschin itself was taken by strong armoured forces. Westwards beyond here the situation is unclear; our impression is that only a few strongpoints are still holding out along the railway and the main road from Posedin to Barnim. A group of 40 to 50 tanks have been reported on the road from Barnim to Alt Trebbin. Herrenhof is under attack but the position there is not known.

In the 5th Light Division's sector all attempts to cross over have been driven back, with the exception of a bridgehead at Zäckerick. The perimeter of this bridgehead is not firm and is under attack. The local reserves of the division have stood up to a lot during the day, especially from heavy fire. At certain points they have undergone two and a half hours of heavy bombardment and concentrated fire. There has been a considerable expenditure of ammunition. Between 40 to 50, perhaps 60 tanks are attacking and aircraft are attacking in waves, currently also in depth.

Our own losses in armoured vehicles are not inconsiderable, especially with the XI SS Panzer Corps. Ammunition holdings are down to 54 percent of first line issues. The infantry and armoured troops have taken the most losses. Tomorrow will see the resumption of the attack, and our losses will be even heavier.[20]

From this report it can be seen that the Soviet main and secondary thrusts had been clearly identified by the defence, but the German shortage of reserves and fuel meant that they would not be able to provide the flexible response that the situation demanded. Everything now depended upon the ability of the troops already deployed to continue to hold out. Defence resources appeared adequate on the flanks, but the pressure on Seelow and Wriezen was a real cause of concern.

In contrast to what was happening on the 1st Byelorussian Front, Marshal Koniev's operation had gone very well on its first day, and his forces were now threatening to break through the German lines well ahead of Zhukov's.

The site chosen for the 1st Ukrainian Front's main attack was along an eighteen-mile stretch of the Neisse River, extending from astride the little town of Forst to just above the even smaller town of Muskau, and about fifteen miles from a roughly parallel stretch of the Upper Spree River between Cottbus and Spremberg. Both rivers were up to fifty yards wide in this sector, winding through narrow valleys whose sides climbed steeply to almost a hundred feet in the south but petered out into marshland in the north. The area between the rivers was almost entirely covered in dense forest cut by broad sandy rides, allowing easy passage for vehicles, but in the middle there was a large patch of open-cast mines, some of which were flooded. From the centre of the Soviet lines near Triebel the autobahn from Liegnitz led tantalisingly across the Neisse to Berlin via Forst and Cottbus, marred only by its blown bridges.

The 4th Panzer Army's defensive system consisted of three main lines, the first and third following the west banks of the Neisse and Upper Spree respectively, and the second extending between Peitz and Weisswasser to incorporate the open-cast mines.

Although the German defences were particularly strong in this area, crossing the Neisse further north would have led them into the Spreewald pocket and a complicated network of waterways forming an almost impenetrable barrier from Peitz to Lübben, but here all three lines of defence could be tackled in one short operation while the Soviet forces were still concentrated and had maximum artillery support.

The opening bombardment began at 0415 hours, smashing down on the initial objectives with the same ferocious intensity experienced on the Oder Front. The 2nd Air Army's 6th Guards Air Corps simultaneously began bombing the German rear areas and centres of communication.[21]

After the first 40 minutes the infantry then started across, swimming, floating, rafting and boating, under a flat trajectory hail of heavy machine-gun and artillery fire aimed at the west bank. By 0515 hours the first bridgehead had been secured and the engineers were working with frantic haste to ferry across tanks and self-propelled guns to support them, even dragging some 85mm guns across the river bed by cable.[22]

These crossings were effected under cover of a dense smokescreen, for which the climatic conditions happened to be ideal. It was laid and maintained by fighter aircraft over a distance of 240 miles in order to confuse the enemy for as long as possible. As this smokescreen also obstructed the Soviet artillery observers, great pains had been taken beforehand to plot all possible targets and zero in the guns to them.[23]

After a deafening two hours and forty minutes the preliminary bombardment ended at 0655 hours, by which time 133 of the 150 planned crossings had been secured. The first echelon had taken only an hour to get across, and as soon as the bridgeheads were secured, the bridges followed. Light pontoon bridges were ready in fifty minutes, thirty-ton capacity bridges in two hours, and the sixty-ton capacity bridges for the heavy tanks in four to five hours, but the tanks to support the infantry were brought across much earlier by ferry. None of the tank armies' bridging capacity was used, as this was reserved for the Spree crossing.[24] The 3rd Guards Tank Army and the 25th Tank Corps were now fighting in and around Forst, the 13th Army in the centre near Bahren, and the 5th Guards Army with the 4th Guards Tank Corps around Köbeln, just north of Muskau. The air attacks on Forst had proved particularly effective in demoralising the defence and facilitating the work of the ground forces.[25]

The artillery was then switched to blasting swathes through the enemy lines for the troops to follow. Unfortunately the woods caught fire, creating an unexpected hazard for both sides alike, and a Russian general was killed when his vehicle ran into some German troops in the ensuing confusion.[26] The effect of these fires on flying conditions over the battlefield was such that the pilots could no longer see their targets, so the air support was diverted to the German third line of defence on the Upper Spree.[27]

The Luftwaffe was much weaker in this sector, but still did its best to counter the Russians, losing forty aircraft in thirty-three sorties that day. Towards evening German tanks were observed to be gathering near the third line of defence, so as soon as it was dark, formations of PO-2 bombers were sent to harass the concentrations at Cottbus, Gross Ossig, Neuhausen and Spremberg.[28]

The morning thus went quite well for the Russians, with the Germans reeling back stunned and confused, but in the afternoon General Gräser's 4th Panzer Army rallied and counterattacked in strength to slow the Russian advance, using tanks and motorised infantry. Among the forces committed were the 21st Panzer, 'Führer' Security and 'Bohemia' Panzergrenadier Divisions.[29] Koniev's reserves, the 28th and 31st Armies transferred from the 2nd Byelorussian Front, were still not quite ready for action, so, being anxious to maintain momentum, he decided that the following morning he would send in his two tank armies, whose leading brigades were already across the Neisse.[30]

Unlike Zhukov's precipitate decision to use his tanks ahead of schedule, Koniev knew that he was now engaged against the last of the 4th Panzer Army's reserves, and that by using the full weight of his armour to punch his through and over the Upper Spree he was accomplishing his primary objective of destroying the enemy forces south of Berlin.[31] The German V Corps on the northern flank was isolated in the Spreewald pocket, where it could easily be contained, and therefore posed no immediate threat. Koniev's southern thrust towards Bautzen was strong enough to deal with any problems likely to arise in that area and he could therefore feel confident in the outcome of this operation.[32]

The 17th was a day of hard fighting on both fronts, a day of attrition, with the marshals spurring their men on to even greater efforts, themselves spurred on by Stalin's caustic tongue. The slaughter was appalling, for again the tactics used were attacks in mass to overrun positions remaining after the preliminary barrages. On the 1st Byelorussian Front the manpower situation became so desperate that they were compelled to round up every available man from the rear services to send into the line as infantry.[33]

On the main line of attack the 8th Guards Army continued to exploit the advantage gained on the right flank to lever away at the Seelow defences, while at the same time attacking the 'Hardenberg-Stellung' fiercely all along its front. Seelow was penetrated, the Germans forced back on the right flank beyond Werbig and the breach at Ludwigslust deepened to Friedersdorf, but the German line from Dolgelin to Mallnow held fast.

The 5th Shock Army overran Gusow and Platkow, pushing the shattered 9th Parachute Division back. The situation was such that the OKW released its only reserve, the 18th Panzergrenadier Division, to the LVI Panzer Corps, and Heinrici sent his reserves, the SS 'Nederland' and 'Nordland' Panzergrenadier Divisions, to the aid of the 9th Army, where they were allocated to the XI SS Panzer and LVI Panzer Corps respectively. However, before they could arrive, changing circumstances caused both to be directed to the latter formation. In the meantime the pressure on General Weidling's LVI Panzer Corps Headquarters forced him to move it twice that day, losing contact with General Busse in the process.[34]

By evening the 3rd Shock Army had closed up to the Friedland Canal, the last water obstacle across its front before the Seelow Heights, and was preparing to attack the Metzdorf–Kunersdorf sector of the 'Hardenberg-Stellung' next day with the assistance of its integral 9th Tank Corps. Like the other combined-arms armies, it was now well behind schedule for, according to the master plan, it should have been two-thirds of the way towards Berlin by this stage.

Although the 'Hardenberg-Stellung' had been penetrated at several points, the day's results for the combined-arms armies was meagre in terms of ground gained, no progress had been made on the extreme flanks, and the tank armies remained impotently entangled with the infantry.[35]

With fog and low cloud reducing visibility to about 500 yards, the air forces were unable to play an effective part all day, although the Luftwaffe claimed to have destroyed two bridges across the Oder. However, the overall effect on the Germans was beginning to tell; casualties in men and equipment were mounting steadily and could not be replaced, and the repeated devastating bombardments were wearing down the survivors.[36]

Again Koniev's forces in the south had made better progress, both groups having smashed through the main line of defence and beyond. In fact by noon fighting was going on between and at all three lines of defence, with retreating and counterattacking enemy units and forest fires adding to the confusion on the ground. Nevertheless, determined leadership prevailed and the second line was penetrated early in the day in both the 5th Guards and 13th Armies' sectors, opening the way for the armour to push on to the Upper Spree with an eager Koniev following close behind. The 3rd Guards Tank Army found some unmarked fords and started crossing immediately. The 4th Guards Tank Army was turned back by heavy opposition further south and was then summoned downriver to cross by a ford adjacent to the 3rd Guards Tank Army; this was the kind of manoeuvre that Koniev was to repeat later in the battle, cutting his losses and reinforcing his successes without hesitation. Ferries and bridges were brought forward and put into operation with the utmost speed, and by nightfall the bulk of both tank armies were across and breaking out to the west and northwest.[37]

That evening when Koniev reported the events of the day over the radio-telephone, Stalin made the impractical suggestion that Zhukov's armour should be brought south to exploit the breach opened by the 1st Ukrainian Front, but Koniev was able to suggest that his armies make for Berlin instead. After a short deliberation, Stalin agreed but, significantly, failed to inform Zhukov of this important decision.[38]

The orders that Koniev produced that night in confirmation of his verbal instructions included the following points and show his determination to beat Zhukov into Berlin:

In keeping with the orders of the Supreme High Command, I order:

1. Commander 3rd Guards Tank Army: on the night of 17 Apr 45 the Army will force the Spree and advance rapidly in the general direction of Vetschau, Golssen, Baruth, Teltow and the southern outskirts of Berlin. The task of the Army is to break into Berlin from the south on the night of 20 Apr 45.

2. Commander of the 4th Guards Tank Army: on the night of 17 Apr 45 the Army will force the Spree north of Spremberg and advance rapidly in the general direction of Drebkau, Calau, Dahme and Luckenwalde. By the end of 20 Apr 45 the Army will capture the area of Beelitz, Treuenbrietzen and Luckenwalde, and on the night of 20 Apr 45 Potsdam and the south-western part of Berlin. When turning towards Potsdam the Army will secure the Treuenbrietzen area with the 5th Guards Mechanised Corps. Reconnaissance will be made in the direction of Senftenburg, Finsterwalde and Herzberg.

3. The tanks will advance daringly and resolutely in the main direction. They will bypass towns and large communities and not engage in protracted frontal fighting. I demand a firm understanding that the success of the tank armies depends on the boldness of the manoeuvre and swiftness of the operation.

4. Point 3 is to be impressed on the minds of the corps and brigade commanders.[39]

Meanwhile the 4th Panzer Army fell back to the third line of defence, concentrating its reinforcements at Cottbus and Spremberg, which had the only bridges along this stretch of the river capable of taking heavy tanks, but for which the Russians no longer had any requirement.

Hitler now decided that the situation called for offensive action and ordered Field Marshal Ferdinand Schörner to mount a strong attack with his Army Group 'Mitte' reserve from the area of Görlitz, with the object of smashing Koniev's subsidiary thrust and threatening the main thrust's communications in the flank. In conjunction with this, the 9th Army would provide the other half of the pincers to trap Koniev by mounting an attack southwards to meet up with them. Field Marshal Keitel, appreciating that the 9th Army lacked the resources to both comply with this instruction and hold on to its current positions, opposed the plan but was unable to prevent General Krebs, the Army Chief-of-Staff, from issuing the orders.[40]

Keitel had a theory that if the German defences could continue to hold out for three consecutive days the Russians would be obliged to call off their offensive. The 4th Panzer and 9th Armies were still holding firm and inflicting heavy casualties, giving reasonable cause for encouragement. There was even an air of optimism in the Führerbunker that night.[41]

The sound of the guns had been heard in Berlin since the attack began, but the population was so dulled by the effects of the incessant air raids and Goebbels's propaganda that its significance made little impression. For most people the struggle for existence went on in the usual state of resignation.

On the official side the preparation of defensive positions within the city was accelerated, barricades were hastily erected and the second category of Volkssturm called up and assigned to their posts. Additional rations were made available on an extensive scale and in some districts as much as 15 pounds of meat were issued per head. The newspapers continued to appear, but irregularly.

A French doctor described the atmosphere in one of the central districts on 17 as follows: 'No excitement, no groups talking on the streets, housewives queue in front of the shops, men go to work, the squares are full of children at play.'[42]

6

Breakthrough

On the morning of 18 April Marshal Rokossovsky's 2nd Byelorussian Front opened its offensive against General Hasso von Manteuffel's 3rd Panzer Army between Schwedt and Stettin two days ahead of the original plan and virtually off the march. This was a particularly difficult operation, involving the crossing of the east and west branches of the Oder, which were separated by a two-mile wide strip of flooded marshland bordered by dikes.[1] Under these circumstances the effectiveness of the artillery support was seriously reduced and it fell to the air forces to make up this deficiency.[2]

The initial phase of crossing the two branches of the Oder took two days to accomplish, so that it was not until 20 April that the Russians were able to come to grips with the German defences. Although this operation played no direct part in the taking of Berlin, it successfully prevented the 3rd Panzer Army from intervening in the main operation and contributed significantly to the final collapse of the German Armed Forces.

For the 1st Byelorussian Front 18 April was again a day of attrition, with the 8th Guards Army making most of the headway, although at great cost. Casualties, and the failure of the 69th Army to advance, caused Chuikov to drop off the 28th Guards Rifle Corps's two leading divisions to protect his open left flank while he concentrated the efforts of the 4th and 29th Guards Rifle Corps on the main axis astride the Seelow–Müncheberg highway, and the German defence was able to hold firm along the crest line Carzig to Dolgelin until midnight.[3]

Marshal Zhukov turned his attention to the north, where he ordered a dawn barrage on the Alt Friedland-Wriezen sector in support of the 3rd Shock and 47th Armies, whose performance so far had been disappointing. In the early hours the 79th Corps of the 3rd Shock Army, supported by 9th Guards Tank Corps of the 2nd Guards Tank Army, crossed the Friedland Canal and attacked the Kunersdorf and Metzdorf positions, a task that had originally been set for the evening of the 16th.[4] The southern wing of the 3rd Shock Army went on to storm the Heights, reaching the vicinity of Batzlow by the evening.

On the morning of the 18th the Germans surprised the Russians with a strong counterattack backed by the Luftwaffe outside Diedersdorf. As the leading tanks emerged from the village, creeping along nose to tail along the highway, they were met by a storm of fire from the 'Stein-Stellung' in what amounted to an ambush. The 39th Guards Rifle Division had to be brought out of the 8th Guards Army's reserve to called out to save the situation, but the Germans were not driven back until they had inflicted severe casualties.[5]

The depth and intricacy of the German defence continued to prevent the breakout or deployment of the Soviet armour, and the presence of the latter in the forward area remained a hindrance and embarrassment to the infantry, whose battle it was. The Diedersdorf episode must have registered this point with Zhukov, for that evening he issued the following orders, which provide an interesting insight into the problems confronting him at this stage:

1. All Army, Corps, Division and Brigade commanders will visit their forward units and make a personal investigation of the situation, viz:

    a. Location and nature of the enemy forces.

    b. Location of own units and supporting arms, and what exactly they are doing.

    c. Ammunition states of supporting arms and their fire control organisation.

2. By 1200 hours 19 Apr 45 units will be put into order, tasks clearly defined, cooperation between units organised, and supplies of ammunition replenished. At 1200 hours a combined artillery and air preparation will commence and the enemy then attacked in conformity with the artillery preparation, the advance being developed according to plan. Coordination of action in the 3rd Shock and 2nd Guards Tank sector will be the responsibility of the commander of the 3rd Shock Army, and in the 8th Guards and 1st Guards Tank Armies sector that of the commander of the 8th Guards Army.

3. A traffic control service will be organised forthwith to ensure strict order on the roads.

4. All transport vehicles of armoured brigades and corps and those of corps and brigade rear services will be immediately taken off the roads and put under cover. In future the mechanised infantry will move on foot.

5. In order to maintain coordination of action between the rifle divisions and tank brigades, the Military Councils[6] of the 3rd Shock Armies and 8th Guards Armies will have their own responsible officers with means of communication in each tank brigade of the 1st and 2nd Guards Tank Armies, and the 1st and 2nd Guards Tank Armies will have theirs in the rifle divisions.

6. All officers who have shown themselves incapable of carrying out assignments and have displayed lack of resolution will be replaced by able and courageous officers.

However, these orders were not received by the 8th Guards Army until the early hours of the 19th, and in fact several days were to elapse before an opportunity arose enabling the 8th Guards and 1st Guards Tank Armies to regroup and implement the coordinating instructions properly.[7] The coordinating instructions were long overdue and it is surprising that they had not been issued as part of the main battle plan, looking ahead to the street-fighting phase.[8]

Heinrici now sought to withdraw the 9th Army from its exposed position before it was completely cut off, and while it was still relatively intact, but Hitler could not see the situation in the same light and insisted that they remain on the Oder, refusing to countenance a withdrawal.[9]

The pressure on the 9th Army was now such that no attention could be given to Hitler's order to mount a southerly attack to the relief of the 4th Panzer Army. General Busse appealed for four of the Berlin battalions to bolster the defence of his line, which was agreed at the morning conference on 19 April. Von Oven, a Propaganda Ministry official, provided an interesting background to this decision in his diary entry for that day:

The battle of the Oder has reached a critical stage. The result of an offensive is usually determined on the third, fourth or fifth day. The Minister and his immediate entourage passed the day in a state of highly nervous tension.

The Minister keeps in constant telephone communication with General Busse. He has promised him every possible support and assistance he can give. For instance, as when Busse urgently requested a trained battalion from Berlin on the night of Tuesday/Wednesday (17/18 April). The railway as a means of transport would have been too slow, being under constant air attack, so the Minister immediately had a convoy of Berlin buses and other city transport assembled, and just a few hours later the required soldiers were in position.

On Wednesday (18 April), the third day of the battle, the situation became critical when the Soviets succeeded in gaining the strategically important Seelow Heights near Buckow, the so-called Märkische Schweiz. Our reserves went straight into a counterattack and were able to clear the enemy off the Heights. A new Soviet attack succeeded and the Heights changed hands repeatedly. The day ended in eventful, extremely violent fighting, costing both sides many casualties. The anxious question then arose: 'Would it be possible to stop the enemy in front of Berlin, or would it perhaps soon come to a fight within the Reich capital itself?'[10]

That evening the 8th Guards Army reached the line Trebnitz–Marxdorf, and on their right flank the 5th Shock Army reached the line Wulkow–Neu Hardenberg. Further north the 3rd Shock and 47th Armies were slowly making their way up and over the escarpment in the dogged fighting described by von Oven, and the 47th also enlarged its bridgehead north of Neu Lewin opposite Wriezen, the town being abandoned by the defence that evening. However the armies on the flanks were still unable to report any satisfactory progress.[11]

In general the situation was steadily improving for the 1st Byelorussian Front, despite the difficulties being experienced, the heavy casualties and the disappointing performances on the flanks. The combined-arms armies had all had a successful day and the German defences were crumbling rapidly before them. Achievement of the main aim in this phase of the operation – the opening of breaches to enable the breakout of the armour – could be expected at any moment, albeit three days behind schedule.

Meanwhile Koniev's armour was hastening towards the main objective. In accordance with the instructions to bypass towns and built-up areas and to avoid protracted frontal fighting, Colonel-General P.S. Rybalko's 3rd Guards Tank Army advanced 18 miles that day along its assigned Vetschau–Golssen–Baruth–Teltow axis from its start point on the Upper Spree, and Colonel-General D.D. Lelyushenko's 4th Guards Tank Army did even better with a 28 mile advance along its Calau–Dahme–Luckenwalde axis.[12]

Naturally the tanks commanders were concerned about their lines of communication, so Koniev pulled the 13th Army forward across the Spree to fill the widening gap on the right flank, leaving the 3rd and 5th Guards Armies to finish mopping up the area between the two rivers and to face up to some particularly fierce counterattacks on their flanks. However, by the end of this third day of fighting Koniev's Front could claim to have destroyed the best part of four enemy formations – the 'Brandenburg' Panzergrenadier, 615th Special, 342nd and 545th Infantry Divisions – that had been holding the sector, and to have destroyed 155 enemy aircraft. Casualties on both sides had been very heavy in men and material.[13]

On the northern flank the German V Corps was now isolated from the rest of the 4th Panzer Army in the Spreewald pocket and was obliged to swing round one of its divisions to cover the threat to its rear from the 3rd Guards Tank Army. What remained of the 4th Panzer Army was now concentrated in the two pockets centred on the fortified towns of Cottbus and Spremberg, on which the 3rd Guards and 5th Guards Armies respectively could now turn their full attention.

The subsidiary thrust further south had also been very active that day, taking the fortified town of Niesy in the morning and then being struck by the flank attack of Army Group 'Mitte' which pushed it back some two miles off course before it was able to resume progress towards Bautzen.[14]

That same day, 19 April, Berlin saw its second influx of refugees of the year with sad columns streaming in from the south and east, this time from towns and villages abandoned nearby. Some of the city's inhabitants also started to depart discreetly to seek shelter elsewhere. The roads around the capital were filling with people on the move, their precious belongings loaded on farm carts, bicycles, prams, and pushcarts of all kinds, making it difficult for military and other official traffic to get through.[15]

Goebbels's concern over events on the Oder Front is shown in von Oven's diary entry for that day:

Next morning, Thursday 19 April, the Minister held a telephone conversation with Colonel Hölz, Chief-of-Staff of the 9th Army, who asked for at least four battalions from the Berlin defence to save the important threatened situation at Buckow.

From this the Minister approached the basic question of whether Berlin should be defended on the Oder or in the city itself. If the view is that the Russians should be struck on the approaches to Berlin with the assistance of the forces that have been prepared for the defence of the capital, then he is resolved to strip Berlin of troops completely. However, he is against sending only four battalions if Busse does not use them, as this would imperil the defence of Berlin.

Feverish conferences begin. The Commandant of Berlin, General Reymann, says that the Berlin Defence is so weak that he cannot be answerable for the despatch of four battalions. This statement shows him to be a defeatist and lacking in courage, and he should be replaced by a younger, more aggressive officer.

Nevertheless, every level-headed and sober-minded person knows that he is right. The Berlin SA-Führer, Graentz, who is responsible for the Volkssturm, shares Reymann's opinion. All that we have available in Berlin is the Guard Regiment, 30 Volkssturm battalions (only partly armed) and some police, Flak and Hitlerjugend units of little account.

Should the 9th Army's request for four battalions be agreed, the question of the defence of Berlin will be decided with it. The Minister does not want to bear the responsibility alone. He therefore asks General Burgdorf, Hitler's Chief Adjutant, to get the Führer's decision on this matter right away.

The question was raised at the briefing on Thursday (19 April) and Hitler decided on strengthening the Oder Front. That is how the dice have fallen. If the enemy is not stopped in front of Berlin, the Reich capital will fall into their hands more or less without a fight.[16]

That morning, 19 April, Marshal Zhukov resumed the offensive with his combined-arms armies, which were now beginning to feel the effects of the prolonged and intensive breakthrough battle. In conformity with his orders of the night before, the 8th Guards Army launched an attack on the line Dahmsdorf–Münchebeg–Behlendorf at 1030 hours after 30 minutes of heavy artillery and aerial bombardment. The troops eventually succeeded in clearing a way through the last of the 9th Army's defences to allow the 1st Guards Tank Army to break out on the main axis. A subsidiary thrust to the south reached as far as Fürstenwalde before it could be held and driven back. The 5th Shock Army completed the rout of the 9th Parachute Division and broke through the last line of the defence near Buckow.[17]

Complementing this success, the 3rd Shock Army tore through the last of the CI Corps's defences to clear a passage for the 2nd Guards Tank Army, while the 47th Army circumvented Wriezen. Three of the 1st Polish Army's divisions then passed through the town to take up the pursuit to the west, their arrival north of the town assisting the two other divisions to force the Alte Oder and the 'Hardenberg-Stellung' behind.[18]

The LVI Panzer Corps was forced to withdraw westwards along a twelve-mile front open at either end, but exacting a heavy toll from the pursuing armour, in this phase alone accounting for 118 of the 226 tanks that the 9th Amy claimed to have destroyed that day. Back at the Führerbunker the collapse of the 9th Parachute Division was cited as yet another Luftwaffe failure, causing Göring to react by dismissing the Parachute Division's commander, General Bruno Bräuer, and replacing him with Lieutenant-Colonel Harry Herrmann. This was done under the calumnious pretext that Bräuer had suffered a nervous breakdown when he requested twenty-four hours to regroup the shattered remains of his command. Herrmann was promoted to full colonel on the 20th.[19]

Although the original plan had been for the 2nd Guards Tank Army to provide the northern armoured pincer enveloping Berlin, a complete change of plan was found to be necessary, the three component corps being allocated individually to the three combined-arms armies in that sector. The 9th Guards Tank Corps now had the task of pushing straight through to the Havel in support of the 47th Army, the 1st Mechanised Corps was to assist the 3rd Shock Army, and the 12th Guards Tank Corps the 5th Shock Army. The reason for this decision was no doubt the exhausted state of these combined-arms armies following the hard fight to break out of the bridgehead. It is clear that the armour set the pace for this next phase of the operation, with the combined-arms armies keeping up as best as they could.[20]

With this group went some airfield construction and service units from the 16th Air Army who were to secure the airfields at Eberswalde, Werneuchen and Strausberg.[21]

This fateful day left a breach nineteen miles wide in the 9th Army's lines from Wriezen to Behlendorf. The remains of the CI Corps, with its southern flank and rear suddenly exposed, was obliged to withdraw into a bridgehead around Eberswalde, south of the Finow Canal, thus opening the way westwards for the 61st and 1st Polish Armies.[22] Severed from this northern group, and also from the LVI Panzer Corps, which now constituted the army reserve and was fighting its own rearguard action as it screened Berlin, General Busse's command was reduced to the remains of the XI SS Panzer Corps, the Frankfurt Garrison and the V SS Mountain Corps, still trying to hold on to their original positions. With Hitler's instructions to hold firm on the Oder, Busse was forced to adopt an all-round defensive position, initially extending his northern flank through Lietzen, Heinersdorf and Fürstenwalde, and moving his headquarters into the Spreewald, where thousands of civilians were already seeking refuge among his units in the woods and marshes. That night the V Corps, consisting of the 21st Panzer, 35th SS Police Grenadier, 36th SS Grenadier, 275th and 342nd Infantry Divisions, was transferred to his command from the 4th Panzer Army in a logical regrouping.[23]

With Hitler's permission, the eastern suburbs of Frankfurt-an-der-Oder were abandoned to the Russians so that Colonel Biehler's garrison could concentrate on defending its positions around the main part of the city on the west bank.[24]

During the course of the day General Busse made an urgent appeal for the Berlin forward defence line to be manned by whatever forces were available as a fall-back position for his collapsing front. Consequently, General Reymann was ordered to despatch ten Volkssturm battalions and a flak battalion of the 'Grossdeutschland' Guard Regiment from his meagre resources forthwith.[25] These reinforcements were again rushed forward in commandeered buses and taxis reminiscent of the Battle of the Marne. Von Oven wrote in his diary for the 20th:

> The situation deteriorated during the night. The Minister was in lively, earnest telephone conversation with General Burgdorf, saying that the reinforcement of the Oder Front with four battalions was simply not enough and that the Führer must now decide finally whether to despatch all the Berlin forces to the Oder Front. No doubt he also realises that should the 9th Army's Front be broken, quite clearly the 9th Army could no longer be counted upon defending Berlin.
>
> The Führer's replay arrives early in the morning. It is that Berlin is to be defended outside the city boundary. Immediately all the soldiers available in Berlin are to be sent to the Front in convoys of buses standing by. Our warmest wishes go with them.[26]

By the end of this fourth day of fighting the Russians estimated that they had destroyed over 400 German aircraft and were confident that the Luftwaffe would now pose no problem during the attack on Berlin itself.[27]

Meanwhile Koniev's tank armies, backed by 75 percent of the 2nd Air Army's aircraft, continued to make steady progress northwards, although not fast enough to satisfy Koniev, who was still hoping to get into Berlin ahead of Zhukov. Apart from a few local Volkssturm units, there were no troops around to oppose the Russians in this area and yet the 3rd Guards Tank Army, concerned about enemy forces on its right flank, made only about eighteen miles on 19 April in comparison with the thirty-one miles made by the 4th Guards Tank Army.[28]

The 5th Guards Army with the 4th Guards Tank Corps continued clearing the Upper Spree defences, crossing the river and completing the encirclement of the Spremberg group. The 3rd Guards Army were having a difficult time, being still under attack both in the Forst area and around Cottbus on the Spree defences, but was able to contain these attacks and steadily improve its own position without having to commit its reserves.[29]

In order to protect the 3rd Panzer Army's southern flank from the threat posed by the Russian breakthrough, Heinrici decided to use SS-Obergruppenführer (Lieutenant-General) Felix Steiner's III 'Germanic' Panzer Corps Headquarters, which commanded the 3rd Panzer Army Reserve. He therefore ordered Steiner to move his headquarters forward to near Eberswalde and to take over the remains of the CI Corps and the 25th Panzergrenadier Division, with the task of holding the line of the Finow Canal. To supplement these meagre resources, Heinrici ordered the 3rd Naval Division to come down by rail from Swinemünde on the Baltic coast, and also assigned Steiner the 45th SS Police Grenadier Division, which was supposed to be forming in the area. Finally, he added all the odd units he could find, including some Luftwaffe battalions, some emergency units formed from clerks and storemen, and some local Volkssturm units. Steiner was immediately concerned with extending his front westwards to keep pace with the Soviet advance on the south side of the canal, and in finding sufficient man-power to meet his task.[30]

The 19 April was the day that Hitler belatedly decided to make Army Group 'Weichsel' responsible for the defence of the capital by placing the Berlin Defence Area under its command. Heinrici immediately assigned the Area to the 9th Army, but General Busse argued the point and the order was rescinded, the Berlin Defence Area remaining directly under Army Group Headquarters. However, with the 3rd Panzer Army preparing to face up to the 2nd Byelorussian Front's offensive in the north, and the remains of the 9th Army coiling back on themselves in the south, the only resources left to deal with this commitment were the remains of the LVI Panzer Corps, already fully stretched and in imminent danger of losing contact with the formations on its flanks.[31] In Heinrici's opinion, Hitler's instructions for the 9th Army to remain on the Oder had condemned it to extinction, and he therefore decided to concentrate on saving the 3rd Panzer Army from a similar fate, in essence leaving the problem of Berlin to General Weidling's LVI Panzer Corps.[32]

As a means of compensating for the depletion of the garrison, the 'Friedrich Ludwig Jahn' RAD Division of Wenck's 12th Army was reassigned to the Berlin Defence Area, but no one in Berlin seemed to know where this division was, or what it consisted of, and such was the state of communications that despatch riders had to be sent out to find it. Eventually the divisional headquarters were traced to a village north of Trebbin and General Reymann set out to visit them.[33]

The threat to the capital that night was sufficiently serious for Hitler to authorise the evacuation of various government departments to take place the following night by road, involving the use of much valuable transport and fuel. Advance parties had already reconnoitred a route west and south through the territory occupied by Wenck's troops. However, the Propaganda Minister had no intention of joining this exodus and, that evening, seemingly ignoring the seriousness of the general situation, to which he made but passing reference, he broadcast his customary eulogy of the Führer on the eve of Hitler's birthday, just as he had done every year since 1933. Nevertheless, the Berliners were becoming increasingly uneasy as evidence of the true state of affairs percolated through to them.[34]

They had good reason, for Koniev's forces were approaching rapidly from the south against negligible opposition.[35] General Rybalko remained highly apprehensive about his 3rd Guards Tank Army's vulnerability to flank attack, and kept dropping off roadblocks to seal off the Spreewald pocket, much to the annoyance of Koniev, who sent him the following signal:

> Comrade Rybalko, you are moving like a snail. One brigade is fighting, the rest of the army standing still. I order you to cross the Baruth-Luckenwalde line through the swamps along several routes and deployed in battle order. Report fulfilment, Koniev.[36]

To deal with this threat to his communications posed by the Cottbus and Spremberg strongholds, Koniev concentrated 1,110 guns and 140 mortars in support of an all-out attack on Spremberg by the 5th Guards Army scheduled for 0900 hours that day. The 33rd Guards Rifle Corps assaulted the town itself, and the 32nd Guards Rifle Corps, in conjunction with the 4th Guards Tank Corps, attacked the defences north of the town, advancing some 12 miles beyond the Upper Spree. The third component of this army, the 34th Guards Rifle Corps, was strung out over the 37-mile gap between the front's main and subsidiary thrusts. Then, with Spremberg out of the way, Koniev went to see General Gordov of the 3rd Guards Army and ordered him to plan a similar assault on Cottbus for the next day, promising him heavy reinforcement with guns and aircraft. Meanwhile two corps of the 13th Army were following up behind his two tank armies, while the third corps sealed off the exits from the Spreewald pocket.[37]

With Koniev's exhortations urging them on, the 3rd Guards Tank Army succeeded in covering 37 miles on 20 April, taking Baruth during the course of the afternoon and almost reaching Zossen before disaster struck.[38] The leading brigade of the 6th Guards Tank Corps ran out of fuel and was then destroyed piecemeal by Panzerfausts.[39]

This occurred close to the 'Maybach' bunker complex, where the bulk of the OKW and OKH had anxiously been awaiting permission to evacuate all day. The camp guard company, together with six to eight tanks from the nearby Wünsdorf training establishment, had been sent to block the crossroads at Luckau. By 0600 hours that morning, however, they were already reporting being bypassed by Soviet armour, and by nightfall the ten survivors of this 250-strong unit were back in Zossen, apparently unaware of the cause of the delay in the Soviet advance. This, presumably, had been due to the intervention of a local Volkssturm or Hitlerjugend unit. Permission was then received from Führer Headquarters to evacuate but, before leaving, Lieutenant-General August Winter, Jodl's deputy, addressed the assembled staff on the occasion of Hitler's birthday and for the first time publicly admitted that the war might end badly for Germany. The staff then packed in such haste that there was no time to destroy any documents and equipment left behind, and the Russians were able to take over these comprehensive items intact next day, including the still functional 'Zeppelin' command signals bunker.[40]

That evening General Reymann returned to Berlin with the news that the 'Friedrich Ludwig Jahn' RAD Division, while still forming up on the parade-ground at the Wehrmacht's main ammunition depot that day, had been surprised and scattered by Russian tanks. Some of the men from two of the regiments had been saved but nearly all the artillery had been lost and the divisional commander, Colonel Klein, had been captured while trying to re-establish contact with the missing third regiment. Shortly afterwards Colonel-General Krebs telephoned instructions to send this division together with the 'Wünsdorf' Tank Unit to drive back the enemy spearheads approaching Berlin from the south. These Führerbunker orders, committing the remains of two badly shattered regiments and a handful of tanks that had already been destroyed to repulse two Soviet tank armies, Reymann could only ignore, and he ordered the survivors back to Potsdam.[41]

On the left flank the 4th Guards Tank Army came up against some resistance in the Jüterbog-Luckenwalde area but were still able to cover twenty-eight miles in daylight, and one group pushed on through the night for a further twenty-one miles until it reached the southern obstacle belt of the Berlin defence system.[42]

Meanwhile the centre and right of the 1st Byelorussian Front was also on the move. The northern flank force hastened to assume its role in support of the 2nd Guards Tank Army's thrust with the advancing combined-arms armies. In the centre the 1st Guards Tank Army moved cautiously ahead of the 8th Guards Army, only too well aware of the effectiveness of the hand-held anti-tank weapons liberally supplied to the German infantry and Hitlerjugend, which continued to exact a heavy toll.[43] In accordance with Heinrici's instructions, the LVI Panzer

Corps managed to delay the Russians along the city's outer defence line in a desperate bid to maintain contact with the 9th Army on its southern flank, but only briefly, being unable to cover the whole of its exposed front, which fell short of Werneuchen on the northern flank. Consequently, the 2nd Guards Tank Army had little trouble in overcoming the Volkssturm and Luftwaffe units deployed before it.[44]

The 1st Mechanised Corps pushed on as far as Elisenau, just south of Bernau, that day, and the 12th Guards Tank Corps formed up in the woods southwest of Tiefensee and attacked towards Werneuchen, Hirschfelde and Wegendorf, breaking through to Altlandsberg that night. Meanwhile the 32nd Rifle Corps of the 5th Shock Army took Strausberg, which was to house Marshal Zhukov's headquarters for the remainder of the operation. Neither the forward defence line, nor the obstacle belt, could check the Soviet advance.[45]

From Map 4 it can be seen how the armoured spearheads cleared the way for the combined-arms armies without heeding the planned boundaries. In similar manner the 4th Polish Infantry Division, operating on the southern flank of the 1st Polish Army, was to clear Bernau for the 47th Army next day, 21 April.[46]

Progress was sufficient on the 20th to enable the long-range artillery of the 79th Rifle Corps and the 1st Battalion, 30th Guards Artillery Brigade, of the 3rd Shock and 47th Armies respectively to fire the first salvoes into the city perimeter in what was more of a defiant propaganda gesture than a tactical measure. However, railway engineer units were hard at work preparing the main line from Küstrin and the railway bridges there, which had been destroyed by the Luftwaffe on the 17th, to take some heavy siege artillery captured in the Crimea that could fire shells weighing half a ton each.[47]

Colonel-General Heinrici spent most of the day personally trying to restore order in the Eberswalde area, where there was utter confusion among the units scattered by the Soviet breakthrough. The belt of the woodland south of the Finow Canal was swarming with disorganised troops and by nightfall he had established some form of front along the line of the autobahn, although it could be regarded only as a temporary expedient. He appealed to the OKH for troops to hold the line of the Havel between Oranienburg and Spandau as a fall-back position and was allocated the 'Müller' Brigade, consisting of a few understrength infantry battalions from the Döberitz Training Area, for this purpose.[48]

The 2nd Byelorussian Front had started its assault across the west branch of the Oder with an hour-long artillery and aerial bombardment that morning, but it was bad flying weather with poor visibility, much to the advantage of the defence. Only General Batov's 65th Army managed to establish a bridgehead of reasonable size that day, the 49th and 70th Armies making little progress in what were extremely difficult circumstances.[49]

Hitler rose at 1100 hours on 20 April and throughout the day received congratulatory calls from his court on the occasion of his 56th birthday. Among those who came to pay tribute to their Führer were Goebbels, Grand Admiral Dönitz, Speer, von Ribbentrop, Göring, Axmann and Himmler, as well as members of his staff, such as Field Marshal Keitel, Generals Jodl, Krebs and Koller, and the diligent Bormann. At one stage in the afternoon he climbed the steps to the Chancellery garden to review a parade of Hitlerjugend who had distinguished themselves in the recent fighting and air raids. He shook hands and patted the cheeks of the youngsters before the cameras in this, his last public appearance, but left the distribution of awards to his subordinates.[50]

At noon the Americans joined in the salutations with a 1,000-bomber raid lasting two hours and conducted from such a height that the city's flak could not reach them. To Keitel, Dönitz and their wives watching from a garden in Dahlem, it seemed as if the silver bombers were on parade, dropping their bombs in perfect unison. Berlin was left stunned and silent in its desolation, the gas, electricity and sewage services disrupted yet again and water now available only from the street pumps, so that queuing for water in the open was to become a necessary hazard for survival during the rest of the battle. After the bombers had gone, some low-flying 'Mosquitoes' of the Royal Air Force pestered the flak defences until dusk, when the Red Army Air Force made a short raid. That night the British made their last attack on the city and were followed in the morning by a final attack from the American 8th Army Air Force. From then on the sky above Berlin was to be dominated by the Russians.[51]

During the afternoon of 20 April Field Marshal Keitel's private aircraft took off from Tempelhof with his wife, Frau Jodl, Lieutenant-General Winter and Dr Rudolf Lehmann, head of the OKW's legal department, bound for Prague, where a staff car was waiting to take them on to the Obersalzberg. The aircraft was back in Berlin by the evening, awaiting instructions for the anticipated evacuation of other Nazi leaders.[52]

The last big war conference took place in the Führerbunker at 1600 hours that day, and was attended by all the dignitaries assembled for Hitler's birthday. It began with the usual briefing on the war situation, Krebs covering events on the Eastern Front for the OKH and Jodl covering the rest for the OKW. It was a gloomy account at best, with the Russians and Americans closing in from east and West, the British about to enter Bremen and Hamburg in the north, and the Allied armies in Italy already in the Po Valley. They all looked to their Führer for guidance.[53]

From arrangements made ten days previously, when an advance party had been sent to Bavaria to prepare the Berghof for Hitler's arrival, it was generally expected that he would leave Berlin either that night or the following.[54] At the conference Göring, Goebbels, Himmler, Bormann and Krebs all urged Hitler to leave the city before it was too late, but he gave no positive response. Instead he repeated his instructions of 14 April to the effect that, in the event of Germany being split in two, separate commands would be established in the north and south to continue the struggle under Grand Admiral Karl Dönitz and Field Marshal Albert Kesselring respectively.[55] On this occasion he formally transferred authority over the armed forces in the north of Dönitz, but omitted to do the same for Kesselring in the south, which led them to believe that he still intended taking command of the mythical 'Alpine Redoubt' himself. He went on to authorise von Ribbentrop to try and open negotiations with the Anglo-Americans, using Sweden as an intermediary, unaware that Himmler had already begun private talks with Count Bernadotte on these lines, using Jewish lives as his bargaining point.[56]

Having taken their leave of Hitler, the Party elite, armed with special passes, began making their exodus from Berlin by road and air, their staff cars mingling with the trucks loaded with files and office equipment from the various government departments on the move. Grand Admiral Dönitz headed north for Plön to establish his headquarters there.[57]

Himmler went to his castle at Ziethen to continue his treasonable plotting,[58] and Speer went to Hamburg, where he secretly recorded a speech with the connivance of the city Gauleiter, Erich Kaufmann. The speech was to be broadcast in the event of the death of either himself or Hitler, and was in fact broadcast on 3 May, exhorting the people not to despair, but to keep going and salvage as much as they could. Kaufmann's complicity in this matter resulted from his disillusionment with the Party leadership following Hitler's refusal to visit the city and commiserate with the survivors after the terrible air raids of July 1943, in which 30,000 inhabitants died and three-quarters of the city was destroyed.[59]

Göring made a final call at the Führerbunker at 0100 hours to say farewell and then was caught in an air raid on his way to the Luftwaffe Headquarters at Werder, outside Potsdam, and was forced to take cover in a public shelter, where his relief at being able to get away expressed itself in good-humoured jokes against himself. At the Luftwaffe Headquarters in Werder he met up with the convoy of trucks carrying the personal treasures he had saved from 'Karinhall', his favourite residence on the Schorfheide, just north of Eberswalde, before blowing it up.[60]

He then left the headquarters compound at the head of his convoy in such haste that he did not even bid farewell to his saluting Chief-of-Staff, Lieutenant-General Karl Koller, who, together with Major-General Eckhardt Christian at the Führerbunker, was to represent him in his absence.[61]

That night 713 bombers of the 18th Air Army and Po-2s of the 16th Air Army bombed German positions north and northeast of the city, softening them up for the advancing ground troops.[62]

The state of the troops after the prolonged fight for the Seelow Heights obliged Marshal Zhukov to review his plans for the encirclement of the city.[63] The 3rd Shock Army, which he had intended to use for the arc from Bernau to Spandau, was now assigned a far smaller segment in the northeast. The 47th Army, whose original role had been to cover and expand the operation westwards from the Havel, was reinforced with both the 7th Guards Tank Corps from the 2nd Guards Tank Army and the 7th Cavalry Corps from his Front Reserve and given the additional tasks of securing Spandau and the airfield at Gatow. The remaining two corps of the 2nd Guards Tank Army were assigned to the northern sector of Berlin.[64]

Meanwhile General Busse was trying to cover the exposed northern flank of his truncated 9th Army as best as he could. The Soviet thrust towards Fürstenwalde threatened the rear of the 169th and 712th Infantry Divisions which, with the Frankfurt Garrison, were still trying to hold on to their forward positions. He had only the remains of the 'Kurmark' and SS 'Nederland' Panzergrenadier Divisions, the latter having been cut off from the LVI Panzer Corps in the battle for Müncheberg, to both cover his exposed rear, which hinged on the 156th Infantry Division's position at Lietzen, and to counter the Soviet thrusts on his front.[65] Inevitably the three infantry divisions began to reel back to the southwest as the situation rapidly deteriorated, with the Panzergrenadier divisions fighting to keep open the escape routes over the Spree at Fürstenwalde. In order to cover the line west of this point, part of the 32nd SS '30. Januar' Grenadier Division was pulled out of the line to establish a screen from Fürstenwalde to the Müggelsee along the Oder–Spree Canal/Spree River barrier.[66]

7

Encirclement

During the early hours of 21 April, a small nucleus of personnel from Zossen reported in by telephone from Wannsee in southwest Berlin and were directed to establish temporary headquarters for the OKH at the Luftwaffe Academy at Gatow, and for the OKW at the barracks at Krampnitz nearby. The main body headed south for the Obersalzberg and later in the day had the misfortune to be attacked by some of their own aircraft, who mistook the convoy for a column of Soviet tanks.[1]

On the morning of 21 April, the 2nd Guards Tank Army crossed the autobahn ring on the northeast side of Berlin, brushing aside the opposition, and advanced on the city along a broad front. The 12th Guards Tank Corps's component brigades advanced with the 48th Guards Tank Brigade on the Axis Mehrow–Ahrensfelde–Hohenschönhausen; the 66th Guards Tank Brigade on the axis Eiche–Marzahn; the 49th Guards Tank Brigade on the axis Eiche–Kaulsdorf; and the 34th Motorised Rifle Brigade swung around through Dahlwitz to attach through southern Kaulsdorf into Lichtenberg. A counterattack of battalion size supported by 12 tanks was beaten back at Hönow, and by the evening the 12th Guards Tank Corps and 32nd Rifle Corps of the 3rd Shock Army were firmly established in the suburb of Hohenschönhausen. Similarly, on their northern flank, the 1st Mechanised Corps reached the suburb of Weissensee with some other elements of the 3rd Shock Army.[2] The Soviet troops easily submerged the small pockets of resistance that had been set up in accordance with the original defence plan by local Volkssturm detachments. A witness from one of the outermost suburbs related:

> Twelve assault tanks appeared, flanked left and right by infantry, approximately one company, armed with submachine-guns and spraying the walls of houses whilst moving from door to door at the double. They were followed by anti-aircraft guns. Behind these assault troops came carts drawn by two or four horses, containing food and ammunition as well as loot.[3]

That evening the Soviet troops were briefed on the severe kind of fighting they could expect to encounter in the more densely built-up areas of Berlin, and preparations were made to adapt to this kind of warfare.[4]

It is not proposed to expound on the atrocities that followed the fighting. On this subject all accounts are agreed without exception: the ransacking of cellars and shelters, the summary executions, immediate looting and the rape of women, from young girls to the very oldest and the infirm, were a standard corollary to all the fighting in the city. These facts were known to all the defenders and in several accounts mention is made of the demoralisation caused when they heard the screams of women being raped at night. Ilya Ehrenburg had written in his manifesto to the Red Army:

> Kill! Kill! None of the Germans are innocent, neither the living nor those not yet born! Follow the advice of Comrade Stalin and wipe out the Fascist Beast in his lair for ever! Break the proud racial pride of the German women brutally! Take them in just revenge![5]

Although this policy had been revoked, it still represented the basic attitude of the Soviet soldier towards the German population.

The 8th Guards and 1st Guards Tank Armies, which were advancing westwards in the Rüdersdorf–Erkner area, now received orders to approach the city from the south and southeast. However, these orders took time to implement, for the troops were already fighting in built-up areas and it was not easy to extricate them. The nature of the terrain with the many lakes and waterways in this particular area not only helped concentrate the defence, but also channelled the lines of approach, while the built-up areas were seen to absorb troops like sponges.[6]

The LVI Panzer Corps had been forced back into the Rahnsdorf–Neuenhagen area by the Soviet advance, losing contact with its parent 9th Army in the process, and during the course of 21 April was obliged to withdraw even further to the line Köpenick–Marzahn. General Weidling's headquarters in Kaulsdorf apparently made no attempt to get in touch with the Führerbunker in accordance with the Führer-Order of 21 January,[7] although this should have been possible on the civilian telephone network. Somehow the rumour had spread that the corps had withdrawn to Döberitz on the western side of Berlin, and when General Busse and Hitler heard of it they both ordered Weidling's arrest and execution.[8]

Meanwhile Weidling was having disciplinary problems of his own with SS-Major-General Jürgen Ziegler, who was apparently piqued at finding himself under a Wehrmacht general and unilaterally wanted to extricate his SS 'Nordland' Panzergrenadier Division from the LVI Panzer Corps's left flank and rejoin Steiner's command. Weidling suspended Ziegler from duty, but he was able to resume command next day when Hitler ordered the division back into Berlin without reference to the corps commander.[9]

The extraordinarily chaotic atmosphere that prevailed at the senior German command level at this stage comes out quite clearly from the various exchanges recorded between senior officers on 21 April. Disruption of communications contributed to the chaos, but could not be held responsible for the air of fantasy and sheer lack of realism that dominated proceedings and were translated into decisions and orders, which were then enforced under penalty of death.

Before the noon conference Hitler formally placed SS-Major-General Wilhelm Mohnke in command of the central government area, which included the Reich Chancellery and Führerbunker. However, Mohnke's interest does not appear to have extended to the whole of 'Zitadelle' as originally foreseen in General Reymann's plan.[10]

At 1130 hours the Russian siege and heavy field artillery started shelling the city centre from the mass of railway sidings east of the Schlesischer Railway Station (today's *Ostbahnhof*). This shelling introduced a new dimension of horror and discomfort to life in the city. The fairly regular pattern of air raids, which hitherto had enabled people to go about their business between alerts, had ended. Shells arrived without warning, sending shrapnel tearing along the streets and creating havoc. More buildings collapsed, streets were torn up and old debris churned over by the force of the explosions. In the affected area, the central districts in particular, people were obliged to take to the shelters permanently, emerging only occasionally for vital supplies of food and water. Only the main flak towers had their own water supplies; elsewhere the plumbing had already been shattered by the bombing, the toilets no longer functioned and people had to relieve themselves wherever they could in the densely packed shelters, adding a nauseating stench to the already appalling conditions. For food and water people had to risk their lives queuing in the streets.

The solid fuel stocks at the city's power stations being almost exhausted, the authorities were obliged to shut down the factories to conserve enough electricity for lighting and essential services. Cooking by electricity was now forbidden on pain of death.[11]

When the firing started Hitler telephoned Lieutenant General Karl Koller at Werder asking the Luftwaffe to locate and destroy the guns concerned. He would not believe it when Koller reported back that the flak towers were already engaged with enemy batteries firing from the eastern suburb of Marzahn. The towers counted over 500 incoming shells that day, mainly from what they suspected were 152mm guns with a range of nine miles.[12]

That afternoon Hitler telephoned Koller again asking for details of Luftwaffe operations south of Berlin, but Koller could only reply that communications with the operational units were now so unreliable that they would have to wait until the next 24-hour report arrived to get the information. Shortly afterwards Hitler telephoned again to complain about the failure of some jet fighters to arrive from Prague. He was told that the German airfields were now so closely covered by enemy aircraft that it was often impossible to take off.[13]

Field Marshal Ferdinand Schörner arrived in Berlin that day in time for the afternoon war conference. He briefed Hitler on Army Group 'Mitte', whose counterattack against Koniev's southern group was delaying Soviet progress towards Dresden to such an extent that Koniev had sent his new Chief-of-Staff, Colonel-General I.E. Petrov, to put some more zest into the operation.[14]

Another caller during the course of this conference was General Walter Wenck, who came to report the XXXIX Panzer Corps's progress in the Harz Mountains, unaware that as he spoke it was being eliminated in the forlorn attempt to rescue elements of the 11th Army trapped there.[15]

During this conference Hitler looked for some means of stemming the Soviet advance. First he decided to pull back the LVI Panzer Corps into the city, not realising that it was already fighting on the city boundary, for it had been out of touch since 2000 hours the previous evening, and to get it to link up with Steiner's group in the north. He then seized on Steiner's name, for Steiner had conducted a successful counterattack against the 1st Byelorussian Front in Pomerania in February, and perhaps could do the same thing again. All available resources would be allocated to him, forming Army Detachment 'Steiner', which would mount an attack southwards from Eberswalde next day in conjunction with an attack northwards by the 9th Army, thus nipping off the head of Zhukov's advance. It was emphasised that the matter was to be pursued with the utmost vigour and that the Luftwaffe was to support the operation with every aircraft still capable of taking to the air. The orders to Steiner concluded:

> It is expressly forbidden to fall back to the west. Officers who do not comply unconditionally with this order are to be arrested and shot immediately. You, Steiner, are answerable with your head for the execution of this order. The fate of the Reich capital depends upon the success of your mission.
> Adolf Hitler[16]

None of those present dare raise any objections to this plan, and the next twenty-four hours were spent in frenzied activity. The bulk of the manpower came from the Luftwaffe, who found 12,000–15,000 men from the ground services in the northern region, regrouping them by their companies and battalions into larger formations under the command of Luftwaffe-General Johannes Stumpf. Other units were formed from cadets, railway troops, the Berlin Fire Brigade, police, Volkssturm and even convicts. Thus the manpower equivalent of about one and a half divisions was raised virtually overnight, but of course lacking the necessary training, cohesion, communications, heavy arms or equipment for the intended role. The Motor Transport Department was given the task of getting them into position but at first there was considerable confusion on this point, as Steiner's location and requirements were unknown to the Berlin-based organisers. Eventually Steiner was located at Oranienburg and the troops sent off to the Finow Canal, using fuel requisitioned from vital airfield supplies.[17]

In typical fashion Steiner received his orders direct from the Führerbunker, bypassing Army Group 'Weichsel' to which he was accountable. He was appalled at what was expected of him and the type of troops available for the task, and immediately telephoned Army Group Headquarters to report his dilemma. Of all the troops assigned to him, only those that Heinrici had previously transferred from the 9th Army were in any way capable of mounting a military operation. Moreover, the remnants of the 5th Light, 25th Panzergrenadier and 606th Infantry Divisions were already fully committed along the line of the Finow Canal and could not be redeployed until relieved by the 3rd Naval Division, which had been delayed by air attacks on the railways and had yet to arrive from the coast. The so-called 4th SS Police Division so far amounted to only two unarmed battalions.

When Krebs eventually briefed Heinrici on Steiner's mission by telephone, Heinrici took the opportunity of once more asking him to impress upon the Führer the urgent necessity of withdrawing the 9th Army from its present position without further delay. Zhukov's southern thrust towards Königs Wusterhausen had already isolated the 9th Army from the city, and should Hitler continue to refuse this request, Heinrici asked to be relieved of his command. He said that he would rather serve as a simple Volkssturm soldier than continue to bear the responsibility for ordering it to hold on any longer. Krebs merely replied somewhat stuffily that the Führer alone took responsibility for this order. Shortly afterwards Heinrici was informed that his Chief-of-Staff, General Eberhardt Kinzel, was to be replaced by a Major-General Thilo von Trotha, reputed to be a convinced Nazi, who had previously served under Heinrici in this capacity.[18]

That evening scouts of the 3rd Guards Tank Army reached Königs Wusterhausen from the south, thereby effectively completing the encirclement of the 9th Army, although as they were on the other side of the water complex from the 8th Guards Army, the troops of the two Soviet fronts remained unaware of the proximity of each other. The orders from Moscow were to have the 9th Army surrounded by 24 April,[19] so Marshal Koniev ordered forward the balance of the 28th Army to seal off the Spreewald pocket in place of the 13th Army, which he wanted for other tasks. His orders to the 28th Army, which was allocated all the front's available transport for the move, included placing two infantry divisions in the Baruth area as a counterattack force in case of an attempted breakout. The screening force was to block off the exit routes with strong defences against tanks and infantry to thwart any possible breakout to the west or southwest. Koniev was highly conscious of the vulnerability of his main communications route, the Dresden–Berlin autobahn, to attack from the 9th Army.[20]

For his part, in compliance with Moscow's instructions, Marshal Zhukov moved the bulk of the 69th Army from its ineffective deployment on the Oder and despatched it together with the 3rd Army from his reserve to apply pressure on the 9th Army from the north, while at the same time protecting his southern flank. By the evening of the 21st the Soviets had a bridgehead across the Spree west of Fürstenwalde in the area where part of the 32nd SS '30. Januar' Panzergrenadier Division was hastily trying to establish a defensive screen.[21]

General Busse's Spreewald concentration also became a focus of attention for Air Marshal Novikov, who devoted a large part of his resources from the 2nd, 16th and 18th Air Armies to the harassment of the 9th Army pocket around the clock, with as many as 60 to 100 aircraft at a time.[22] The night of 21 April over 700 aircraft from the 16th and 18th Air Armies attacked targets in the northern outskirts of Berlin in preparation for the 2nd Guards Tank Army's operations the next day.[23]

With the 9th Army were tens of thousands of refugees from the eastern provinces who had been camping out in the woods since their arrival during the winter, their numbers now augmented by inhabitants of the combat zone that had fled their homes. Although there was sufficient food for everyone, communications rapidly deteriorated, and troops and civilians became hopelessly mixed in their predicament. Ammunition and fuel were in particularly short supply, and when the artillery ran out of shells on the 21st, General Heinrici advised General Busse to find some means of disengaging from the enemy and to forget Hitler's orders about holding on to the Oder.[24]

At 2030 hours Hitler called Lieutenant General Koller to say that the 'Hermann Göring' Division stationed at 'Karinhall' was to be sent to the front at once. From 'Karinhall' Koller established that in fact only one battalion of the division remained there. When he reported this to Hitler, he was abruptly told to assign the battalion to Steiner's command and then he was cut off. At this stage Koller knew nothing about either Steiner or his mission, although presumably Major-General Christian had represented the Luftwaffe at the meeting in the Führerbunker when Hitler had issued the relevant orders. Koller therefore telephoned the 'Hermann Göring' Division (presumably a rear headquarters in its barracks at Tegel, now the *Julius-Leber-Kaserne*), and obtained an outline of the plan with the information that Steiner had last been seen at Schönwalde that afternoon accompanied by only one staff officer.[25]

Koller then tried to get information from the Führerbunker, eventually contacting Krebs. While he was asking where he was to despatch the men he was supposed to be mustering for Steiner, Hitler broke into the conversation with:

'Do you still doubt my orders? I thought I had made myself quite clear. All Luftwaffe forces north of the city are to join Steiner and take part in a ground attack. Any commander that holds his men back will pay for it with his head within five hours. You are responsible with your life for seeing to it that every last man gets into battle!'

Krebs then added that the attack would be from Eberswalde southwards and that Koller was to throw in every man he had.[26]

Next Koller telephoned the OKW to see if it had any more information to offer but it had none, promising to contact him as soon as it had found Steiner, who was believed to be based upon Oranienburg.[27]

Then Colonel von Below, Hitler's Luftwaffe Aide-de-Camp, called with orders for air activity to be concentrated on the gap in the 4th Panzer Army's line between Cottbus and Spremberg, and for the 'Spremberg' Unit to be supplied by air. Once again no one knew exactly where or what the 'Spremberg' Unit was.[28] In fact, the 5th Guards Army had completed mopping up the Spremberg area that day, and within twenty-four hours the 3rd Guards Army, with powerful air support, was to do the same to the Cottbus pocket.

At about midnight Koller spoke with Hitler again, saying that he could not possibly air-supply a unit whose location was unknown, and then went on to say that the Luftwaffe men he was assembling for Steiner's operation were both untrained and insufficiently armed for ground combat. Surprisingly Hitler did not take umbrage at these remarks, but expressed optimism about the outcome of the operation, adding: 'You will see; the Russians are about to suffer the bloodiest defeat of their history at the gates of Berlin!'

Eventually, uncertain what to do for the best, Luftwaffe contingents were sent to both Oranienburg and Eberswalde in the hope that at least some would arrive at the right place at the right time.[29]

The 22 April began with a distinct aura of optimism in the Führerbunker. Hitler kept asking for news of Steiner's attack, but there had been a total disruption of communications over the past twenty-four hours and any news that did arrive was uncertain and contradictory.[30]

At 1100 hours General Heinrici telephoned General Krebs to say that unless the 9th Army was allowed to withdraw it would be split in two by nightfall. This time his words must have had some effect, for at 1430 hours Krebs telephoned back with permission for the Frankfurt-an-der-Oder Garrison, whose commander, Colonel Biehler, had been conducting a most successful defence, to abandon the city and fall back on the 9th Army, thus allowing some adjustment to the latter's overextended disposition.[31]

At this stage the 9th Army's northern flank was still firm from Frankfurt to a bridgehead north of Fürstenwalde. From there it followed the line of the Spree to a point north of Prieros, where it cut down to a chain of lakes, with strong roadblocks across the Berlin–Frankfurt autobahn. On gaining control of the V Corps, General Busse had immediately ordered it to leave only a light screen in the Neisse positions and to establish a line of defence from Lübben to Halle. He had also taken its 21st Panzer Division under the direct command of his Army Headquarters and sent it to establish a line of defence along the chain of lakes between Teupitz and Königs Wusterhausen, but it had since been driven back to the other chain of lakes between Teupitz and Prieros, where it was able to hold out against further attacks.[32]

Hitler's orders for the 9th Army, which were received by Heinrici at 1720 hours, were to hold on to the existing line from Cottbus to Fürstenberg, and from there to curve it back to via Müllrose to Fürstenwalde. At the same time a strong front was to be established between Königs Wusterhausen and Cottbus, from which repeated, vigorous and coordinated attacks in cooperation with the 12th Army could be made on the deep flank of the enemy attacking Berlin from the south.[33]

However, General Busse had already started making preparations for the breakout suggested by General Heinrici. The re-disposition of the V Corps was part of this plan. As soon as the Frankfurt Garrison withdrew into his lines, the V Corps and V SS Mountain Corps would start a simultaneous withdrawal from their Oder–Neisse positions in two bounds back either side of Friedland to the line Straupitz–Beeskow – the junction of the Spree and Oder–Spree Canal.[34]

Meanwhile Steiner, as he had explained to Army Group Headquarters the previous day, as yet had no means of implementing Hitler's ambitious instructions and remained primarily concerned with meeting his initial commitment of covering the 3rd Panzer Army's southern flank. The pressure from Zhukov's northern flank group and its air support caused him to evacuate his own headquarters northwards out of Oranienburg during the day, when the town suddenly became part of the front line. Not only did he have to concern himself with the defence of Oranienburg but also with preparations for the extension of his right flank westwards along the Ruppiner Canal, for, although the town had some natural strength as a defensive position, the promised 'Müller' Brigade had failed to appear from Döberitz, and the line of the Havel south of the town remained unmanned.

Marshal Zhukov naturally expected the Havel to prove a major obstacle in the path of his northern encircling thrust. His northern flank group, having recovered from its bad start, was pushed hastily forward to keep abreast of this thrust and to support the main crossing with diversionary attacks in its own sectors. Spearheaded by the 9th Guards Tank Corps and the 47th Army's 125th Rifle Corps, the armoured thrust led through Zepernick, Schönlinde, Mühlenbeck and Schönfliess, then on to the bridge at Hennigsdorf. Meanwhile the 1st Polish Army had cleared the centre strip between Wiesenthal and Bernau, its 4th Infantry Division having taken Bernau to ease the 47th Army's passage, and passed on to close up to the canal in front of Oranienburg. The 61st Army on the extreme northern flank cleared the south side of the line of the canals, but also had to contain the bridgehead at Eberswalde, and two minor ones at Zerpenschleuse and Kreuzbruch.[35]

On the night of 22/23 April, supported by artillery, rocket-launchers and bombing attacks from the air, the 1st Polish Army attacked Oranienburg and the 61st Army attacked across the Oder–Havel Canal between Friedrichsthal and Kreuzbruch. Much to its surprise, the main crossing at Hennigsdorf by the 47th Army met with only light resistance and the armour was able to cross the bridge there without much difficulty. This spearhead was closely followed by the 7th Guards Cavalry Corps, which was to be used extensively in the scouting role in the next phase of the operation.[36]

Steiner was under considerable pressure around Oranienburg and was forced to commit the two newly arrived battalions of the 3rd Naval Division to assist in the defence of the town. These two units were the only ones to get through from the coast and Steiner had hoped to use them to release his combat-experienced troops at the eastern end of the line, which he badly needed if he was to mount the counterattack demanded by Hitler.[37] A member of the Oranienburg Hitlerjugend described his experiences a few days later:

> Our leader and the police fetched us from our homes and we had to assemble in the SS barracks and the Schlossplatz. Then we were divided up by our companies and attached to the SS and the Volkssturm. We first saw action to the northeast of the town. Most of us were killed by infantry fire because we had to attack across open fields. Then the fighting in the town; two days of it. In two days and two nights Oranienburg changed hands four times. That finished off another part of us. Then the Russians started bombarding the town with Stalin-Organs, and when we wanted to give up and go home, we were stopped and made to join the escape over the canal. My platoon leader, who refused, was strung up on the nearest tree by a few SS and an SA man, but then he was already 15 years old.[38]

Both the 3rd and 5th Shock Armies seem to have spent the day of 22 April preparing for the street-fighting role that was to follow. Their artillery shelled the city, but little attempt was made at further penetration. That evening, their shepherding role completed, the 2nd Guards Tank Army's 1st Mechanised and 12th Guards Tank Corps pulled out on a wide flanking march around the northern suburbs that brought them to their allotted sectors for the envelopment of the city as a united formation once more.[39]

The same day the 8th Guards and 1st Guards Tank Armies entered the south-eastern suburbs of Dahlwitz, Schöneiche, Fichtenau and Rahnsdorf, their leading elements getting as far forward as Friedrichshagen and Wendenschloss on either side of the Müggelsee. The enterprising 269th Guards Rifle Regiment of General Pankov's 88th Guards Rifle Division crossed two rivers that day, first swimming across the Spree to reach the peninsular between the Müggelsee and the Dahme that morning, then using boats found at Wendenschloss to cross the Dahme under cover of darkness to take Grünau and Falkenberg before dawn.[40] The resistance encountered north of the Müggelsee was minimal following the withdrawal of the LVI Panzer Corps, as was later related by one of the local forces:

> After the middle of February, Sergeant-Major Gümpel and ten men from the Field Replacement Battalion cadre of the Grüneheide Administrative Unit were made responsible for directing the construction of fortifications east of Friedrichshagen and to the north of the Müggelsee, a sector about three kilometres in width. Manpower was recruited from the local Friedrichshagen population and from workers in the local factories, as many as 500 workers a day being provided. A continuous trench was dug and permanent emplacements prepared. The construction of shelters was begun under the supervision of an expert from Friedrichshagen but none were completed before the fighting began. It had been planned to occupy the position with a force of 250 men, comprising elements of the Field Replacement Battalion and Volkssturm. With the approach of the Russians the force holding the position disintegrated and the position was left virtually unmanned. Only the battalion commander and about 25 men offered resistance. The defence was quickly overcome, after which Sergeant-Major Gümpel and his men were tasked with rounding up stragglers.[41]

General Weidling summoned his regimental commanders to a conference at corps headquarters in Biesdorf, where he told them that General Busse had threatened to have him shot if he failed to link up with the 9th Army, and Hitler had threatened him with the same fate if he did not go to the defence of the city. They all agreed that to go into the city would mean the end of the corps, and decided that they should try to hold on to their present positions in the south-eastern suburbs to enable the 9th Army to withdraw in their direction.[42]

Marshal Koniev's armour made rapid progress on 22 April, the lack of natural obstacles and a widely scattered and uncoordinated defence all contributing to their success. The southern obstacle belt and the scanty city perimeter defences with their Volkssturm and Hitlerjugend defenders were easily overcome, the tanks bypassing the barricades, infiltrating the built-up areas, silencing any resistance they encountered and pounding on down the main roads as fast as they could, supported all the while by powerful air-strikes, having completely outstripped their ground support.[43]

In the 4th Guards Tank Army's sector, the 5th Guards Mechanised Corps began forming a protective screen along the line Beelitz–Treuenbrietzen–Kropstädt, where it would be reinforced by the bulk of the 13th Army, whose 6th Guards Rifle Division reached Jüterbog that day. The 6th Guards Mechanised Corps reached Beelitz that evening and rested prior to pushing on further to link up with the 1st Byelorussian Front's 47th Army in the encirclement of the city, and to probing towards Brandenburg. On its right, the 10th Guards Tank Corps swept through Saarmund and Schenkenhorst to seal off the eastern approaches to Potsdam at Caputh and Babelsberg by the evening, and Army Headquarters were established in the village of Schenkenhorst.

The 3rd Guards Tank Army had fought throughout the previous night, forcing the Notte Canal near Zossen. During the course of 22 April it fanned out to advance on Berlin along a broad front. By evening the leading elements of the 7th and 6th Guards Tank Corps had reached the Teltow Canal at Stahnsdorf and Teltow respectively, while on their right the 9th Mechanised Corps, having crossed the autobahn ring at 0900 hours, was well into the southern suburbs of Lichtenrade, Marienfelde and Lankwitz by nightfall.

A French prisoner-of-war saw them arrive:

At midday on Sunday, 22 April 1945, the sky was a lovely cloudless blue and the sun bathed us in its spring warmth. A peaceful calm reigned in Stalag III-D-500, only broken by the familiar sounds of comrades preparing their food.

At about 1630 hours the first fighting started in our area. Six Russian aircraft circled and machine-gunned from a low altitude. No defence activity spoilt their evolutions during the 20 minutes of their appearance. Soon we could pick out quite clearly the crackle of machine guns or automatic weapons perhaps 10 kilometres south of the camp. Several German soldiers fled towards the city along the Berlin–Wittenberg railway tracks that passed close by. Then some bullets whistled over the camp.

The Volkssturm company based on the camp had left that morning. No German defence existed near us, except that some 500 metres away a tank buried up to its turret in the road beside a synthetic rubber factory assured some resistance. A section of young boys normally billeted at Lankwitz occupied the factory with the task of putting up a defence. Within a radius of three kilometres there were three of these tanks with only their turrets serviceable that could enfilade the streets with their anti-tank guns. Barricades made out of tree-trunks stacked one and a half metres high and one metre wide cut the roads leading into the city. One of these tree-trunk barricades was opposite our camp on the Heinersdorf–Lichterfelde road.

At about 1700 hours the first Russian appeared. He was walking straight ahead, stooped, and with his machine gun at the ready, advancing along the ditch bordering the road. He did not pay the least bit of attention to the camp,

I think that they were like that all along the front, with one man every 20 to 50 metres, each man in sight of the others.

I could not see more because of the bushy terrain. He passed our camp unconcernedly, then engine noises announced the presence of tanks nearby. When they reached the barricade several burst of machine gun fire were directed at the disinfection building belonging to our camp that was normally occupied by three Germans. This fire was not returned. The tanks went round the barricade, passing between the trees bordering the road and coming into our sight. There were two tanks of about 30 tons each, well rounded and of an imposing mass, each armed with a machine gun and a light canon. They were being directed by a Russian or Ukrainian prisoner-of-war sitting on the top. No shots were fired into our camp.[44]

A single Russian got down from one of the tanks, abandoning his advance, and interested himself in our camp, revolver in his hand. I led him to the German shelters, where only one sentry was on duty at the entrance. He dropped his rifle and raised his arms. The sergeant-major responsible for the Russian prisoners-of-war, who had lately shown himself full of solicitude for them, came out of the shelter bare-headed. No harm or hurt was done to them. The Russian ordered them to leave the camp. They left quite happily, but no doubt uneasily.

The gun in the German tank turret then fired two or three shells into the building that normally housed the Germans. One shell went into a window-frame, making a hole in the woodwork and breaking two or three panes of glass. Four Russians crept up cautiously, quickly spotted the turret, and in an instant set up three mortars in the ditch bordering the road and fired at top speed for five minutes.

Peace then returned. The camp gates were closed again and a guard placed to prevent anyone going in or out. The tanks followed the road closely without making a noise. They did not fire, nor did they meet with any resistance. Ten minutes later a light gun appeared in front of the camp drawn by a kind of jeep, something like one of our 37mm anti-tank guns. It did not intervene, and moved on again.

At 1730 hours we were liberated. About ten Russians at the most came into sight without bothering themselves about us. The French flag flew at the gate.

Until 1900 hours no further troop movements were seen. The first Soviet officer then appeared at the gate. Night was beginning to fall. He was dressed in black overalls and appeared to have come on foot, as no vehicle had stopped in front of the camp. He asked to see us and urged us to leave the camp, for the wise precaution that the number of Russian troops was insufficient to stop a German counterattack, and we stood the chance of being recaptured.

In this camp there were many Russian prisoners. All were quickly incorporated into the Soviet units and took part in the battle after simply being given a submachine gun or a rifle.[45]

The same sort of treatment was experienced in all the prisoner-of-war camps, the local knowledge of ex-prisoners being used to guide the combatants and, later on, the looters. As for the Western Allied prisoners, most were invited to leave the battlefield and head for camps further to the rear. This usually involved long journeys on foot before reaching the extremely badly organised repatriation centres.[46]

On the night of the 22nd Marshal Koniev ordered the 3rd Guards Tank Army to prepare to attack across the Teltow Canal on the morning of the 24th. To assist it in this operation he assigned it additional infantry in the form of the 128th Rifle Corps from the 28th Army and the artillery reserves from the 5th Guards Army, which were ordered to travel only by night to avoid detection. The artillery formations concerned were the 10th Assault Artillery Corps and the 25th Assault and 23rd Anti-Aircraft Artillery Divisions, while air support was to be provided by the 2nd Air Fighter Corps. In the meantime, the 3rd Guards Tank Army was to secure the suburb of Buckow on its right flank and to try and establish contact with the 1st Byelorussian Front, whose troops were expected in that area.[47]

Koniev had beaten Zhukov to the southern suburbs of Berlin, but he needed the day of the 23rd to amass sufficient strength for his attack on the city proper, which he intended supervising in person. A major threat to his lines of communication having been removed with the elimination of the Cottbus stronghold, the 3rd Guards Army was ordered to turn its attention to the western flank of the German 9th Army.[48]

The daily war conference in the Führerbunker took place at 1500 hours with only Bormann, Keitel, Jodl and Krebs in attendance. Shortly after it began, shells started landing in the area of the Chancellery up above. The generals drew out the meeting for as long as possible, but when Hitler realised that Steiner had not yet even issued orders for the attack he was supposed to have led that day, he flew into a terrible rage, raving about betrayal, cowardice, ignorance and corruption destroying all that he had done and planned for the Third Reich and the German people. Eventually he recovered sufficiently to declare his intention to remain in Berlin to the bitter end. All attempts to dissuade him failed, even pleas by telephone from Dönitz and Himmler. Finally he announced that he would remain with Goebbels and that everyone else could go. He stated that he would take personal charge of the defence of the city, saying: 'I order an immediate radio proclamation to the people of Berlin of my resolve to remain with them to the end, whatever may happen.'[49]

Hitler then withdrew to his private quarters, leaving the others to discuss the import of his decision with the rest of the staff. The whole affair had been so emotional that they found it difficult to assimilate, and now they had to make up their minds whether to leave or stay. Meanwhile Hitler telephoned Goebbels and invited him to move into the Führerbunker with his family. Goebbels agreed and they arrived soon afterwards by the tunnel that connected with the Propaganda Ministry across the street. They discussed the situation together and both Goebbels and his wife said that they would stay and commit suicide rather than be captured. Frau Goebbels added that she would first poison the children and remained adamant on this point, despite Hitler's protestations.[50]

Hitler then went through his papers. Those items he wished to preserve for posterity he had packed in metal boxes, and the rest were burnt by his Aide-de-Camp in the Chancellery garden. Meanwhile some 40 members of the Chancellery staff had decided to take advantage of the opportunity to leave for Berchtesgaden, and these, together with the documents, were assembled and driven out to various airfields around the city, from where they were flown out that night. This operation, organised by Hitler's personal pilot, General Hans Baur, was known as 'Seraglio'. Nine of the ten aircraft involved reached Munich safely, although the departure of one from Gatow was delayed by the baggage handlers scattering the luggage all over the tarmac in protest against this privileged evacuation. The aircraft carrying Hitler's documents crashed, killing all but the rear gunner.[51]

At 1900 hours, Hitler summoned Keitel and Jodl for another conference at which he formally announced his intention of committing suicide in the event of the city falling to the Russians, and rejected all their protestations. Accustomed to the immovability of his decisions once they were made, they then asked for his final orders, but Hitler replied that he had no further orders to give them and referred them to the Reichsmarschall. This dismayed them, for not only did this statement constitute an abdication of his authority and responsibility with regard to the Armed Forces still fighting elsewhere, but they were fully aware that Göring was now generally regarded as an object of ridicule. When they told Hitler that no one would fight for Göring, Hitler commented that it was no longer a question of fighting, but of negotiation, for which Göring was best suited.[52]

However, Hitler had not given up all hope, for, prompted by his generals, he then turned to his maps and began discussing possible means of saving the situation. It was agreed that the 12th Army had nothing to fear from the Americans, who clearly had no intention of crossing the Elbe, and therefore could afford to turn its back on the river and march to the relief of Berlin. Simultaneously, the 9th Army could send its strongest division westwards to meet up with the 12th Army, mopping up any enemy formations encountered on the way, and then make a joint thrust on the capital. Field Marshal Keitel would deliver the orders to General Wenck in person, while Jodl would see to the organisation of the OKW staff in Krampnitz in preparation for their move to Plön, where they would serve both Dönitz and Hitler. General Krebs would remain as Hitler's military adviser. The conference broke up at about 2000 hours.[53]

At about 2300 hours SS-Lieutenant-General Professor Karl Gebhardt, Himmler's personal physician and his nominees for the vacant post as head of the German Red Cross, arrived at the Chancellery to receive confirmation of his appointment. He brought with him the offer of Himmler's 600-man guard battalion, which Hitler gladly accepted, assigning them to the 'Zitadelle' force. Gebhardt then offered to arrange the evacuation of the remaining women and children from the bunker, but Hitler said that all those now remaining were doing so of their own free will.[54]

Hitler's decision to assume personal command of Berlin's defence relieved Army Group 'Weichsel' of that responsibility, and Goebbels took advantage of this opportunity to have General Reymann, who he regarded as somewhat lacking in spirit, removed from his appointment to take command of the Potsdam Garrison and to have a Colonel Ernst Kaether appointed in his place. Kaether had made a name for himself as a regimental commander on the Eastern Front and had since held the appointment of Chief-of-Staff to the Wehrmacht's chief National Socialist Officer, or political commissar. However, Kaether's appointment was to be brief.[55]

Reymann left by car for Potsdam and found the Avus racetrack section of the autobahn crowded with vehicles of all kinds as people sought to leave the city by the only route still open to them. In the distance he could hear the sounds of tanks in action, and it was obvious that even this route would soon be closed. His command in Potsdam was called Army Group 'Spree', although it was no more than a weak corps of two divisions, including the remains of the 'Friedrich Ludwig Jahn' RAD Division. Helped by the terrain, for Potsdam is virtually an island surrounded by vast expanses of water connected by rivers and canals, Reymann was able to maintain an effective defence, even when completely surrounded and despite enemy penetrations into the town itself, until 28 April, when an avenue of escape was opened for the garrison by the 12th Army.[56]

One of the people to leave Berlin that day was Beate Uhse, then a Luftwaffe captain in an air delivery squadron, who had flown into Gatow the day before in an Arado 66, with the object of rescuing her 2-year-old son and his nanny from their home in Rangsdorf. However, when she returned to Gatow with them, she found that the Arado had been destroyed. Fortunately, she then encountered an aircraft mechanic she knew, who told her of a twin-engined 5-seater aircraft belonging to some general that was in a hangar there. She managed to persuade the colonel in charge of the airfield to let her have some fuel for it to enable her to return to her squadron at Barth, and flew out at 0555 hours that morning with her son, the nanny, mechanic and two wounded soldiers, arriving safely at Barth an hour later.[57]

8

Siege Preparations

The night of 22/23 April marked an important stage in the development of the battle, when both sides found themselves obliged to reappraise the measures required to deal with the situation. The Russians had had their first experience of what the next phase of the operation would entail and needed to reorganise their forces accordingly. Belatedly the Germans had to adapt to the implications of a siege.

In the city Goebbels's propaganda efforts produced a noticeable stiffening of the defence.[1] To back up his words, teams of Feldgendarmerie, police and SS, assisted by Party members and cadets for the police and SS schools, set up roadblocks in the suburbs and city centre to check for deserters and to prevent the population from fleeing. They also searched cellars and shelters, querying the identities of the occupants and arresting suspects. Some civilians became so afraid of these visits and the possibility of being accused as accomplices that they even refused shelter to wounded combatants. Those unfortunate enough to be found wanting usually received a short parody of a trial, and were promptly hanged from a nearby lamppost and adorned with labels such as:

'I have been hanged because I was too much of a coward to defend the Reich capital.'
'I was hanged because I was a defeatist.'
'I was hanged here because I did not believe in the Führer.'
'I am a deserter; because of this I will not see the change in destiny.'
'All traitors will die like this one'.

However, these measures still did not prevent several thousand deserters from going into hiding until they were found and taken prisoner by the Russians.[2]

Goebbels appreciated that the people needed more than just exhortations and discipline to keep going, so his staff were tasked with providing something upon which they could base their hopes. It was thus decided to treat the announcement that General Wenck's army was marching to the relief of Berlin as an accomplished fact, and tracts addressed to Wenck's troops were deliberately released in Berlin, as if in error, with the following text:

Führer's Order of 23 April 1945

To the Soldiers of Wenck's Army!

An order of immense importance has removed you from your combat zone facing the enemy in the west and set you marching eastwards. Your task is clear. Berlin must remain German. The objectives given to you must be achieved whatever the circumstances, for operations are in progress elsewhere to inflict a decisive defeat on the Bolsheviks fighting for the capital, and from this the situation in Germany will change completely. Berlin will never capitulate to Bolshevism!

The defenders of the capital have found renewed courage with the news of your rapid progress, and are fighting with bravery and determination in the certainty of soon hearing your cannon. The Führer has summoned you, and you have gone forward into the attack as in the days of conquest. Berlin awaits you! Berlin encourages you with all the warmth of her heart.[3]

This hope in Wenck's army, and the news that Hitler was directing the battle in person, gave heart to many and was the theme for newspaper articles that continued to appear until the 28th. Encouragement also came from outside the city: a British correspondent based in Sweden reported in the *Daily Mail* of 24 April a broadcast by Radio Hamburg:

'Hitler is with you!' (repeated several times) 'Hold out, Berliners! The reserves of the Reich are on their way. Not just the reserves of a fortress, but the reserves of our great Reich are rolling towards Berlin. The first reinforcements arrived in the early hours of today, anti-tank gun after anti-tank gun, tank after tank, rumbled through the streets in long columns. The troops that man them understand the gravity of the hour.'

Then came a report by a front-line reporter:

'Approaching Berlin I can see the huge fires in the centre and hear the boom of the Russian artillery. Grenades and shells whistle through the air. Flames light up the night. The guns are rumbling in this hellish battle. Our Führer is under shellfire!'

'Up, Berliners, and rally round the Führer!' shouted another spokesman. 'As a tower of strength he is amongst us at this critical hour in the history of the Reich capital. Those who desert him and his city are swinish cowards!'

Said another speaker: 'Berlin trusts the Führer! Berlin fights on, though the hour is grave!'

With words and effects such as these, the population and the soldiers were encouraged to continue their resistance to fate at the behest of leaders who had long since lost any contact with reality. Even Field Marshal Keitel, who was to spend the next few days touring the battle area, visiting units and headquarters, attempting to organise and encourage relief operations, remained insensible and impervious to the evidence before his own eyes as to the truth of the situation.[4]

Keitel reached General Wenck's headquarters in the woods east of Magdeburg with some difficulty at about 0100 hours on 23 April. He first briefed Wenck on the general situation as he knew it, and then gave him Hitler's orders for the 12th Army. Keitel waited for Wenck to draft out his orders, as he wanted to take a copy with him back to the Führerbunker, and he also wanted to deliver the orders for General Karl-Erik Koehler's XX Corps, which was to provide the bulk of the attacking force. At dawn he reached one of its divisions, which was already preparing for the operation, and addressed the assembled officers.[5]

What Keitel failed to realise was that Wenck, unlike his immediate superiors, had formed a very clear appreciation of the situation and had no illusions about the future, which he saw as a simple choice between captivity in either the east or the west. There was no doubt in his own mind which was the preferable, and he regarded his primary task as that of holding the door open for a general exodus from what would become the Soviet Zone of Occupation. He was already doing all he could to facilitate the passage of refugees through his lines, including giving them food. He therefore interpreted his instructions as enabling him to attempt the rescue of some of the thousands of men and women trapped with the 9th Army and helping them to escape across the Elbe with his own troops. He certainly had no intention of allowing his forces to become engulfed in Berlin in pursuit of a hopeless cause.[6]

Wenck was fortunate in that many supply barges from all over the country had been trapped and stranded in his sector, so that he had no shortage of supplies, including motor fuel. Although he had dutifully reported this, no attempt had been made by the OKW to have this windfall redistributed.[7]

Keitel went on to call on Lieutenant-General Rudolf Holste, whose XXXXI Panzer Corps, being the weakest of Wenck's formations, was to be detached from the 12th Army to continue surveillance of the line of the Elbe west of Berlin. However, during the course of their discussion, Holste agreed with Keitel that the Americans apparently had no intention of crossing the river.[8]

By 1100 hours Keitel was back in Krampnitz, where he conferred with Jodl and had a brief rest before they set off to return to the Chancellery together. At the afternoon war conference Keitel reported on his trip to Hitler, and Krebs announced that the 12th Army was already on the move. Hitler asked if the 9th and 12th Armies had established contact yet, but there was no information available on this point and Krebs was directed to tell the 9th Army to get on with it. Before leaving, Keitel again tried to persuade Hitler to leave Berlin, but without success.[9]

This conference clearly illustrates the air of fantasy in which Hitler and his staff operated, and which Keitel did nothing to dispel. He must have been fully aware that neither army was ready to act immediately, and yet he said nothing to this effect. In fact Wenck did not expect to be ready until the 25th, by which time his formations would be redeployed for the attack and he hoped to have recovered some of his armour from west of the Elbe to assist him. In the meantime he was acutely conscious of the threat from the southeast, where the 1st Ukrainian Front was making rapid progress in his direction.

When Keitel and Jodl returned to Krampnitz there were rumours of Russian cavalry patrols heading south across the Döberitz Training Area. Much to Keitel's annoyance, the camp commandant had already ordered the destruction of the vast ammunition dump containing Berlin's reserves in his charge but for which there were no guards available. Keitel set off westwards to see what he could do to expedite the relief operation, and shortly afterwards Jodl was obliged to evacuate the OKW Headquarters to one of Himmler's bases at a camp hidden in the woods at Neu Roofen, a small village between Rheinsberg and Fürstenberg about 50 miles to the north of Berlin and behind the still relatively intact 3rd Panzer Army.[10]

Keitel found Wenck still trying to recover some of his armour from west of the Elbe, and his other units hastily preparing for the forthcoming offensive. At midnight on 23 April Keitel was back in Holste's headquarters, where he gave orders for the XXXXI Panzer Corps to ignore the Elbe front and concentrate on protecting Wenck's northern flank in his drive on Berlin.[11]

In the meantime some reinforcements had got through to the city, although by no means on the scale or with the equipment indicated in the Radio Hamburg broadcast. Grand Admiral Dönitz even had a battalion of sailors flown in from Rostock, but they turned out to be trainee technicians taken off a radar course, equipped only with rifles and with no idea of infantry work. Nevertheless, they were allocated to 'Zitadelle' and assisted with the defence of the Reichstag.[12]

Presumably it was at this stage that orders for blowing the city's bridges were issued. Not all the bridges were destroyed immediately, some being retained as reserve demolitions, such as the Frey Bridge on the Heerstrasse and the Mussehl Bridge over the Teltow Canal, but access from one part of the city to another was severely curtailed. As Speer had warned, the blowing of these bridges also disrupted the surviving main service arteries, the most serious being the consequent lack of drinking water at a time when the air was constantly filled with smoke and dust.

Some wagons of arms and ammunition that had arrived by rail during the previous two or three days were unloaded by civilian labour and distributed among the population on Goebbels's orders amid considerable confusion. The Volkssturm units of the inner districts were kept busy improving their fortifications.[13]

The northern and eastern suburbs were evacuated as far as it was possible and the inhabitants willing but, as the last escape routes were cut off to the west, the refugees had to find shelter elsewhere in the city as best they could. Among them were deserters from the Volkssturm and Wehrmacht looking for civilian clothes and a place to hide until the fighting was over. The streets became lined with military vehicles, trucks, field-kitchens, ambulances, gun-limbers, etcetera, all mixed up with farm-carts and even prams abandoned by the refugees. All were immobilised through lack of fuel or the disappearance of their owners.[14]

Dr Hans Fritsche, a senior radio commentator who was to become involved in the surrender negotiations a few days later, described the scene:

> One could already see many shell craters on the Unter den Linden, and as one went further eastwards the noise of battle increased. Fresh debris and broken electricity cables littered the dead streets. Here and there some women threaded their way along, sheltering from building to building, whilst little groups ran alongside the walls clutching their wretched belongings.
>
> Even Alexanderplatz was empty and abandoned, except at the entrance to the big concrete shelter, which was packed tight with human buildings. A member of the Volkssturm, wearing a brassard but without a rifle, told me that the shelter could take several hundred people, but was in fact packed with thousands of them living in intolerable conditions.
>
> Further off the sounds of battle resounded and fires flared in the dusk. In Danziger Strasse there were only two soldiers armed with Panzerfausts, but the adjacent streets were littered with destroyed vehicles and the bodies of dead soldiers and civilians.[15]

The possibility of the enemy infiltrating by means of the U-Bahn and S-Bahn tunnels had been considered at the Führerbunker, and orders had been issued stopping traffic through these tunnels on the 21st so that barricades could be set up at various points. As the lines ran under the Spree and the Landwehr Canal, consideration was also given to the deliberate flooding of these tunnels as a defensive measure. The SS staff responsible for 'Zitadelle' took over the plans and control installations, and began their preparations for flooding in an altercation with the railway engineers, who were primarily concerned with the thousands of people sheltering in the tunnels and underground stations. There were also four hospital trains filled with wounded and their attendants, and another four trains reserved for civilian casualties, parked in the S-Bahn tunnel between Potsdamer Platz and the Unter den Linden. One civilian engineer tried to stop the boring of holes for demolition charges near the Spree embankment and was shot for his pains.[16]

The LVI Panzer Corps moved across the Spree and the southern branch of the Teltow Canal during the night of 22/23 April into the suburb of Rudow. Sometime on the 23rd telephone contact was re-established with the 9th Army Headquarters and General Weidling spoke to the Chief-of-Staff, Major-General Artur Hölz, who gave him orders to secure the 9th Army's northern flank. From another source Weidling learnt that a general had been sent to Döberitz to arrest him on Hitler's instructions, so he tried to contact Krebs for an explanation. Eventually he was summoned to report to the Führerbunker at 1800 hours, where he saw Krebs and General Burgdorf, who received him most coolly at first, but once they had heard his account they agreed to put his case to the Führer immediately.[17]

Weidling then told them that he was moving his corps south towards Königs Wusterhausen that night in support of the 9th Army in accordance with General Busse's instructions, but Krebs said that these orders would have to be cancelled, as the LVI Panzer Corps was needed in Berlin. Weidling saw Hitler shortly afterwards and was shocked by the latter's appearance and obvious deterioration. When he emerged from his interview, Krebs informed him that, with immediate effect, he was to take over the defence of the south-eastern and southern Defence Sectors 'A' to 'E' on the arc Lichtenberg–Karlshorst–Niederschöneweide–Tempelhof–Zehlendorf.[18]

Weidling therefore decided to set up his command post in the administrative buildings at Tempelhof Airport and ordered his formations to disengage from the enemy and redeploy as follows:

1. 9th Parachute Division to Lichtenberg ('A').
2. 'Müncheberg' Panzer Division to Karlshorst ('B').
3. SS 'Nordland' Panzergrenadier Division to Tempelhof ('D').
4. 20th Panzergrenadier Division to Zehlendorf ('E').
5. 18th Panzergrenadier Division in reserve just north of Tempelhof Airport.
6. Corps Artillery to concentrate in the Tiergarten.[19]

All but the 'Müncheberg' Panzer Division, which was caught up in a fierce tank battle in Rudow, were able to disengage and redeploy as instructed during the night of the 23rd/24th. Then at 1100 hours the following morning Weidling was summoned to the Führerbunker once more and told by Krebs that he had so impressed the Führer the previous evening that it had been decided to appoint him overall Commandant of the Berlin Defence Area forthwith. Major-General Hans Mummert of the 'Müncheberg' Panzer Division would relieve him as Corps Commander.[20]

Weidling's request to have sole authority for the issue of orders for the defence of Berlin was ignored; he would be directly responsible to the Führer. Consequently the same profusion of orders emanating from Hitler, Goebbels and other lesser Nazi dignitaries was to continue to confuse the conduct of the defence. In any case it was too late to rectify the damage already done by the muddled system of command. The Sector Commanders were now fully involved with the enemy and, for lack of coordinating instructions, had to decide for themselves how to utilise their severely limited resources. They simply did not have the manpower to implement the full concept of General Reymann's original plan. Some tried to hold on to the perimeter and interim strongpoints, while others fell back rapidly to positions covered by canals or the inner defence ring. In all cases they were handicapped by poor communications both vertically and laterally. This was further aggravated by the difficulties of movement now that many of the bridges had been blown, and the streets were under shellfire and no longer being cleared of debris, so that for a messenger to travel a few hundred yards could sometimes take hours.[21]

Weidling moved to the Berlin Defence Area Headquarters on Fehrbelliner Platz and tried to appraise the situation in which he now found himself. He decided that his first priorities were:

1. To re-site his headquarters more centrally, either at the Zoo Flak-tower or at Bendlerstrasse. He eventually chose the latter for its proximity to the Führerbunker, and the overcrowding of the former.
2. To use his corps's communications units to bolster the defence communications system.
3. To augment the Berlin Defence Area Headquarters staff with officers from his own corps's staff.
4. To completely reorganise the Defence Sector staffs.[22]

The staff responsibilities were then split between two Chiefs-of-Staff. Colonel Theodor von Dufving of the LVI Panzer Corps being responsible for all military matters, and Colonel Hans Refior for liaison with the civilian authorities as a natural continuation of his previous role as Chief-of-Staff to the Defence Area Commander.[23]

It is not possible to establish exactly what forces Weidling has at his disposal with his new command, as no one had the chance to take stock. However, rough estimates place the strength of the LVI Panzer Corps as 13,000–15,000 men at this stage, the equivalent of two divisions, the Waffen-SS forces under SS-Major-General Mohnke as half a division, and the remaining miscellany of units as equating to some two to four divisions, a total of four to five divisions in all, with about 60,000 men and some fifty to sixty tanks.[24] Of this force only the LVI Panzer Corps formed a cohesive and reasonably equipped entity, the component formations now being as follows:

1. 18th Panzergrenadier Division, which was still relatively intact under Major-General Josef Rauch.
2. 20th Panzergrenadier Division, which was severely reduced and whose commander, Major-General Georg Scholze was to commit suicide a few days later.[25]

3.   'Müncheberg' Panzer Division, of which only one-third survived the Rudow battle to take part in the defence of the city.

4.   9th Parachute Division under Colonel Harry Herrmann, which had taken considerable punishment in the battle for the Seelow Heights and was now severely reduced in effectiveness.

5.   SS 'Nordland' Panzergrenadier Division, which was still in reasonable shape, although its commander, SS-Major-General Joachim Ziegler, was proving troublesome and would shortly be replaced.

For artillery, Weidling had at his disposal the surviving integral units of these formations, the city's flak batteries, and some locally raised units under the garrison's artillery commander, Lieutenant-Colonel Edgar Platho. The local artillery consisted of seven light and seven heavy batteries of foreign guns manned by Volkssturm and soldiers of all arms, but few experienced gunners, and a further six batteries of German guns which Platho had had assembled from dismantled exhibits in the local ordnance training establishments.[26] The foreign guns were limited to about 100 rounds per battery and all the crews lacked training. Colonel Hans-Oskar Wöhlermann, the commander of the LVI Panzer Corps's artillery, who remained as Weidling's artillery chief, related:

In the afternoon I contact the artillery commander of the Berlin Defence Area, Lieutenant-Colonel Platho, who was stationed in a flak-tower. At the same time I inspected various strongpoints, a difficult task in that mass of debris, and also several batteries that had been placed in position in the meantime. Altogether four artillery regiments had been posted in the various divisional sectors of Berlin but, as far as I can remember, there were only some eight to ten motorised units. In addition we had the guns of our own four divisions and of the 408th Volks Artillery Corps, though what few guns we had left were almost useless for lack of ammunition. Had I not been born a Berliner and known the places like the back of my hand, I should have found it impossible to site the batteries in the very short time I had been given. As it was, I knew where to go without having to bother too much with the map. As most of our guns were low-firing there were not too many places to choose from; the Tiergarten and some of the larger squares, such as Lützowplatz, Belle-Alliance-Platz [now *Mehringplatz*], the Lustgarten, Alexanderplatz, etcetera, and the railway sidings between the Potsdamer and Anhalter Stations in the centre of the city. We also placed a few mortars on Belle-Alliance-Platz, Lützowplatz and Steinplatz, and guns on the railway tracks. Towards evening I visited a 15cm battery in the Botanical Gardens near my Berlin apartment.[27]

Shortage of ammunition was common to all units, supply being a matter of chance or relying on the ingenuity of the unit commander, although there were in fact ample supplies of standard German ammunition within the city. Large depots existed at three locations, one in the Jungfernheide Volkspark next to the Siemensstadt complex, one in the Grunewald near the War Academy construction site,[28] and one in the Hasenheide Volkspark next to Tempelhof Airport. The three main depots had been stocked to 80 percent capacity before the fighting and measures taken to secure the stocks against dissipation to other fronts. On the approach of the Russians two-thirds of the Jungfernheide depot's stores were evacuated to the Grunewald but, in the event, all three depots were soon overrun.[29]

The miscellany of units on the ground meant that the Soviets were able to bypass the more effective units, isolating them and reducing them at leisure, and it was later noted that they seemed to pick on the weaker Volkssturm units for attack, although it was in fact Party policy, and widely practised, to mix the different types of combatants into composite units. Nevertheless, Weidling kept his LVI Panzer Corps units intact for use on the 'fire brigade' principle.[30]

For the Russians, adjustment to the new circumstances mainly entailed reorganising their forces for the street-fighting role, and the coordination of the various arms into combat teams in the style previous tried out by the 8th Guards Army. It was decided to utilise the artillery resources left over from the initial breakthrough phase of the operation to augment the integral artillery formations, allowing the divisional and corps artillery to be split into small detachments and allocated to individual combat teams, while the army and front artillery took over the counter-bombardment role and harassed the central districts.[31]

A particular problem arose in the joint 8th Guards Army and 1st Guards Tank Army sector as they entered the street-fighting phase. Marshal Zhukov's orders of 18 April concerning cooperation had not yet been fully implemented for lack of opportunity, but now suddenly units of the two armies found themselves chaotically entangled with each other in the narrow streets and something had to be worked out quickly. Although they appear to have cooperated efficiently thereafter, the relationship remained somewhat strained, and it obviously could not have been easy for one army commander to subordinate himself to the other without some feeling of resentment that would have continued down the chain of command.[32]

In order to facilitate air support, Air Marshal Novikov established two control centres, the principal one being based on the headquarters of the 16th Air Army under the Deputy Commander, General S.A. Senarov, east of Berlin, and a secondary one in the north under General B.K. Tokarev, responsible for controlling the ground-attack operations. All air units and individual aircraft operating over Berlin had to keep in touch with these centres and could only attack targets with their permission. There was such a pall of smoke hanging over the city that these measures were imperative. Observers stationed on the rooftops directed the aircraft to their targets with the aid of radio, light and rocket signals.[33]

The combat teams that were organised generally consisted of a platoon of infantry, one or two tanks, some sappers, some man-pack flame-throwers, a section of anti-tank guns, and two or three field guns, usually 76mm but sometimes even 150mm guns or 203mm howitzers were used in this role when particularly strong positions had to be overcome. In this direct support role, the guns advanced with their combat teams, firing over open sights at ranges of up to 400 yards down the axes of the main streets. At these ranges the gunners inevitably took many casualties from infantry fire, and it was a particularly trying time for the artillery observers with the leading infantry, who frequently needed relief from the strain and fatigue of their role.

For the mass artillery the main problem was finding sufficient open space to deploy and operate from, and in some places the guns were packed so close together that it seemed their wheels must be touching. The Katyusha rocket-launcher units found a solution to this problem by detaching the launching frames from the truck beds and reassembling them on convenient rooftops. All these artillery concentrations were protected by a profusion of anti-aircraft guns.[34]

A pattern gradually emerged by which all the artillery combined in a massive hour-long bombardment of the day's first targets first thing every morning. This was first experienced at 0515 hours on 24 April and gradually increased in intensity as more guns were brought into play on subsequent days. At night the shelling did not actually stop but diminished considerably.[35] The effects of deliberate, concentrated and sustained artillery bombardment were particularly severe in comparison to that previously produced by Allied bombing raids, reducing building after building to swathes of churned-up rubble. Some of the avenues leading into the city centre became corridors of destruction as the Russian guns literally blasted a way through for their combat teams. As Colonel-General Berzarin of the 5th Shock Army was later to comment: 'The Allies dropped 65,000 tons of bombs – we fired 40,000 tons of shells in two weeks!' One of the German combatants related:

> Gradually we lost all human appearance. Our eyes burned and our faces were lined and stained with the dust that surrounded us. We no longer saw the blue sky; everywhere buildings were burning, ruins falling, and the smoke billowing back and forth in the streets.
>
> The silence that followed each bombardment was merely the prelude to the roar of engines and the clank of tacks heralding a new tank attack.[36]

For several days the Soviet pressure on the city remained very uneven as the various formations closed in to take up their positions around the defence perimeter and adjusted themselves to the new fighting conditions.

9

Encirclement Completed

On 23 April the 3rd Panzer Army was still desperately holding on to its Oder positions, although hard pressed. It was obvious to Colonel-General Heinrici that General Hasso von Manteuffel's troops could not hold out much longer, and he was in fact planning their withdrawal to the other side of the Elbe to enable their surrender to the Western Allies. On the southern flank Steiner continued to hold the line of canals but the outflanking of Oranienburg meant that he had quickly to man the line of the Ruppiner Canal at the expense of the town, whose fall was imminent. Nevertheless, that day Heinrici received orders from Field Marshal Keitel, on behalf of the Führer, for Steiner to mount an immediate attack southwards to relieve the pressure on Berlin and to sever Zhukov's thrust across the Havel. He was promised reinforcements in the form of the 7th Panzer and 25th Panzergrenadier Divisions, neither of which was yet available, and in any case the latter was coming from the eastern end of his own line, where he had been given permission to abandon the Eberswalde bridgehead. At the same time the XXXXI Panzer Corps was ordered to block the Soviet advance westwards.[1]

The force that crossed the Havel at Hennigsdorf on the night of 22/23 April consisted of the 47th Army with the 9th Guards Tank Corps of the 2nd Guards Tank Army and the 7th Guards Cavalry Corps under command. This force had the dual task of completing the encirclement of the city and of providing a protective screen for the operation as far west as possible. The 9th Guards Tank Corps appears to have been shared out in brigade groups among the rest of the force, whose main body advanced nearly 15 miles to reach the outskirts of Nauen on the 23rd. The 125th Rifle Corps, supported by the 50th Guards Tank and 33rd Guards Mechanised Brigades, closed up to the defences of Spandau and Gatow Airfield but made no attempt to penetrate the town that day. The 77th Rifle Corps's 328th Rifle Division, supported by the 65th Guards Tank Brigade, headed south to link up with the 4th Guards Tank Army, while the cavalry fanned out between these main groups, scouring the countryside for signs of resistance, and it was their appearance on the Döberitz Training Area that had caused the hasty evacuation of the OKW from Krampnitz.[2]

During the course of the 23rd the encircling formations worked their way slowly into the northern and eastern suburbs of Berlin, gradually accustoming themselves to the conditions and learning the techniques of street-fighting from practical experience. Of course, these suburbs did not have the solid blocks of multi-storied structures common to the older parts of the city and therefore did not present exactly the same kind of problems that would be encountered later. For the most part these suburbs consisted of orderly groups of bungalows and villas set in individual gardens. There were also many garden colonies among these suburbs, allotments belonging to the city apartment dwellers who had constructed small summer houses and huts for their weekend leisure, many of them now permanently occupied as a result of the bombing.

The Russians advanced cautiously, but not always wisely. Mistakes were made on both sides. Chuikov writes of tank commanders sending their tanks through the streets in columns, only to be blocked in at either end by flank attacks and then destroyed piecemeal by Panzerfausts and Panzerschrecks.[3]

The Germans, firm believers in the doctrine that attack is the best means of defence, even used their ad hoc units in repeated counterattacks that only sapped their morale and strength uselessly against the more experienced Soviet troops, when fighting from behind cover would have been far more effective with such inexperienced resources.

The outer ring at Tegel was held by a Plant Protection Unit, whose commander, a Major Schwark, reported:

> The position sector was bounded on the left by the northern tip of the Tegeler See, from where it extended to the right along the Tegeler Run, also called the Nordgraben. This ditch held very little water and was more a line on which to build fortifications then an actual obstacle itself. The position consisted of a shallow fire trench without barbed wire or mines.
>
> The Battalion Commander had been familiarised with the terrain and had participated in two map exercises. The position was occupied by the Plant Protection Battalion, which comprised four understrength companies armed with rifles, hand grenades and a few Panzerfausts. Most of the men were veterans of the First World War and, because of their service with plant protection units, were accustomed to order and discipline. The Russians avoided a frontal attack, using infiltration instead, especially at night. Such tactics were aided by the poor visibility afforded by the terrain. Particular trouble was caused by roof-top snipers in front of and behind the German lines. Nevertheless it was still possible to keep the men together. When the battalion was almost surrounded after three days of fighting, it withdrew and occupied a new position in the Wittery Bakery plant, where the writer was seriously wounded.[4]

This unit was fortunate in that the 1st Mechanised Corps, in coming down through Hermsdorf, Waidmannslust and Wittenau, had bypassed them, and its assailants appear to have been members of the 47th Army detailed to secure the Hennigsdorf crossing point by clearing the area down as far as Tegel. Further east the 12th Guards Tank Corps swept down through Lübars, Blankenfelde and Rosenthal, where its arrival was described by a witness:

> Rosenthal was taken after an artillery barrage, followed by an advance of tanks supported by helmet-less infantry, excellent fighters. As soon as they arrived, the men dug individual foxholes and took care of their wounded and their weapons. No uniforms to speak of. Then the looting and the rape. No discipline at all for most of the troops, as admitted by several Soviet officers, but this was only after the fighting was over.[5]

The 12th Guards Tank Corps pushed on, working its way through Reinickendorf District with the 79th Rifle Corps of the 3rd Shock Army on their left flank in Niederschönhausen.

The 12th Guards Rifle Corps's experience in Pankow, as recounted by a member of the Volkssturm opposing it, seems fairly typical:

> We were in two companies of Auxiliary Police of about 45 men armed with Italian rifles. On the 23rd the Russians appeared in the houses and gardens in Breite Strasse opposite Pankow town hall. House to house fighting lasted until four Russian tanks advanced to within 400 metres of us along Breite Strasse. Two were put out of action by an infantry NCO with a Panzerfaust, and the others turned back.
>
> A counterattack was then mounted by combatants from the Police, Auxiliary Police and Hitlerjugend, but this failed. Our losses amounted to 40 percent and, as we lacked both food and ammunition, on the 25th we pulled back to Charlottenburg, where I was allowed to go as I was over 60 years old.[6]

Evidently the infantry-tank cooperation had yet to be perfected by the Russians in this case, but the unskilled defenders stood little chance when used in the open against them. However, a nucleus of resistance was to remain in Pankow until the very end of the battle and appears to have been centred around an air raid shelter.

The 7th Rifle Corps at Hohenschönhausen was still not ready to move, but the 5th Shock Army closed up to the fall-back position in Defence Sector 'A', taking Kaulsdorf and Biesdorf without difficulty. The 9th Rifle Corps on its right flank started moving in a south-westerly direction and took Karlshorst with its engineer training barracks.[7]

Further south the 4th Guards Rifle Corps of the 8th Guards Army took the industrial suburb of Oberschöneweide and prepared to cross the Spree to Johannisthal 'island'. That evening the Dnieper Flotilla arrived to assist with the impending river crossings, the intention being to place the combined 8th Guards and 1st Guards Tank Armies, together with the 9th Rifle Corps and an armoured brigade of the 5th Shock Army in a position to attack Berlin from the south.[8]

In the early hours of the 23rd, the 29th Guards Rifle Corps took intact the railway bridge leading south across the Spree into Adlershof and promptly began moving across to the west bank. During the day the 39th Guards Rifle Division cleared Köpenick with its bridges across the Spree and the Dahme, thereby assuring the two armies' communications routes through this area. Consequently, by the day's end, the 28th Guards Rifle Corps on the left flank was concentrating in the Grünau-Falkenberg area below the southern spur of the Teltow Canal, the 29th Guards Rifle Corps was on the central 'island' facing Johannisthal Airfield, and the 4th Guards Rifle Corps was still on the east bank of the Spree.[9]

That night the Military Council of the 1st Byelorussian Front called for an all-out effort to speed up the fall of Berlin. They were way behind schedule, Stalin was pressing them and Zhukov must have been apprehensive about the progress of Koniev's forces.[10]

The 3rd Guards Tank Army spent the 23rd regrouping south of the outer defence ring between Stahnsdorf and Lichtenrade, allowing the main body to catch up with the leading troops. The presence of these 1st Ukrainian Front troops was still apparently unsuspected by Zhukov, although Air Chief Marshal Novikov and his staff must have been fully aware of their location. There was very little waiting to oppose them, as Volkssturm Lieutenant von Reuss reported:

> Preparations for the defence of the Teltow Canal included the construction of works along the northern bank and the organisation of a bridge demolition team. A fire trench was laid out at a varying distance from the canal and machine-gun emplacements established 500–600 metres apart. Each emplacement was connected with a protected shelter by means of a communication trench.
>
> The trenches led partly through marshy terrain and interfered greatly with troop movements. A machine-gun emplacement protected with concrete slabs was constructed in the grounds of an asbestos factory. There were no artillery emplacements to the rear, although two anti-aircraft guns had been brought into position. A rocket-launcher had also been set up.
>
> The only complete unit that figured in this sector was the Kleinmachnow Volkssturm Company, which was joined by a few stragglers from the Wehrmacht.
>
> The platoon was armed with only one machine gun of Czech manufacture that went out of action after having been fired only once. In addition, there were rifles of various foreign makes, including even some Italian Balilla rifles.

The Lieutenant went on to say that the neighbouring Volkssturm platoon packed up and went home for the night after its first encounter with the enemy, returning in the morning to resume the fight![11]

However, Marshal Koniev's estimation of the opposition here was 15,000 men at 1,900 per mile, 250 guns and mortars, 130 tanks and armoured vehicles, and 500 machine guns.[12] To counter this he was amassing some 3,000 guns and mortars to cover his attack lines along the canal, giving an extraordinary density of 1,050 guns to the mile. In addition, a large number of guns of all calibres were allocated to the direct-fire role in support of the crossing and follow-through. His main problem was the nature of the obstacle before him; his infantry could easily swim the canal under the covering fire available, but once across they would require armoured support. New bridges could not be built under these circumstances and they would have to rely on the few remaining standing.[13]

During the day elements of the 128th Rifle Corps of the 28th Army continued to arrive to take part in the operation, but one of them, the 152nd Rifle Division, was caught up near Mittenwalde in what was thought to have been a breakout attempt by the 9th Army, but which might well have been the redeployment of the 21st Panzer Division. Whatever the cause, the 152nd Rifle Division was still fighting in the Mittenwalde area that night and does not appear to have rejoined its parent formation for another day or two. The two other main elements of this army, the 3rd Guards and 20th Rifle Corps, were also heading north towards Berlin, but were diverted to assist with encirclement of the 9th Army.[14]

The 4th Guards Tank Army continued closing in on Potsdam and closing the gap with the 47th Army, but made no attempt to cross the line of the Havel, which appears to have been the operational boundary. The 6th Guards Mechanised Corps alone pushed on westwards from Beelitz towards Brandenburg and Paretz, taking Lehnin that day.[15]

By the end of 23 April, the 13th Army had almost reached the Elbe at Wittenberg. Koniev decided to detach its 350th Rifle Division to the 4th Guards Tank Army to assist with the screening of Potsdam, and to take over its reserve rifle corps at Luckau as his Front Reserve and move it to Jüterbog, where it would be more centrally located to meet anticipated contingencies.[16]

Further south, the bulk of the 5th Guards Army closed up to the Elbe near Torgau on a wide front that day. Koniev decided to leave only its 34th Guards Rifle Corps in that area to await the arrival of the Americans on the opposite bank, and pulled back the 32nd Guards Rifle Corps and 4th Guards Tank Corps into the second echelon preparatory to striking a counterblow on the German forces that had penetrated some 20 miles towards Spremberg, splitting apart the 52nd Soviet and 2nd Polish Armies and creating havoc in their rear areas.[17]

Although he had just sufficient troops to cope with this emergency in the south, it is clear that Marshal Koniev's forces were extremely finely stretched at this stage. His active northern front extended in a great loop from Cottbus

in the east to Wittenberg in the west, via Berlin, Potsdam, Brandenburg and
Beelitz, and had only a very small reserve in the centre to counter the viable
threat posed by the German 9th and 12th Armies. In addition to these problems,
he was also responsible for the 6th Army, which was not actually involved in the
Berlin operation but impatiently besieging Breslau way behind his lines in Upper
Silesia.[18]

Meanwhile the Nazi leaders continued to play out their heedless melodrama.
On the 23rd General Koller arrived at Berchtesgaden and briefed Göring on
the general situation and the events in the Führerbunker of the previous day,
stressing that Hitler had apparently abandoned leadership of the government
and Armed Forces and had said that Göring should sue for peace. Koller urged
Göring to act, but Göring was reluctant to do so, as he had been out of favour for
some time and thought that Bormann might well have been chosen to take over
from Hitler. However, Göring had been nominated Hitler's successor in the Law
of Succession of 1941, and Reichsleiter Dr Hans Lammers, head of the Reich
Chancellery, advised him that this law was still valid. Eventually it was decided to
send the following signal to Hitler in code:

> Führer!
> In view of your decision to remain at your post in the fortress of Berlin, do
> you agree that I take over, at once, the total leadership of the Reich, with full
> freedom of action at home and abroad, as your deputy, in accordance with the
> decree of 29 June 1941? If no reply is received by 2200 hours I shall take it for
> granted that you have lost your freedom of action, consider the conditions of
> your decree as fulfilled and act for the best interests of our country and our
> people. You know what I feel for you in this gravest hour of my life. Words fail
> me to express myself. May God protect you and speed you quickly here in spite
> of all. Your loyal,
>
> Hermann Göring[19]

When the signal arrived at the Führerbunker, Bormann deliberately kept it to
himself for two or three hours until he could catch Hitler in a nervous, irritable
mood. He then showed the signal to the Führer, suggesting that Göring was trying to seize power for himself. Hitler flew into a rage and denounced Göring
as a traitor. He then sent two signals to Göring, one forbidding him to take any
action, and a second ordering him to resign from all his posts if he wished to
avoid trial for treason. Separate orders were sent to the SS guards, placing Göring
and his staff under house arrest.[20]

A surprise witness to Hitler's rage and the drafting of these signals was Albert
Speer, who had flown into Gatow from Rechlin that evening, and then flown
on by Fieseler 'Storch' to land on the East-West-Axis by the Brandenburg Gate.

Speer had come for the curious reason of confessing to Hitler all that he had done to obstruct the 'scorched earth' policy, an act which could well have cost him his head, but which only evoked an unusually mild response from Hitler under the circumstances, for he told Speer that all was forgiven and forgotten.[21]

In another conversation that evening, Speer tried with Bormann and Ribbentrop to persuade Hitler to leave Berlin, but Hitler refused, saying: 'I shall not go out of the bunker to meet my death at the barricades, for I would risk being wounded and taken alive by the Russians. I will shoot myself here with my own revolver. My body must not fall into enemy hands; they would be sure to use it for propaganda. I have made arrangements for it to be burnt.'[22]

Speer stayed until 0400 hours on the morning of the 24th before flying out again the way he had come eight hours earlier.[23]

On the 24th Steiner at last managed to launch simultaneous attacks southwards from his minor bridgeheads at Kreuzbruch and Zerpenschleuse, using a total of seven battalions. It was a feeble gesture when measured in terms of Hitler's expectations, but little short of miraculous under the circumstances. These twin attacks caught the 61st Army by surprise, and both groups were able to advance about four miles, as far as the villages of Zehlendorf and Klosterfelde respectively, before the Russians rallied and drove the survivors back to the canal. The Luftwaffe supported this operation in accordance with Hitler's instructions, and also attacked the long lines of vehicles backing up the 47th Army's advance westwards, but the Russians had established good ground-to-air liaison with their own air force and were able to call in superior numbers to drive the German aircraft off before too much harm was done.[24]

The 47th Army continued exploiting further to the west and south, with the 76th and 60th Rifle Divisions of the 125th Rifle Corps attacking Spandau simultaneously from the north and west, while the 175th Rifle Division concentrated on Gatow Airfield. Goebbels's propaganda had been effective, and they met determined resistance everywhere. Although they used heavy fire support, progress was slow and costly. A French prisoner-of-war gave the following account of an attack on a barricade outside the Schultheiss Brewery in the northern part of Spandau:

The roadblock's defenders were bombarded by heavy mortars set up in some ruined houses nearby. Then the Russians set up a 75 or 105mm gun several hundred metres from the barricade.

The Russian gunners were completely exposed and, at the cost of several casualties, succeeded in getting some shots on the target, destroying the barricade and killing a number of Germans.

Then the Soviet infantry, about 100 strong, charged in screaming, quickly swamped the remaining defenders, opened the barrier and regrouped on the street corner opposite the brewery.

German losses were increased by the bitterness of the Soviet soldiers, who seemed to be drugged, and rarely took prisoners. We found numerous German corpses, civilians and soldiers, when we were able to get out of the brewery.[25]

At the end of the day the Soviet penetration of Spandau had failed to dislodge the defence, and the situation was so confused that the troops appear to have withdrawn to safer lines for the night and called for aircraft to bomb the town.[26]

The situation at Gatow Airfield was somewhat different. It was an important Luftwaffe establishment, in which were based the Officer Training, Engineering and Staff Academies, whose remaining students participated in the defence of the airfield. Major Komorowski, who commanded a composite battalion on the outer defence ring here, reported:

The battalion, as part of a regiment, defended a section of the first position located along the western perimeter of Gatow Airfield, which was to be protected from attack from the west. If the first position was lost, the troops were to cross the Havel in boats lying in readiness, in order to occupy the second position on the far side of the lake.

The position consisted of a well-built, continuous trench. The battalion was composed of construction and Volkssturm troops, none of whom had any combat experience. They were armed with captured rifles and a few machine guns, and only had a limited supply of ammunition. The infantry were supported by a 88mm anti-aircraft battery and a heavy infantry gun platoon, although the latter had never fired its weapons. Support was also received from the Zoo Flak-tower. On the evening of the first day of battle all the Volkssturm troops deserted, and the gap was filled by recruiting stragglers. In two days of fighting all the defenders were either killed or captured.[27]

Despite the fighting, the airfield remained in operation until actually overrun, as we shall see.

During the day the garrison's last reinforcements to come by road arrived. SS-Major-General Dr Gustav Krukenberg brought in some 350 volunteers, mainly French, from his old command, the SS 'Charlemagne' Panzergrenadier Division. This division had just been disbanded in the interest of questionable future loyalty now that General de Gaulle, as Head of State, was fielding a proper national army against the Germans. The survivors of this formation had been offered the choice of either being employed on construction work or volunteering for a last-ditch stand in Berlin, and it was the latter that he had brought with him. Krukenberg himself, a superb commander of mercenaries, came in response to General Weidling's request for someone to replace the troublesome Ziegler.

When they found their route from Nauen blocked at Wustermark, Krukenberg led them by a roundabout route along country roads with which he was familiar. Near Ketzin they saw Russian infantry converging on them cautiously from north and south, but were able to get through unscathed by holding their fire and keeping the enemy in doubt as to their identity. At Falkenrehde some Volkssturm blew the canal bridge as they arrived, mistaking them for Russians and obliging them to continue on foot. On their way via Krampnitz, Glienicke and Pichelsdorf, they came across no defenders except three Hitlerjugend boys, armed with Panzerfausts and riding bicycles. They passed through the still unmanned roadblocks on the Frey Bridge, where the Heerstrasse (East-West-Axis) crosses over the Havel, and arrived at the Olympic Stadium at 2200 hours. Presumably the Russians must have pulled back for the night from their attacks on Gatow Airfield, as otherwise Krukenberg's group would have run into the fighting there.[28]

On 24 April, the 1st Mechanised Corps and 12th Guards Tank Corps continued their movement south, crossing the Jungfernheide heath[29] to close up to the line of the Hohenzollern Canal during the course of the afternoon. Under the cover of the woods lining the north bank they quickly prepared a strong crossing operation, which took place that evening. By nightfall several combat groups had established themselves on the edges of Siemensstadt, the big modern industrial suburb founded by the Siemens Company. However, their shortage of infantry placed them at a serious disadvantage in this type of fighting, and they were to suffer very heavy casualties as a result of this deficiency.[30]

The 3rd Shock Army's 79th Rifle Corps was not so lucky, for, having come through the southern part of Reinickendorf and swung as far west as the deserted Luftwaffe 'Hermann Göring' Barracks (now *Julius-Leber-Kaserne*) before turning south for the Hohenzollern Canal, it came under heavy fire from the direction of Plötzensee Prison and the Westhafen warehouses, and was unable to effect a crossing that day.[31]

The 12th Guards Rifle Corps began working its way down through the old working class district of Wedding with its enormous tenement block complexes, each a mass of connecting courtyards. An improvement in tactics is indicated in the following witness account of events in Müllerstrasse:

> A dozen tanks penetrated our street in the direction of the town hall. Infantry slipped through in the same direction. They were on either side of the street and about 20 metres apart. The firing stopped after about half an hour, and the soldiers then went from house to house searching the cellars.[32]

Where the main roads from Tegel (Müllerstrasse) and Pankow (Reinickendorfer Strasse) converged at Wedding S-Bahn station on the inner defence ring, the

Russians encountered fierce resistance from well prepared positions, which held them up for a while until the powerful Soviet artillery support was able to overwhelm the defence. However, units on the 12th Guards Rifle Corps's left flank came up against the Humboldhain Flak-tower position, which proved a formidable obstacle. An arc of railway cuttings forming a dry moat across the front of this position, plus the open parkland with the supporting control tower behind, all helped to keep the attackers at bay. The Soviets could only contain and bypass this position, which remained in action until the very end of the battle.[33]

Wolfgang Karow, an infantry NCO on leave in Berlin, had been mustered into an ad hoc unit based on the Humboldthain Flak-tower only the previous day, and gave the following account of activity on the 24th:

We first came under fire from the Hertha BSC football ground and then pushed off to Bellermannstrasse, where we took over an apartment block. We had to get the occupants out of the cellars to unlock the apartment doors for us. The other side of the street was already occupied by the Russians, and a brisk exchange of fire was opened up between us.

Our Lieutenant and combat team leader was a good comrade. We knew as well as he did that this was all 'five to twelve' and that the war would be over in a few days. His orders were therefore considerate, and he was careful not to take risks with anyone unless it was necessary.

So we pulled out, quit the apartment block and made for Humboldthain Flak-tower. There we were put into reserve and were able to get to know the interior of this vast bunker. We experienced the violent shaking when all eight 125mm anti-aircraft guns fired a salvo at the Russians, feeding them a violent form of respect.

Their artillery fire was particularly fierce against the walls of the bunker since their infantry could not get in. The brave gunners were being killed mercilessly at their posts, and they were nearly all young Flak Auxiliaries, 14 to 16-year-olds. These brave youngsters continued to serve their guns fearlessly, and several were felled before our eyes.

An assault group was formed from our reserve combat team, including myself. We were ordered to try and get some sweets from the Hildebrandt Chocolate Factory in Pankstrasse, which was nearby in no-man's land, so we put on some large Luftwaffe rucksacks and set off. We arrived without any trouble, but then had to detain a NSDAP (Party) official, who tried to prevent us entering at gunpoint. We were able to fill our rucksacks with chocolates and return to the bunker without suffering any casualties, and were warmly received by our comrades.[34]

The 7th Rifle Corps advanced through the Prenzlauer Berg district, which was similar in character to Wedding, working its way down the two main roads leading into Alexanderplatz, Prenzlauer Allee from Blankenburg and Greifswalder Strasse from Weissensee, and through the inner defence ring without encountering any serious opposition.[35]

The 26th Guards and 32nd Rifle Corps of the 5th Shock Army, strongly supported by armoured elements, continued their advance astride Frankfurter Allee on the East-West-Axis and cleared the Central Cattle Market and abattoir area just inside the inner defence ring, which does not seem to have represented much of a problem to them.[36] However, progress became uneven when those units that came under fire from the Friedrichshain Flak-tower were brought to an abrupt halt, as was the case with those advancing along Frankfurter Allee. Progress along this main artery was henceforth marked by the systematic destruction of every building, and it was along this avenue that the most damage appears to have been caused.

The third component of the 5th Shock Army, the 9th Rifle Corps, crossed the Spree into Treptow Park during the early hours of morning with the assistance of the 1st Brigade of the Dnieper Flotilla. Ten craft, described as semi-hydrofoils, had been delivered to Berlin by road, and these, together with pontoons, were used to get 16,000 men, 100 guns and mortars, 27 tanks and 700 supply trucks across the Spree under fire.[37]

According to Soviet accounts, the river crossing was opposed in strength, which was the result of the engineer battalion of the SS 'Nordland' Panzergrenadier Division assisting the local defence in this area.[38] On its way, the 301st Rifle Division took the large Rummelsberg power station not only intact but operating, a fact that delighted the Soviet command and won its commander an award.[39] The division then spent the rest of the day clearing Treptow 'island', and we have the following account of events on the southern flank on the road to Britz:

> The defence was the work of the Volkssturm and some SS using snipers. The Russians did their mopping up very cautiously and burnt with petrol all the houses from which they had been fired upon. Here the Russians used the following tactics; by day aircraft flew over the buildings where resistance was suspected and where they had spotted snipers posted on the roofs, dropping small-calibre bombs, or possibly clusters of hand grenades. Simultaneously the tanks advanced, slowly opening a passage with their fire. Behind the tanks came the infantry, usually about 30 to 40 men armed with submachine guns. Behind the assault troops came other shock troops, who searched the houses to left and right. As soon as a cellar or building had been visited, the assault troops passed on, leaving one or two sentries.
>
> In Baumschulenstrasse there were one or two machine guns manned by two men firing towards the station, and one or two armoured cars were dodging about in one of the side-streets. These two pockets of resistance held up the Russian advance for about four hours.[40]

The 8th Guards Army, with the 1st Guards Tank Army under command, and therefore Marshal Zhukov's strongest striking force, was busy that day side-stepping to the west to get into position to attack Berlin from the south. However, their plans were unexpectedly modified as a result of a surprise encounter, which must have created a tremendous upheaval at Front and Army command levels. In the early hours of the morning, some of Chuikov's troops traversing Schönefeld Airfield came across several tanks from the 3rd Guards Tank Army, thus linking up with the 1st Ukrainian Front. According to Chuikov, Zhukov did not apparently learn of this encounter until the evening and then acted disbelievingly, insisting that Chuikov send officers to discover what units of the 1st Ukrainian Front were involved, where they were located and what their objectives were.[41]

If, as it appears, this was Zhukov's first intimation of Koniev's participation in the battle for the city itself, one can imagine the consternation this report must have caused. Apart from the blow to Zhukov's pride, this incident clearly demonstrates the lack of communication between the Soviet leaders and their continuing mutual distrust. Having had his hand revealed, Stalin then laid down the inter-front boundary, which was to run from Lübben through Teupitz, Mittenwalde and Mariendorf to the Anhalter Railway Station. Within the city, this meant the line of the railway leading north from Lichtenrade.

Koniev had obviously been aware of this when he issued his orders on the night of the 22nd for the attack across the canal and for the 71st Mechanised Brigade to cover the right flank and establish contact with the 1st Byelorussian Front. Somehow, though, this GHQ order had been withheld from Zhukov, despite the fact that it was effective from 0600 hours (Moscow Time) on the 23rd, and his balance of forces and his reported reactions to the news of this encounter at Schönefeld clearly demonstrate how unprepared he was for this eventuality.[42]

Significantly, Chuikov states: 'the 8th Guards Army, in whose front of advance formations of the 1st Guards Tank Army were also operating, was diverted by order of the Front Commander to the northwest – against the central sector of Berlin.'[43] This diversion led to the 28th and 29th Guards Rifle Corps wheeling right through Rudow, Buckow and Lichtenrade into Mariendorf, and closing up to the line of the Teltow Canal on the 24th, while the 4th Guards Rifle Corps crossed the Spree to clear the Königsheide part of Johannisthal 'island' before deploying in Britz that evening. Cooperation with the 1st Guards Tank Army units was improved (Chuikov's choice of words does not indicate a happy relationship) and the night generally spent preparing for the attack across the canal next day.[44]

The 3rd Guards Tank Army's assault across the Teltow Canal began with a 55-minute bombardment at 0420 hours on the 24th, each of the three corps having an attack line of about one mile. On the right flank in Lankwitz the attack by the 9th Mechanised Corps and 61st Guards Rifle Division had initial success, but was then beaten back by German tanks and infantry, the bridgehead being eliminated with heavy loss. However, in the centre at Teltow, the 6th Guards Tank Corps's operation went well. Leading elements of the 22nd Guards Motorised Rifle Brigade went across the canal first in boats or by scrambling over the remains of a destroyed bridge. They established themselves on the opposite embankment and were joined by the rest of the brigade at 0500 hours. The 48th Guards Rifle Division then followed and enlarged the bridgehead. By 1100 hours the engineers had the first bridge ready to get guns and tanks across, and by the end of the day the corps had penetrated some one and a half miles, securing the southern half of Zehlendorf. Nearby on the left flank at Stahnsdorf the 7th Guards Tank Corps also succeeded in establishing a small bridgehead but against such fierce opposition that it was decided not to try and expand it after the already partially destroyed bridge over the canal finally collapsed.[45] Koniev, who was directing the operation in person, did as he had done at the crossing of the Upper Spree and channelled all three corps through the successful bridgehead, even ordering the 10th Guards Tank Corps of the 4th Guards Tank Army to get its right wing across by the same route to cover the attack on Potsdam.[46]

The resistance encountered at the Teltow and Stahnsdorf was due to the arrival of the remains of the 20th Panzergrenadier Division as part of the redeployment of the LVI Panzer Corps for the defence of the city. However, the result of this encounter was to force this division back on to Wannsee 'island', where it was effectively isolated from the rest of the defence. Depleted to a strength of only 90 men as a result of the deliberate misdirections of 'Seydlitz-Troops' during the retreat from Seelow, this division, together with elements of the Potsdam garrison and Volkssturm, nevertheless continued to preoccupy the 10th Guards Tanks Corps until the very end of the battle.[47]

In its advance on Potsdam the 10th Guards Tank Corps took the eastern suburbs without difficulty but found all the bridges leading across the Havel into the main part of the town to have been destroyed. Further west, the 6th Guards Mechanised Corps continued its advance and penetrated the eastern suburbs of Brandenburg, taking the prison and releasing some prominent German Communists incarcerated there.[48]

In the south the 13th Army reached Wittenberg on the Elbe that afternoon but ran into the encamped 'Ulrich von Hutten', 'Theodor Körner' and 'Scharnhorst' Divisions, which reacted so violently that Koniev was led to believe that Wenck's 12th Army was launching its anticipated counterattack, and therefore called in part of the 5th Guards Mechanised Corps and the 1st Air Attack Corps to assist. In fact General Wenck was not yet ready to launch his attack, but the news of the fighting caused some concern in the 4th Guards Tank Army.[49]

Meanwhile there was a surprise development in the sector of the 33rd Army, whose bridgeheads had been firmly contained by the V SS Mountain Corps against all attempts to break out since the beginning of the operation. That morning the 2nd Brigade of the Dnieper Flotilla laid a smokescreen across the Oder opposite Fürstenberg and supported an attack by marine infantry and some troops of the 33rd Army on the town. The withdrawal of the V SS Mountain Corps had already begun, so presumably there could not have been much resistance, if any, to this assault.[50]

On 24 April, General A.V. Gorbatov's 3rd Army of the 1st Byelorussian Front linked up with the 1st Ukrainian Front's 28th Army at Teupitz, thereby completing the encirclement of the German 9th Army in accordance with Stavka orders. Also that day the 2nd Air Army moved all its bomber bases forward across the Neisse, the bombers still having ample range capacity for their operations in support of the 1st Ukrainian Front.[51]

Further south the intervention of the 5th Guards Army group under Koniev's Chief of Operations, who, in addition to the Chief-of-Staff, had been sent to resolve the situation, succeeded in checking Field Marshal Schörner's disruptive drive towards Spremberg. However, several more days of hard fighting were to ensue before the Germans were driven back. General Baranov's 1st Guards Cavalry Corps took no part in this episode, for it was engaged on strictly private cavalry business. That day it reached the Elbe and prepared to make a foray across to recover the entire stock of one of the largest pedigree stud farms in the Soviet Union, which had been removed from the Northern Caucasus by the Germans in 1942. The mission had been initiated by the famous Marshal Budyonny, an old and influential friend of Stalin's.[52]

As already mentioned, General Weidling's redeployment of the LVI Panzer Corps into the city the previous evening had helped to bolster the pitifully weak defence structure that he had found there upon taking up his new appointment. The 20th Panzergrenadier Division having been caught off balance and forced back on Wannsee 'island', the 18th Panzergrenadier Division had to be taken out of reserve to plug the gap in the south-western suburbs. It then deployed along the chain of small lakes extending from the Wannsee part of the Havel near the Nikolassee towards the Westkreuz S-Bahn station at the northern end of the Avus. It was thus in thick woodland, completely outside the built-up area, but with the divisional headquarters still co-located with Defence Sector 'E's headquarters in the Zoo Flak control tower.

The 9th Parachute Division was deployed in the northern sectors, based upon the Humboldthain Flak-tower, from where it made a most useful contribution in blocking the 12th Guards and 7th Rifle Corps of the 3rd Shock Army. The 'Müncheberg' Panzer Division was assigned to assist with the defence of Tempelhof Airport but, being the only armoured formation, inevitably lost some of its few remaining tanks to other areas in difficulties, while the SS 'Nordland' Panzergrenadier Division deployed in Neukölln and the eastern end of Kreuzberg.[53]

Hopeful rumours continued to circulate, and an officer of the 'Müncheberg' Panzer Division noted in his diary for that day:

News and rumours from the Air Ministry of a successful attack towards Berlin by Wenck. Wenck's artillery can already be heard on the Havel. Another army is breaking through to us from the north.[54]

In fact, as we know, Wenck's army had yet to make a start and Steiner's seven battalions had already been routed.

Late that evening Hitler made some command decisions that showed that he had completely recovered from his breakdown of the 22nd. He drafted an order for publication the next day that read:

1. The OKW is responsible to me for the conduct of all operations.

2. It will issue orders in accordance with my instructions, which I shall transmit through the OKH Chief-of-Staff now with me.

3. Command Staff 'A' under Grand Admiral Dönitz will not assume its function until notified by me.

4. The main task of the OKW is to re-establish contact with Berlin by attacking from the southwest, northeast and south, thus bringing the battle of Berlin to a victorious conclusion.

Hitler was to remain Supreme Commander, while Command Staff 'B' (South) was to go to Lieutenant General Winter, not to Field Marshal Kesselring as previously considered, and would be directly subordinate to the OKW. These decisions, which ended the illogical OKW/OKH division of responsibilities, were greatly to Jodl's satisfaction as he had been trying to achieve this for some time, particularly as it made him, as OKW Chief-of-Staff, virtual head of the Armed Forces.[55]

That evening Colonel-General Robert Ritter von Greim, commanding the 6th Air Fleet based on Munich, received orders from Hitler to report in person to the Führerbunker. He was puzzled by these instructions as he had not heard of Göring's downfall, and first telephoned Koller, whom he knew to be at Berchtesgaden. Von Greim then decided that he should consult with Koller in person before attempting the hazardous flight to Berlin, but was unable to get away until the following morning as continuous enemy attacks on his airfields were preventing aircraft from taking off.[56]

The same evening Field Marshal Keitel revisited the XXXXI Panzer Corps, where General Holste blamed the tardiness of his redeployment to the east on lack of transport.[57]

Back in Berlin General Weidling did his best to improve the existing defence structure by sacking incompetent commanders and reducing the number of

Defence Sectors, but could do little that was effective at this late stage. Most of the remaining military and governmental establishments closed down, sending their personnel into the line and even recruiting female personnel into Battle Group 'Mohnke' to assist with the defence of 'Zitadelle'. The 5,000 boys of the Hitlerjugend Regiment, commanded by Obergebietsführer Dr Schlünder, with a few experienced officers and NCOs, were sent to hold the two southernmost of the four bridges leading over the Havel into Spandau with the primary aim of keeping the route open for Wenck's army's entry into the city.[58]

The Russians appointed the commander of the 5th Shock Army, Colonel-General Nikolai Erastovitch Berzarin, Soviet Commandant of Berlin and Commander of the Berlin Garrison. In Hermsdorf they set up their first civil administration with a German mayor.[59]

The Russian encirclement of the city still contained many gaps. Despite their considerable numbers, admittedly depleted though they had been in the fighting so far, the sheer size of the city made complete peripheral control impossible at this distance from the city centre. For instance, the 3rd Shock Army's three rifle corps appear to have fought their battles in isolation from each other. The 79th Rifle Corps was separated from the rest by the Schiffahrts Canal and there was a considerable gap between the 7th Rifle Corps advancing on the Alexanderplatz defences and the 12th Guards Rifle Corps in the centre. The latter seem to have adopted their normal open-country tactics in this situation, using the S-Bahn ring as a firm base line from which to strike out at the enemy, in this case concentrating their efforts on the right wing down the Chausseestrasse axis. This left a considerable area of no-man's land for the antagonists to move around in, as we shall see, and one Soviet group claims to have penetrated as far as the Unter den Linden and to have held out for a week insight of the Brandenburg Gate, well inside 'Zitadelle'.

10

The Noose Tightens

On the morning of 25 April Colonel-General Heinrici visited General von Manteuffel, whose 3rd Panzer Army was now strained to breaking point trying to hold the 2nd Byelorussian Front on the Oder. He then went on to the headquarters of the 25th Panzergrenadier Division, where he found Colonel-General Jodl trying to persuade Steiner to launch an immediate attack to the relief of Berlin. Both Keitel and Jodl were primarily concerned with the relief of Berlin and the rescue of Hitler, and were counting on the 3rd Panzer Army to hold firm in order to enable Steiner to attack south-eastwards towards Spandau. Steiner was decidedly reluctant, producing many reasons why he could not comply immediately, much to the annoyance of the OKW leaders. He still had to receive two of the formations promised him – the 3rd Naval Division, which was strung out along the railway from Swinemünde, and the 7th Panzer Division, which had arrived by sea from Danzig only a few days previously and was stuck in an assembly area near Neubrandenburg for lack of transport and fuel. The fall of Oranienburg had not affected the main issue, and Steiner was doing well, and all that could reasonably be expected of him under the circumstances, in holding the line of canals securing the 3rd Panzer Army's exposed southern flank while keeping both the 61st Army and 1st Polish Army at bay.[1]

The lack of realism displayed by the OKW leaders was in direct contrast with the views of the generals in the field, evoking this comment from Heinrici:

> To get to their new command post from Berlin, Keitel and Jodl had passed interminable columns of fugitives and broken units during the night, and had been mixed up with them again during the course of the morning. During this journey they had probably seen for the first time the true picture known to every combatant, whether at the front or at the rear. If their eyes had not been completely closed to the truth, they would undoubtedly have come to the conclusion there and then that the war had inexorably reached its end.[2]

Upon returning to his headquarters there was an urgent call from von Manteuffel reporting that the Russians had breached his lines south of Stettin. Heinrici promptly authorised withdrawal in accordance with a detailed plan he had worked out previously, but not conveyed to the OKW, and specifically ordered the abandoning of the Stettin Festung. This was all done without reference to the OKW, although he immediately gave instructions that it was to be informed of his decisions, and 48 hours were to pass before a scandalised Keitel was to receive the message.[3]

Some good news for Heinrici that day was the information that Colonel Biehler's Frankfurt-an-der-Oder Garrison had at last succeeded in breaking through to the 9th Army, a full three days after receiving Hitler's permission to do so. General Busse could now attempt his breakout to the west. His concentration was being harassed night and day from both land and air, and it was time to act if the people in his charge were to have a chance of escaping either death or capture at the hands of the Russians.[4]

However, the 25th also saw the historic link of the Russians and the Americans on the Elbe, where the 5th Guards Army's 58th Guards Rifle Division encountered patrols from the 69th Infantry of the American 1st Army near Torgau. Germany was thus split horizontally in two, but when Hitler learnt of this meeting and that the Russians had apparently hesitated before stopping their advance, he immediately concluded that discord reigned among the Allies and predicted an early outbreak of hostilities between the Anglo-Americans and the Soviets.[5]

At noon that day General Weidling issued his revised command organisation instructions for the defence of the city, which were based on the deployment of the LVI Panzer Corps already effected.[6] The Defence Sectors were to be grouped and commanded as follows:

'A' & 'B' (East): Major-General Mummert, now nominal Corps Commander.

'C' (Southeast): SS-Major-General Ziegler of the SS 'Nordland' Panzergrenadier Division.

'D' (Astride Tempelhof Airport): Colonel Wöhlermann, the Corps Artillery Commander.

'E' (Southwest & Grunewald Forest): Commander 20th Panzergrenadier Division, but, due to the developments previously referred to, the same day replaced by Major-General Rauch of the 18th Panzergrenadier Division. (Two days later the remains of the 20th Panzergrenadier Division were transferred to Army Detachment 'Spree'.)[7]

'F' (Spandau & Charlottenburg): Lieutenant-Colonel Anton Eder of Alexander Barracks, Ruhleben.

'G' & 'H' (North): Colonel Herrmann, commanding the 9th Parachute Division.

'Z' (Zitadelle): Lieutenant-Colonel Seifert.

It will be noted that control was now firmly in military hands. Lieutenant-Colonel Seifert, located in the Air Ministry building, presumably remained subordinate to SS-Major-General Mohnke, Hitler's appointee for the command of 'Zitadelle' in addition to commanding the 'Praetorian Guard' of Waffen-SS based on the Reich Chancellery. The parameters of Seifert's function are thus difficult to determine here but, as we shall see, he had a positive role to play in events to come, and later we find him commanding the Western Sub-Sector and SS-Major-General Krukenberg commanding the Eastern Sub-Sector of 'Zitadelle'.[8]

The anticipated meeting between the 4th Guards Tank and 47th Armies also took place that morning, when elements of the 6th Guards Mechanised Corps met up with troops of the 328th Rifle Division and the 65th Guards Tank Brigade near Ketzin, somewhat later than Krukenberg's account would have led us to expect, but again illustrating the extreme caution with which this operation was conducted by troops on the ground.[9]

The 125th Rifle Corps continued with its attacks on Spandau and Gatow Airfield, succeeding in isolating the Spandau defence, which consisted mainly of ad hoc units, Volkssturm and Hitlerjugend under the command of SS-Gruppenführer (Major General) August Heissmeyer, cutting them off from the Havel and the rest of the Berlin defence. The Gatow Airfield defence continued to hold, and it would seem that overall the Soviet forces deployed west of the Havel were inadequate in numbers for their role, the various objectives being too diversified to enable effective strength to be brought to bear in response to the situation.[10]

Air Chief Marshal Novikov mounted a special operation on 25 and 26 April, massing aircraft to maintain heavy bombing of the city in what he called 'Operation Salute'. The first strike was by 100 heavy bombers of the 18th Air Army, followed by waves of bombers throughout the day from the 16th Air Army. In all 1,368 aircraft took part, including 569 PE-2 dive-bombers, which were given specific targets to attack.[11]

The two armoured corps of the 2nd Guards Tank Army were involved in a hard struggle to clear the northern industrial suburb of Siemensstadt. That night they were assigned the 2nd Polish Heavy Artillery Brigade and the 6th Polish Pontoon-Bridging Brigade to support them, but it was to take until 28 April to close up to the line of the Spree.[12]

The 3rd Shock Army's 79th Rifle Corps crossed the Hohenzollern Canal at the Plötzensee Locks at dawn on 25 April under cover of a heavy artillery barrage. They took Plötzensee Prison and cleared the north bank of the Westhafen Canal but found that they could get no further.[13] The Westhafen Canal extended right across their front, and the Königsdamm Bridge, which provided the only practical route forward to Moabit 'island', had been blown. The wreckage had been mined and obstructed so that only five men could cross at a time. The northern embankment was fully exposed to crossfire from the enemy defences, which had been prepared to a depth of 200 yards from the canal to the parallel line of the S-Bahn. The railway stations had been developed as strongpoints, and the burnt-out, towering warehouses on the quays provided further vantage points for the defence. After some suicidal attempts to force the bridge had failed, the Russians were obliged to wait until darkness to provide some degree of cover for their engineers to start clearing the way. During the night artillery and heavy machine guns were brought right up to the edge of the canal in preparation for further attempts the following day.[14]

Meanwhile the 12th Guards Rifle Corps crossed into Moabit by the Fenn Bridge at the Nordhafen, securing the bridge against possible counterattacks from that direction, but not going any further towards outflanking the Westhafen position. Hampered by the Humboldhain Flak-tower in the centre of its lines, it was to spend the rest of the day caught up in costly street-fighting among the factories and densely-packed tenement blocks north of Invalidenstrasse. Reinforced by the remnants of the 9th Parachute Division, the defence in this area proved both tenacious and aggressive.

The 7th Rifle Corps fought its way right up to the edge of Alexanderplatz on the 25th, thereby coming up against the eastern bastion of 'Zitadelle'. Initially the defence proved so ineffective in this area that General Weidling was obliged to commit some of his precious tanks from the 'Müncheberg' Panzer Division, supported by infantry reserves, in a desperate counterattack that checked the Soviet advance but failed to regain any of the lost ground.[15]

On 25 April the 5th Shock Army continued to make slow progress towards the city centre against determined resistance. On the right flank the 26th Guards Rifle Corps worked its way past the Friedrichshain Flak-tower position along Frankfurter Allee (this section has since been renamed *Karl-Marx-Allee*) to the incessant pounding of massive artillery support. In the centre the 32nd Rifle Corps came up against a hard core of defence based on the Schlesischer Railway Station (now *Ostbahnhof*), whose broad expanses of track and sidings provided ample fields of fire for the defenders and enabled them to keep the attacking armour and infantry at bay for several days. The fight for this station was regarded by Marshal Zhukov as one of the 5th Shock Army's two most difficult tasks in this operation (the other being the forthcoming crossing of the Spree in the city centre). On the other side of the river the 9th Rifle Corps forced the Landwehr Canal from Treptow and then became involved in heavy fighting around the Görlitzer Railway Station, which dominated its front.[16]

At dawn on the 25th under cover of a tremendous artillery barrage, Chuikov threw his 8th Guards and 1st Guards Tank Armies, a total of three rifle and four armoured corps, across the Teltow Canal with the seizure of Tempelhof Airport as his main objective. The airfield was roughly one mile square, with a massive arc of hangars and administrative buildings in the northern corner covering a vast complex of underground hangars and cellars, where aircraft were known to be on stand-by to fly out the remaining Nazi leaders.

The airfield defence included a strong Luftwaffe flak unit with its guns readily convertible to the anti-tank role, the normal base personnel organised as infantry, a Hitlerjugend tank-hunting unit mounted in jeeps and equipped with Panzerfausts, plus the bulk of the 'Müncheberg' Panzer Division. The southern edge of the airfield was skirted by the S-Bahn ring, thus forming part of the inner defence ring, and had some of the original garrison's fuel-less tanks dug in along the southern and eastern edges of the perimeter. The inner defence ring and the banks of the canal, which constituted the fall-back position for the defenders of the outer defence ring, were held by the usual miscellany of Volkssturm and ad hoc units. The banks of the canal were lined with industrial premises, and the focus of the local defence here appears to have been astride the Stubenrauch Bridge on the main Mariendorf–Tempelhof road, where the Ullstein printing works on the south bank and the Lorenz factory bunker on the north bank had been turned into strongpoints. These positions appear to have been under harassment from the 3rd Guards Tank Army before the arrival of Chuikov's troops, as German accounts indicate that they held out for two or three days before they fell. There is nothing, however, to indicate that they withstood the overwhelming might of Chuikov's attack.[17]

The attack on the airfield itself was conducted by the 28th Guards Rifle Corps, supported by two brigades from the 1st Guards Tank Army, with the 39th Guards Rifle Division on the left, the 79th Guards Rifle Division on the right, and the 88th Guards Rifle Division mopping up the centre. Artillery fire was used to keep the runways clear and, as the Russians did not know the exact location of the underground hangars and their exits, some combat groups with tanks were given the specific task of ensuring that no aircraft should escape. During the course of the first day the Russians overran the two local defence lines and managed to get on to the airfield, but the main defence held. The 'Müncheberg' Panzer Division diarist recorded:

Early morning. We are at Tempelhof Airport. Russian artillery is firing without respite. We need infantry reinforcements and get motley emergency units. Behind the lines civilians are still trying to get away right under the Russian artillery fire, dragging along some wretched bundle containing all they have left in the world.

The Russians burn their way into buildings with flame-throwers. The screams of the women and children are terrible.

1500 hours. We have barely a dozen tanks and 30 armoured personnel carriers. These are all the armoured vehicles left in the government sector. The chain of command seems all mixed up. We consistently get orders from the Chancellery to send tanks to back some danger spot or other, and they never come back. So far only General Mummert's determination has kept us from being expended. We have hardly any vehicles left to carry the wounded.

Afternoon. Our artillery withdraws to new positions. They have very little ammunition left. The howling and explosions of the 'Stalin-Organs', the screaming of the wounded, the roar of engines and the rattle of machine guns. Clouds of smoke and the stench of burning. Dead women in the streets, killed while trying to get water. But also here and there, women with Panzerfausts, Silesian girls thirsting for revenge.[18]

To the left of the main action, the 29th Guards Rifle Corps, supported by the 8th Guards Mechanised Corps, crossed the Teltow Canal in the sector between the Tempelhofer Damm and the railway line marking the inter-front boundary, while on the right flank the 4th Guards Rifle Corps crossed into Neukölln. It seems that both these flank attacks met only local defence resistance and that the 4th Guards Rifle Corps did not come up against the 11th SS 'Nordland' Panzergrenadier Division until the following day.[19]

Having first reported to Colonel-General Krebs, who sent him on to General Weidling at Fehrbelliner Platz, SS-Major-General Krukenberg was instructed to take over the 11th SS 'Nordland' Panzergrenadier Division from SS-Major-General Ziegler, whom Weidling wanted replaced. The division had started the battle reduced to brigade size with its 23rd 'Norge' and 24th 'Danmark' Panzergrenadier Regiments down to between 600 and 700 men each. Krukenberg's French volunteers from the former 33rd SS 'Charlemagne' Panzergrenadier Division thus made a most welcome addition.[20]

Krukenberg found the divisional headquarters on the Hasenheide heath without difficulty from the number of vehicles parked outside the building, but so had the Russians, for the place had just been bombed and the wounded, including Ziegler, were lying about everywhere. To his horror, Krukenberg learnt that Ziegler had only 70 men on duty in the line, the remainder being exhausted and resting. Krukenberg then sent for his party of 90 Frenchmen from the Olympic Stadium where he had left them, and went to call on the local Volkssturm commander, whom he found in an observation post on Hermannplatz, from where he could see Russian tanks approaching. Krukenberg ordered half of his French anti-tank team to assist the Volkssturm, and by the following morning they had accounted for 14 tanks between them.

There was a hospital for French prisoners-of-war in Neukölln not far from the Landwehr Canal, and one of the doctors recalled the events of the day:

I spent long periods at the window of my observation post. In the street there were several women with shopping bags, some files of soldiers keeping close to the walls, and armoured vehicles passing to and fro. The 88mm gun on Weichselstrasse continued firing ceaselessly. Russian squadrons flew in a sky clear of German aircraft, but towards Tempelhof Airport the light flak was still in evidence. On the right the smoke of an enormous fire hid the two 80-metre-high towers of the large Karstadt department store that dominated the quarter.

The battle was now very close for, particularly on the left, one could hear the rattle of automatic weapons. The Russian attack seemed to be following the two almost perpendicular axes; along the canal towards Tempelhof and along the Ring towards Hermannplatz. In the latter direction the signs of a German collapse were evident, numerous small detachments passing the hospital heading towards the city centre.

We hoped that the decision would not be delayed, as our problems were mounting by the hour. We already had 300 sick prisoners to feed and care for.

The water supplies were running out and we did not know what to do about making the soup. We moved in the cellar with difficulty in almost total darkness. The situation of the seriously ill was particularly bad; they were lying on stretchers or even thin mattresses ranked side by side on the floor. The execution of medical attention or even simple hygiene became extremely difficult. The congestion was made even worse by many German wounded being too ill to move after the initial bandaging.

The operating theatre had to be moved long before because of the shelling, and we had improvised one in the former cloakroom, where amputations were carried out on an old wooden table covered with a mattress. The surgeons operated without gloves, practically without antiseptics, and the instruments hardly boiled. Everything was defective or exhausted. It was impossible to change one's overalls and even washing one's hands became a problem. The oil lamps were dead and the last candles consumed. Fortunately we had found two bicycles equipped with electric lights, and the pedals turned by hand provided sufficient illumination for the operating table. The Germans were grouped in some rooms under the meagre care of some local women who had offered their services.

A young conscript appeared with a broken arm. He had failed in an attempt to escape with two comrades from Tempelhof Airport in a Fieseler 'Storch'. Having a pilot's licence and working for Lufthansa, he had long planned his escape, but some security measures unknown to him had caused him to crash on take-off. He had been imprisoned at Alexanderplatz (Police Headquarters) awaiting trial when the Russian advance resulted in the Germans throwing open the prison doors!

The hospital staff faced up to the situation with courage, volunteers from the sick replacing those few defaulters paralysed with fear that dare not leave the corners where they had gone to ground.[21]

At dusk more tanks rolled on to the airfield carrying infantry to sustain the attack, but the defence held, the hangars and administrative buildings remaining in German hands.

This was a hard but successful day for the 3rd Guards Tank Army as it adjusted to street-fighting in the extensive garden suburbs of southwest Berlin. All night the troops, tanks and guns poured across the main bridgehead and deployed to their respective sectors. There had been no time to train or prepare for this phase. The infantry and armour had to learn to work closely together under novel conditions, the lessons proving expensive in both men and material. Later they would have to adapt to fighting under the more exacting conditions imposed by the densely built-up areas of the central districts.

Gradually, as with the 1st Byelorussian Front, combat teams combining all the arms were evolved. However, sheer weight of numbers told and by the end of the day the 3rd Guards Tank Army was well advanced towards the S-Bahn ring. The 9th Mechanised Corps was through Steglitz and almost into Schöneberg on the right; the 6th Guards Tank Corps, having quickly disposed of the heavy flak battery that opposed them from Königin-Luise-Platz outside the Botanical Gardens, was almost into Schmargendorf in the centre; and on the left the 7th Guards Tank Corps, having secured the southern belt of suburbs as far west as Nikolassee, was heading up through Dahlem, having taken the Luftgau III Headquarters on the way. The fighting in this sector was uneven, some areas having no form of defence whatsoever. Consequently various areas survived virtually unscathed while others suffered serious damage, for the Russians reacted violently whenever resistance was encountered.[22]

The task of covering the left flank of the main force and clearing the Grunewald forests was delegated to Colonel David Dragunsky's 55th Guards Tank Brigade, which was only 1,500 strong and was having to use tank crews that had lost their tanks as infantry, but was later augmented by two companies from the 23rd Guards Motorised Rifle Brigade.[23] It is clear that Koniev was concentrating the 3rd Guards Tank Army in a north-easterly thrust aimed directly at the Reichstag, determined to beat Zhukov to the prize. The rivalry between the two front commanders was reflected in the adjacent army commanders, between whom there was no attempt at liaison or communication of any kind, leading to some extraordinary and absurd situations. Stalin, having made his point to Zhukov by introducing Koniev's troops to the scene, now saw to it that Koniev's ambitions would be thwarted in turn, but neither was to know this yet and the rivalry was to continue in this vein.

The difficulties of aircraft coordination over such a congested battlefield soon became apparent with some embarrassing 'own goals'. An appeal was made to GHQ over the inter-front boundary, which was then altered to run along the line Mittenwalde–Mariendorf–Tempelhof–Potsdamer Railway Station, but by the time this came through the 9th Mechanised Corps was already east of this line and had to be recalled. It seems that GHQ was content to play the role of arbitrator in these inter-front matters, rather than act as coordinator.[24]

The 4th Guards Tank Army continued fighting at the approaches to Potsdam and Brandenburg, and made the long-awaited contact with the 47th Army. The 5th Guards Mechanised Corps and the 13th Army maintained pressure on Wenck's 12th Army's extended lines with the aid of the 2nd Air Army's 1st Air Attack Corps.[25]

During this period the energy of the defence varied considerably, despite Goebbels's efforts with whip and carrot. However, as the lines contracted, the relative numerical strength of the defenders, despite casualties, was gradually increasing, together with the proportion of experienced personnel. One of the officers at the Reich Chancellery reported on the 25th that desertion continued to be rife among the Volkssturm but that the Hitlerjugend gave repeated proof of their courage and devotion, and that the regular units were fighting with calm resolution. It was noticed that the Russians seemed to be deliberately picking on positions manned by the Volkssturm, which they then took fairly easily as a preliminary to attacking neighbouring positions from the flank and rear. They were also suspected of using German deserters as spies and guides.[26]

On the 25th Colonel-General Ritter von Greim visited Lieutenant-General Koller at Berchtesgaden and discussed the situation with him. He did not share Koller's view of Göring's innocence in the affair of the 23rd but promised to deliver Koller's plea of mitigation on Göring's behalf to the Führer in person. He then flew back to Munich, where he recruited a willing companion for this hazardous trip to Berlin, the famous female test pilot, Hanna Reitsch.[27] Hanna, a devotee of Hitler's, flew von Greim to Rechlin that night, hoping to find a helicopter there which could take them on to the Reich Chancellery. However, the only remaining machine had been damaged and they were obliged to wait until daylight for an aircraft and escort to be arranged for them.[28]

The ammunition situation was now desperate for the few guns and tanks remaining. With both Gatow and Tempelhof Airfields under fire, it was decided to clear an airstrip on the East-West-Axis between the Brandenburg Gate and the Siegessäule (Victory Column), which was completed on the afternoon of the 24th. At dawn on the 26th a squadron of Me 109s dropped over 100 ammunition containers in the Tiergarten, but barely a fifth was recovered and the risks involved in getting through the Soviet air defences barely justified this method of delivery, so transport aircraft were ordered to try and land on the airstrip instead. The many craters were hastily filled in and at 1030 hours two Ju 52s landed safely with their cargoes of tank ammunition. They took off again within half an hour, laden with seriously wounded from the Charité Hospital, but one hit an obstruction on take-off and crashed, killing all aboard, so this method of supply was also abandoned.[29]

At 2330 hours on 25 April Jodl received Hitler's detailed instructions supplementing the OKW order of the previous evening. Hitler demanded the fastest possible execution of all the planned relief operations as part of an incredibly optimistic scheme for the restoration of a firm Eastern Front. In the north the 3rd Panzer Army was to retain the 2nd Byelorussian Front while Steiner attacked southeast towards Spandau, cutting off the Russian forces west of the Havel, which the XXXXI Panzer Corps would then mop up; the 9th Army was to maintain a firm front to the east, with which Army Group 'Mitte' would connect in its drive from the south, and at the same time link up with the 12th Army's drive south of Potsdam, so that both armies could advance together on Berlin on a broad front. This plan, as usual, completely ignored the state of the German forces and the strength of the opposition.[30]

Jodl reported back that all relief operations had either already begun or were about to begin. He also informed Hitler of the Russian build-up south of Prenzlau and of a build-up by the British 21st Army Group southeast of Hamburg threatening a drive on Lübeck, which could cut off the northern province of Schleswig-Holstein and the German forces in Denmark. Hitler then authorised the formation of the 21st Army under General Kurt von Tippelskirch from units drawn from the North Sea coast in order to counter the British threat to the 3rd Panzer Army's rear. However, the 21st Army could muster only two regiments and would take at least one or two days to get into position for its role.

Jodl's misleading report on the relief operations caused the 26th to be a day of optimism in the Führerbunker, but outside in the bright spring sunshine the true situation was nothing less than desperate. Heinrici and his army commanders were wide awake to the realities, unlike Hitler and his blind disciples in the OKW, and were all covertly working at the problem of getting the maximum number of their troops back across the Elbe, which meant fending off the Russians and deceiving the OKW about their intentions for as long as possible.

During the night the 25th Panzergrenadier Division had moved into Steiner's bridgehead south of the Ruppiner Canal at Kremmen, from where the roads led southwest to Nauen and southeast to Spandau. However, two-thirds of Steiner's striking force had still to arrive, the 3rd Naval Division being stuck on the railways and the 7th Panzer Division it its assembly area near Neubrandenburg, and his troops were under strong Soviet pressure.[31]

General von Manteuffel had already used up all his available reserves to try and stem the Russian flood in front of Prenzlau, and was now forced to withdraw troops from his flanks to fill the centre of his line. With this contraction of his front, troops were evacuating the Schorfheide in the south, thereby exposing the rear of Steiner's forces. Under these circumstances, Steiner's attack would be suicidal and therefore, sometime before noon on the 26th, Heinrici telephoned Jodl requesting reinforcement of the 3rd Panzer Army by the three divisions assigned to Steiner. Jodl regarded any deviation from Hitler's orders as heresy and refused. Heinrici decided to ignore this rejection and placed an embargo on the 7th Panzer Division without Jodl's knowledge. That night the 3rd Panzer Army withdrew from the north–south line of the Uecker River running through Prenzlau that had provided it with the last opportunity of making a concerted stand.[32]

During the night the survivors of SS-Major-General Heissmeyer's Spandau defenders managed to break out of their encirclement and fight their way back through the ruins of the old garrison town to cross the Havel by the Charlotten Bridge. The Gatow defence continued to hold out on the west bank, and Weidling sent Luftwaffe Major-General Aribert Müller to take charge.[33]

At dawn on the 26th Wenck launched his relief attack with the XX Corps from the line Brandenburg–Belzig, not heading towards Jüterbog as the OKW expected, but towards Potsdam, where the Russian forces did not appear to be quite so strong. The roads were blocked with refugees, so the troops had to move across country. At first all went well, the angle of attack avoiding the prepared line held by the 5th Guards Mechanised Corps and the 13th Army, and caught the 6th Guards Mechanised Corps on an exposed flank. A whole number of Soviet units were captured intact, including tank workshops and supply columns. The young trainees of the 'Clausewitz', 'Scharnhorst' and 'Theodor Körner' Divisions, reinforced by the brand new 'Ferdinand von Schill' Division, fought with all the élan of the German Army during the first years of the war. They covered eleven miles that afternoon and by evening had reached the spa of Beelitz, only 15 miles from Berlin. There they recaptured a German field hospital complete with its doctors, staff, valuable medical supplies and 3,000 wounded who had been in Russian hands for the past three days. Their transport resources, including a commandeered train, were used to establish a shuttle service to evacuate the wounded and refugees the fifty miles back to Elbe.[34]

That same morning Air Chief Marshal Novikov resumed 'Operation Salute' with a raid on the city centre by 563 heavy bombers of the 18th Air Army.[35]

At dawn the 79th Rifle Corps resumed its efforts to get across the Westhafen Canal. The 3rd Battalion of the 756th Rifle Regiment tried to cross the ruined bridge under cover of a massive artillery concentration from corps and divisional artillery, including direct fire from the divisional artillery massed on the northern embankment. However, this attempt also failed with heavy losses, and the few men that managed to reach the southern bank were soon routed by a counterattack.[36]

The Russians tried again with the same artillery support, but sending forward a chemical warfare company instead of infantry, and this time managed to get enough men and equipment across to lay a dense smokescreen to mask the operation. By this means a second wave of troops managed to establish a small bridgehead that was then rapidly expanded. Some close-support artillery was brought across with the infantry, although all the horses drawing the guns were killed in the vicious crossfire on the bridge and the guns had to be dragged into position by hand.

The strongpoint at Beusselstrasse Railway Station was to hold out for a while longer, but this was bypassed and the Russians were well into Moabit by evening. Although losses had been extremely heavy, they had captured over 100 of the enemy and released 1,200 Russian prisoners-of-war, who were promptly armed, fed and sent back into the line as replacements.

The confused close-fighting in the remainder of the area north of the Spree continued from the previous day without any identifiable changes. The guns roared, the debris was turned over yet again, and casualties continued to mount on both sides.

On 26 April Weidling was suddenly informed that his immediate predecessor as Defence Commandant, Lieutenant-Colonel Erich Bärenfänger, who had been assigned to General Mummert's command, had been reinstated by Hitler as a Major-General and was to take over the command of Defence Sectors 'A' and 'B' forthwith. Bärenfänger's successful wire-pulling with the hierarchy, ridiculous as it may seem, was in fact beneficial to the defence, for it enabled Mummert to resume command of the 'Müncheberg' Panzer Division at Tempelhof. It thereby also released Colonel Wöhlermann to return to his command of the defence area artillery and, as we shall see, Bärenfänger was to acquit himself well in the new role.[37]

That morning SS-Major-General Krukenberg's SS 'Nordland' Panzergrenadier Division launched counterattacks in Neukölln and the area of Görlitzer Railway Station against the 4th Guards and 9th Rifle Corps respectively. A Frenchman with the SS 'Charlemagne' Battalion, as they now styled themselves, described his experiences:

> Our men advanced as if on exercise, jumping from doorway to doorway, over walls and rubble, and fell on the Russian infantry, who were spread out on the various floors. The following tanks spurted fire and flames, hardly giving the Russian infantry a chance to fire back. Our attack made progress, and it was then that we received a blow. A reserve section coming from Neukölln town hall, and thinking themselves safe, were still in order of march when suddenly a series of Russian tank shells fell on the street corner. Broken-hearted, I counted about 15 bodies of young soldiers lying in the roadway, which was running with blood.
>
> To our right and left the situation was even more confused. Whilst clearing the area into which we had penetrated, we kept coming across the flanks of friendly units as well as Russians on every side. A strange order then reached us from Division: 'If the attack has not already started, stop and await further orders; if it has, then do your best!'

Three hours after our successful attack had begun we had to pull back. In fact there was no longer any front either alongside us or behind us. 'What shall I do?' I asked myself: 'Surely we should not hold on here. In the meantime, let us make sure that we have not been surrounded.'

The town hall was then occupied as a defensive position by a group of Hitlerjugend who had been sent us as reinforcements.[38]

Fires were spreading unchecked all over the central districts of Berlin on the 26th, as the firemen could not carry out their task under the heavy shellfire that was falling everywhere. The 'Müncheberg' Panzer Corps diarist recorded:

0530 hours. New, massive tank attacks. We are forced to withdraw. Orders from the Chancellery: our Division is to move immediately to Alexanderplatz.

0900 hours. Order cancelled.

1000 hours. Russian drive on the airport becoming irresistible. New defence line Rathaus Schöneberg – Hallesches Tor – Belle-Alliance-Platz. Heavy street-fighting, many civilian casualties, dying animals, women fleeing from cellar to cellar. We are pushed northwest. New orders to go to Alexanderplatz as before. General Bärenfänger has taken over Defence Sectors 'A' and 'B' from General Mummert. The Führerbunker must have false information; the positions we are supposed to be taking over are already in Russian hands. We withdraw again under heavy Russian air attacks. Inscriptions on the walls of buildings: 'The hour before the sunrise is the darkest!' and 'We withdraw but we are winning!' Deserters are hanged or shot. What we see on the march is unforgettable.

Evening. Announcement of a new organisation, Freikorps 'Mohnke'. 'Bring your own weapons, equipment, rations. Every German is needed!' Heavy fighting in Dircksenstrasse, Königstrasse, the Central Market and inside the Stock Exchange.[39] First skirmishes in the S-Bahn tunnels, through which the Russians are trying to get behind our lines. The tunnels are packed with civilians.[40]

This was the first indication of the Soviet use of the underground railway tunnels to assist their advance and was probably the work of the 7th Rifle Corps, which was nearest to Alexanderplatz and finding it difficult to make further progress after an initially rapid advance from Hohenschönhausen.

That day General Weidling went to visit Major-General Bärenfänger, now commanding what amounted to the eastern bastion of 'Zitadelle', and later commented:

Potsdamer Platz and Leipziger Strasse were under heavy artillery fire. The dust from the rubble hung in the air like a thick fog. Shells burst all around us. The streets were riddled with shell craters and piles of brick rubble. Streets and squares lay deserted. Dodging Russian mortars, we made our way to the U-Bahn station by bounds. The roomy U-Bahn station, two storeys deep, was crowded with terrified civilians. It was a shattering sight.

From Platform 'E' we walked through the tunnel as far as Schillingstrasse [the next east along Frankfurter Strasse] to General Bärenfänger's HQ. Bärenfänger reported strong Russian attacks near Frankfurter Strasse. This former Hitlerjugend leader and fanatical follower of Hitler's was full of praise for the valour of his soldiers and their deeds of heroism. A considerable number of enemy tanks had been destroyed in his sector. He now pressed me for more men and ammunition, but I could promise him neither. Most of Bärenfänger's men were Volkssturm troopers that had been sent into the fighting with captured weapons, French, Italian, etc. No ammunition for these weapons could be found anywhere in Berlin.

On my way back I visited one of the hospitals. It was terribly overcrowded. The doctors simply could not cope with the numbers of wounded. There was hardly any light or water.[41]

That evening Chuikov's troops reached Kreuzberg and took the French prisoner-of-war hospital there. The following account describes how the Russians advanced in an area that had not previously been devastated by artillery fire:

That morning I greeted daylight with pleasure. A surprise awaited me. The Karstadt department store towers had vanished and the vast building itself was now on fire.

Several spent bullets whistled up the street. The sound of automatic weapons now came from the right as well as the left and was mixed with the drier, more regular rattlings presumably coming from Russian submachine guns. The 88mm on Weichselstrasse was no longer firing, having been either silenced or removed.

The inhabitants were now staying indoors. The withdrawal towards the city centre was marked by a detachment of police and firemen following the lines of the walls with their packs on their backs, rifles slung across their chests, and suitcases in either hand. And still the wounded were coming into the yard.

At about 1600 hours the retreat was still on but the Russians were already at the end of the street and more and more bullets were whistling past. A light tank went by, covering its retreat with bursts of machine-gun fire.

In the cellar, which had been permanently occupied for the last few days, the atmosphere was stifling. Civilians were packed against the other side of the partition separating our side of the cellar from theirs. The rumour ran around that Tempelhof had been outflanked from both east and west. Surgical patients were stretched out on mattresses wherever there was space; soldiers, old men, women, children, French, Russian, Serb and Italian workers, mixed up side by side and asking for water. There were already a dozen corpses stacked in an old trench shelter nearby. Short cries were mixed with it and gradually as they approached we distinguished the sound of 'Stalin, hurrah!' Anxiety reigned in the cellar. The sick lying on the first landing of one of the stairwells had seen Russian tanks pass. Then a soldier stuck his head through one of the holes in the metal plates reinforcing the porch grill and, no doubt perturbed by this abandoned large building, sent a burst of machine-gun fire into the windows.

It was necessary to act quickly if an irreparable error was to be avoided. A delegation composed of three Frenchmen, the senior doctor, a man we trusted, and our youngest comrade, Medical Lieutenant 'T', who spoke Russian fluently, left the cellar to report to the Russians. We awaited the result of the encounter with impatience. The order had been given for everyone to remain below until the situation had been clarified. Faces were grave. Information was passed round from the men nearest the exits.

Contact was established without incident, and the Russians visited out building for they thought some shots had come from the south wing. The problem was finally resolved by two tank shells fired at the suspect windows.[42]

Heavy fighting in the 5th Shock Army's sector continued to delay its progress but Chuikov's troops, having taken Tempelhof Airport by noon, began to wheel into Schöneberg with their right flank edged up to the Landwehr Canal. Viktoria Park was taken, giving them an elevation on which to mount their artillery, and next day an eye-witness saw 205mm guns being fired from there over open sights at the Anhalter Railway Station less than a mile away.[43] During the afternoon, according to Chuikov's account, his troops were amazed to see a column of about 400 Hitlerjugend carrying Panzerfausts marching towards them as if on parade down Kolonnenstrasse. After some initial hesitation, the Russians opened fire, killing the leaders and putting the rest to flight.[44]

By the end of 26 April the 8th Guards and 1st Guards Tank Armies were up to the line of Potsdamer Strasse on their left, and the 28th Guards Rifle Corps were engaged against a strongpoint commanding the important street junction at the southeast corner of Heinrich-von-Kleist Park. Leading elements of the 34th Heavy Tank Regiment had penetrated even further and were fighting outside the Twelve Apostles Church in Kurfürstenstrasse, having made their way across the Yorckstrasse complex of tracks and marshalling yards serving the Anhalter and Potsdamer Railway Stations.[45]

This penetration westwards by Chuikov's forces put the 1st Byelorussian Front well beyond the Tempelhof–Potsdamer Station boundary established by GHQ the night before, but whether this order had not been transmitted to Chuikov, or it had been decided to ignore it with a view to establishing a firm base for the attack on the central enemy stronghold across the Landwehr Canal. In any case, the 3rd Guards Tank Army remained totally unaware that Chuikov's troops were working across their front.

That same day the 3rd Guards Tank Army started running into the more densely built-up areas of Friedenau and Schmargendorf immediately south of the S-Bahn ring, and had to adjust to the new conditions of street-fighting. The 55th Guards Tank Brigade, after a 15-minute bombardment of German positions on the outskirts of Nikolassee and on the Havelberg, avoided the open expanse of the Avus and advanced up the east bank of the Havel through the Grunewald Forest. On its way it encountered a flak battery firing across the Havel in support of the defence of Gatow Airport and called for air support to destroy it. Eventually the brigade emerged from the woods at the bend in the Heerstrasse section of the East-West-Axis, not far from the Olympic Stadium. Here it turned right towards Charlottenburg and started working its way slowly through the residential areas on either side of that broad thoroughfare against increasing opposition as the defence reacted to its unexpected appearance. Colonel Dragunsky describes the advance with the tanks in column about 100 yards apart, scouts out on the flanks and submachine-gunners going ahead, engineers, artillery and assault groups following the tanks, and his own command group on foot between two tank battalions so that they could see what was going on. All resistance was smothered with heavy concentrations of fire, while long-range artillery shelled the areas yet to be penetrated. By nightfall they had overrun the ammunition dump in the unfinished War Academy near the Teufelssee and occupied the Eichkamp residential area. Brigade Headquarters remained on the edge of the woods under heavy guard, as nothing was known of what enemy forces remained ahead or behind them.[46]

Although Koniev badly wanted to redeploy the 4th Guards Tank Army's 10th Guards Tank Corps to meet the threat posed by the advance of the German 12th Army on Berlin, it remained fully committed in bottling up the remains of the 20th Panzergrenadier Division and other units of General Reymann's Army Detachment 'Spree' on the Wannsee and Potsdam 'islands'.[47]

The 18th Panzergrenadier Division, seeing themselves being outflanked by these manoeuvres, pulled out of its positions along the Grunewald chain of lakes and swung round into Wilmersdorf to meet the main Soviet threat head on.[48]

During the course of the 26th General Weidling moved his headquarters out of Fehrbelliner Platz to the OKH buildings in Bendlerstrasse (now *Stauffenbergstrasse*), as Koniev's troops were getting uncomfortably close from the south. Axmann was also prompted to move his Hitlerjugend Headquarters from No. 86 on the Kaiserdamm to No. 64 Wilhelmstrasse, where he could be closer to the Führer.[49]

The lack of proper communication facilities continued to bedevil the conduct of the defence, and the sector headquarters were now obliged to pick numbers at random from the civilian telephone directory to try and discover what was going on. Sometimes they were answered by Russian voices, and one Soviet officer claimed to have been connected with Goebbels from Siemensstadt and to have conversed cheekily with him in German.[50]

That day the pilot who had previously flown Speer into Berlin and back from Rechlin flew Colonel-General von Greim to Gatow in a Focke-Wolf 190, which had only one passenger seat, so Hanna Reitsch was stuffed into a storage compartment in the tail of the aircraft in order to accompany von Greim on his visit to the Führer. They were escorted by 20 other aircraft and arrived safely with only a few bullet holes in the wings, but at a cost of seven of their number.

Von Greim tried to telephone Hitler from Gatow, but without success. He therefore attempted to fly on to the Brandenburg Gate airstrip in a Fieseler 'Storch' with Hanna behind him in the passenger seat. Their fighter escort held off the attacking Soviet aircraft as von Greim took off and vanished into the murk shrouding the city. While flying over the Grunewald residential area, the aircraft was hit and von Greim badly injured in the foot. Hanna managed to reach the controls over his shoulders and flew on to land safely on the airstrip. They then commandeered a passing vehicle and were taken to the Chancellery bunker, where von Greim had his injuries attended to before they went on to report to Hitler. It then transpired that Hitler had summoned von Greim merely to confer upon him the command of the Luftwaffe in the rank of Field Marshal, something which could just as well have been done by signal. Hitler wanted them to leave again immediately, but von Greim's injuries were both painful and serious, and it proved impossible to fly in any further aircraft for this purpose. Six Fieseler 'Storch' aircraft flown in from Rechlin under fighter escort were all shot down, as were twelve Junker 52 transports bringing in SS reinforcements.[51]

During the course of 26 April Berlin's last telephone links with the outside world, which had been operating only intermittently over the last two days, were finally severed.[52]

1 Marshal Georgi Zhukov, C-in-C 1st Byelorussian Front, in his command post on the Reitwein Spur.

2 Marshal Ivan Koniev, C-in-C 1st Ukrainian Front, left with his 'liberated' staff car.

Left: 3 Marshal Konstantin Rokossovsky, C-in-C 2nd Byelorussian Front.

Below: 4 Colonel-General Vassily Chuikov, GOC 8th Guards Army, in his command post on the Reitwein Spur.

Above left: 5 Colonel-General Gotthardt Heinrici, C-In-C Army Group 'Weichsel'.

Above right: 6 General Theodor Busse, GOC 9th Army.

Right: 7 General Helmuth Weidling, GOC LVI Panzer Corps.

8 Hitler visiting the CI Corps HQ at Schloss Harnekop on 3 March 1945.

9 Soviet infantry crossing the Oderbruch.

10 Oderbruch fighting conditions: a Soviet tank stuck in a drainage ditch.

11 Massed Soviet artillery on the banks of the Oder.

12 A crowded Soviet ferry crossing the Oder with a rocket launcher and jeep.

Above: 13 An 88mm Flak gun in the anti-tank role.

Below: 14 Soviet bridge-building.

Above: 15 German dead from the Soviet bombardments below Seelow.

Right: 16 Lieutenant-General Walter Wenck, GOC 12th Army.

17 Soviet mortars firing in the streets of Berlin.

18 Soviet rocket launchers preparing for action in the streets. The rocket frames were sometimes dismantled and reassembled on rooftops.

19 Göring's Air Ministry building on Wilhelmstrasse before the battle.

20 The ruined Anhalter Railway Station with the flat-topped air raid shelter in the foreground.

21 The devastated central district of Kreuzberg after Soviet artillery bombardments had raked through the bombed ruins.

22 Potsdamer Platz after the fighting with Potsdamer Railway Station in the background.

Left: 23 SS-Major-General Wilhelm Mohnke.

Below: 24 The barricade on the Schloss Bridge on the Unter den Linden. The Arsenal is on the right and through the gap in the barricade one can see the boxed-in statue of Frederick the Great.

Above: 25 General Krebs (back to camera) outside Colonel-General Chuikov's headquarters in Tempelhof while attempting to negotiate an armistice, accompanied by SS-Lt Neilands (in German Army uniform) as his interpreter.

Right: 26 The remains of the Bendler Bridge, where Colonel Theodor von Dufving crossed the Landwehr Canal to arrange the surrender of General Weidling, with the badly damaged Shell Haus in the background.

27 The Charlotten Bridge over the Havel River in Spandau used for the German breakout to the west. The suburb of Stresow on the right is dominated by the massive Deutsche-Industrie-Werke factory producing guns and tanks.

28 The footbridge, incorporated into the Friedrich Strasse Station bridge over the Spree, was used by Reichsleiter Bormann and others in their breakout attempt from the Reich Chancellery.

29 The last armoured personnel carrier of the Waffen-SS Division 'Nordland' destroyed north of the Spree during the breakout attempt from Friedrichstrasse.

30 The 9th Army's last tank, a *Königstiger*, abandoned for lack of fuel in a swamp near Beelitz.

31 An aerial photograph showing the rugged nature of the Reichstag battlefield taken from a reconnaissance biplane. The Customs Yard buildings bottom with the Moltke Bridge beyond leading between the remains of the Diplomatic Quarter and the Prussian Ministry of the Interior leading to the Reichstag.

32 The Moltke Bridge over the River Spree in earlier days with the Customs Yard, Washington Platz and Lehrter Railway Station on the left, Diplomatic Quarter and Prussian Ministry of the Interior on the right.

33 Soviet gun tractors and tanks crossing the Moltke Bridge protected by self-propelled guns firing down Moltkestrasse.

34 Soviet troops in front of the captured Reichstag.

35 The Reichstag still burning on the afternoon of 2 May 1945. Left of the dome, the Prussian Ministry of the Interior, Moltkestrasse, Swiss Legation; to the right, the Lehrter Railway Station behind the remains of the Diplomatic Quarter.

36 The Soviet War Memorial opened on the battlefield on 11 November 1945, with the 2,200 Soviet dead killed in the battle for the Reichstag buried immediately behind the memorial.

11

No Relief

In Kreuzberg the pressure of Chuikov's forces caused the German defence to withdraw over the Landwehr Canal during the night of 26/27 April and consolidate on that line. At the eastern end of the canal the SS 'Nordland' Panzergrenadier Division continued to hold the 9th Rifle Corps back in the Görlitzer Railway Station area. Operating north of here, as far out as Alexanderplatz, were elements of the 'Müncheberg' Panzer Division, whose diarist recorded:

> The night is fiery red. Heavy shelling. Otherwise a terrible silence. We are sniped at from many buildings, probably by foreign labourers. About 0530 hours, another grinding barrage. The Russians attack with tanks and flame-throwers. We withdraw to the Anhalter Railway Station. Defence of Askanischer Platz, Saarlandstrasse [now *Stresemannstrasse*] and Wilhelmstrasse. Three times during the morning we enquire: 'Where is Wenck?' Wenck's spearheads are said to be at Werder [21 miles away on the far side of Potsdam]. Incomprehensible! A reliable release from the Propaganda Ministry that all the troops from the Elbe Front are marching on Berlin.
>
> At about 1100 hours 'L' comes from the Propaganda Ministry, his eyes shining, with an even more reliable release straight from Secretary of State Naumann. There have been negotiations with the Western Allies. We shall have to make sacrifices, but the Western Allies will not stand by and let the Russians take Berlin. Our morale goes up enormously. 'L' says it is absolutely certain that we will not have to go on fighting for more than 24 hours – 48 at the very most.[1]

On 27 April the situation on the 3rd Panzer Army's front deteriorated rapidly when the Russians broke through just north of Prenzlau during the morning. Eventually, late afternoon, Keitel was reluctantly forced to concede to Heinrici's request that the 7th Panzer and 25th Panzergrenadier Division be assigned to relieve the pressure on his front instead of participating in Steiner's attack as originally intended. (By this time the 3rd Naval Division appears to have ceased to exist as a formation, having been caught up piecemeal in the 3rd Panzer

Army's withdrawal.) However, Keitel insisted that these two divisions be used specifically in an attack on the 2nd Byelorussian Front's southern flank, laying down the assembly area, line of attack and objectives, and that they revert to their original task immediately thereafter. Heinrici had no intention of adopting such an impracticable course of action, and gave them orders to dig in on the line Neubrandenburg–Neustrelitz to cover the main line of retreat.[2]

That day Gatow Airfield finally fell and the Russians were able to finish clearing the west bank of the Havel opposite the city. On the way to the Elbe, the leading elements of the 47th Army reached the towns of Rathenow and Fehrbellin, but then paused. They were up against the strong opposition from General Holste's XXXXI Panzer Corps and it was no longer feasible to continue their advance without flanking support. Until more formations could be withdrawn from the city fighting further progress westwards would have to be delayed.[3]

The 1st Mechanised and 12th Guards Tank Corps finished clearing the suburb of Siemensstadt and closed up to the banks of the Spree from its junction with the Havel in Spandau to the Westhafen Canal in the east. All the bridges across their front had been destroyed, apart from a footbridge at the Spree locks. However, part of the 35th Mechanised Brigade managed to cross over to the area of Ruhleben racecourse (now the Ruhleben Waterworks) and this happened to coincide – there was no question of coordination! – with a thrust northwards along the axis of Reichsstrasse by the 55th Guards Tank Brigade. The latter had just been reinforced by 7th Guards Tank Corps's reserves of a battalion of motorised infantry, a rocket-launcher battalion, ten heavy tanks and a company of self-propelled guns, plus two artillery brigades. Colonel Dragunsky's orders were to seal off the defence by reaching the banks of the Spree at Ruhleben, locating the 1st Byelorussian troops and linking up with them. According to Dragunsky, progress was down to 50 yards an hour, with frequent detours due to blocked streets. Map reading proved extremely difficult in these circumstances, their compasses would not function properly with the amount of exposed metal about, and their internal radio communications were also not working.[4]

Eventually, elements of the two brigades met near the Charlottenburger Chaussee at about noon, after which the 35th Mechanised Brigade troops appear to have withdrawn again over the Spree, leaving Dragunsky's troops mopping up and securing the Westend residential area for the rest of the day and night in furtherance of their aim. However, they were under increasing pressure, as General Weidling could not afford to lose this potential escape route to the west and so sent part of the 18th Panzergrenadier Division to assist the local defence. It is clear that Dragunsky did not have sufficient numbers for his task, as German units were able to infiltrate through his lines time and time again, and even his rear echelon of supply vehicles was obliged to seek shelter with the main body that morning after having been forced out of its base at the Reichssportfeld (now Olympia Stadion) U-Bahn Station.[5]

The 79th Rifle Corps had a difficult time fighting through Moabit. The defence was the usual mixed bag of units, and some of the individual strongpoints could be bypassed and eliminated later, but the heavily built-up nature of this district made progress slow and costly. Once isolated, with the lack of water and provisions now being experienced, and the unnerving screams of women being raped at night, the defenders of these strongpoints rarely held out for long. However, among them were some of Vlassov's White Russian units, and these invariably fought with true desperation until the bitter end. Losses continued to be heavy, but the prisons in the area yielded large numbers of prisoners-of-war who were immediately used to replenish depleted units. It can be seen that the 79th Rifle Corps was deliberately heading southeast through Moabit for the big prize, the Reichstag building, leaving the 2nd Guards Tank Army to clear the Beusselstrasse area behind them down to Am Knie (now *Ernst-Reuter-Platz*).[6]

As for the rest of the 3rd Shock Army, the position is far from clear. The 9th Parachute Division was fighting well, and the Humboldthain Flak-tower, Stettiner Railway Station (now *Nordbahnhof*) and other positions in the area were holding out, with street-fighting going on all around them. Wolfgang Karow, the infantry NCO with an ad hoc team based on the flak-tower reported:

> The next operational order was to retake Wedding S-Bahn Station, which had been lost. We only got as far as Schönwalder Strasse on the night of the 27th, for it was impossible to establish who was in front of us, or to the left and right. The command post was in No. 27. Suddenly we heard 'Urrah! Urrah!' and the Russians attacked over the railway embankment. 'Come on, let's get out of here!' The men fired and then we rushed up the cellar steps. Up above the Stalin-Organs met us with a rocket salvo and we could hardly see the yard through the smoke. We reached the street in short bounds and ran down Kunkelstrasse to Schönwalder Strasse. In Schönwalder Strasse we had to cross the bridge over the Panke. It was about four in the morning and all we could see were some shadowy figures. I ran across to ask them where they came from, thinking they were a couple of our chaps, but discovered straight away that they were Russians. The accompanying Volkssturm and myself immediately took cover in the nearest building and opened fire on the Soviet stormtroops.[7]

Marshal Zhukov wrote:

> Our advance did not stop either by day or night. Our every effort was aimed at giving the enemy no chance to organise a defence or new strongpoints. The basic formations of the armies were well organised in depth. By day the first wave would advance and by night the second wave would take over.
>
> Each army taking part in the assault had been assigned to zones of action. The units and smaller elements were assigned specific streets, squares and other

objectives. Behind the seeming chaos of street-to-street fighting was a logical and well thought out system. Its main objectives became targets for devastating fire.[8]

This may have been what was required by the Stavka manuals, but in reality to try and continue the advance by night proved highly impractical for the combat teams. It was a noted characteristic of this battle that most Soviet troops used the nights as opportunities for rest, drunken orgies, looting and rape, leaving the higher echelon artillery to harass the enemy. In the area assigned to the 12th Guards and 7th Rifle Corps the apparent chaos became real, and the situation was so confused that the command was unable to exercise proper control, as becomes evident later.

The street-fighting techniques used by the 1st Byelorussian Front were based on the principle that each street should be tackled by a complete regiment, one battalion working down either side of the street and the third in reserve bringing up the rear. The frontage for a regiment was thus as little as 200 to 250 yards, while that of higher formations varied according to the terrain. Individual units were each assigned immediate tasks, subsequent tasks and an axis for further advance, the depth of penetration expected of it varying according to the circumstances. Usually the troops did not advance down the streets themselves but mouseholed their way through the buildings at various levels, while the supporting artillery pushed its way through the backyards and alleys with engineer assistance. The light infantry guns and dismantled rocket-launchers were manhandled up into the buildings and used with great flexibility. In attacking a heavily defended building the assault group would usually split in two, one part concentrating on quickly bottling up the enemy in the cellars, where they would normally have taken shelter during the preliminary bombardment, and the other clearing the upper storeys.[9]

Throughout the 5th Shock Army's area irregular fighting continued on 27 April. The front was now greatly fragmented with isolated pockets of resistance all over the combat zone. The whole area between Alexanderplatz and the Spree was in uproar, and there was still fighting around the Friedrichshain Flak-tower and Schlesischer Railway Station. On the other side of the river the 9th Rifle Corps continued to advance through Kreuzberg and reached Moritzplatz.[10]

During the 27th the bulk of Chuikov's forces closed up to the line of the Landwehr Canal along the northern front and consolidated their positions. In the centre the 28th Guards Rifle Corps with its strong armoured support continued to clear a firm base for the launching of the forthcoming operation, and appears to have secured the area roughly from Heinrich-von-Kleist Park through Nollendorfplatz to Lützowplatz, although the two latter squares remained in German hands and the battery position on Lützowplatz was to hold out until the very end of the battle. Heavy fighting took place around the Cornelius Bridge on

Budapester Strasse, and some Soviet tanks broke through the Zoo boundary wall and started firing at the flak-towers.[11]

Chuikov established his headquarters in a house at No. 2 Schulenburgring, close to both Tempelhof Airport and Viktoria Park, and began planning the next and final phase of his operation for the crossing of the Landwehr Canal into the main enemy stronghold, 'Zitdadelle'. He decided to use the next day resting his troops while he made his preparations, leaving the artillery and mortars keeping the enemy occupied. In conjunction with the 79th Rifle Corps's attack on the Reichstag building and the 5th Shock Army's push westwards through the city centre, Chuikov was responsible for clearing the southern part of the Tiergarten park as far as the East-West-Axis, and especially for the area of the Potsdamer and Anhalter Railway Stations leading to the Reich Chancellery.[12]

The Russians sent forward reconnaissance parties to probe the German defences, and three of these parties seem to have been in sufficient strength to have caused some concern. Fighting was reported near the Potsdamer Railway Station and two Soviet tanks were knocked out on the Hallesches Tor Bridge. SS-Major-General Mohnke reported that a group of Russian tanks accompanying two Czech tanks bearing German insignia had managed to enter Wilhelmstrasse before being destroyed.

With the pressure increasing, Mohnke deployed some 105mm howitzers on the Gendarmenmarkt to cover Belle-Alliance-Platz, on Pariser Platz to cover the Unter den Linden, and in Leipziger Strasse to cover the Spittelmarkt area, but there were only twelve rounds available per gun and once they had been fired the gunners were ordered to fight on as infantry.[13]

The 3rd Guards Tank Army was now fighting along the line of the inner defence ring. The Germans still held on grimly to their positions, especially at Schmargendorf S-Bahn station and in the adjacent Hindenburg Park (now *Volkspark*), where they had good fields of fire. However, the incessant hammering from the massed Soviet artillery eventually forced them to give ground. There was some bitter fighting around Fehrbelliner Platz, where it took the Russians three days to break through. After a German battery had been eliminated there, a Hitlerjugend tank-hunting unit using Panzerfausts mounted on staff cars carried out a series of raids in the Wilmersdorf District. Soviet casualties continued to be high.[14]

In 'Zitadelle' conditions were gradually deteriorating, as observed by the 'Müncheberg' Panzer Division diarist:

> The new command post is in the S-Bahn tunnels under Anhalter Railway Station. The station looks like an armed camp. Women and children huddle in niches, some sitting on folding chairs, listening to the sound of battle. Shells hit the roof, cement crumbles from the ceiling. Smells of powder and smoke in the tunnels. S-Bahn hospital trains trundle slowly by.

Suddenly a surprise. Water splashes into our command post. Shrieks, cries and curses. People are struggling around the ladders leading up to the ventilation shafts to the street above. Gurgling water floods through the tunnels. The crowds are panicky, pushing through the rising water, leaving children and wounded behind. People are being trampled underfoot, the water covering them. It rises a metre or so then slowly runs away. The panic lasts for hours. Many drowned. Reason: on somebody's orders, engineers have blown up the safety bulkhead control chamber on the Landwehr Canal between the Schöneberger and Möckern Bridges to flood the tunnels against the Russians. The whole time heavy fighting continues above ground.

Late afternoon the command post moves to the Potsdamer Platz station first level, the lower tunnel still being flooded. Direct hit through the roof. Heavy losses among wounded and civilians. Smoke drifts through the hole. Outside stocks of Panzerfausts explode under heavy Russian fire. Terrible sight at the station entrance, one flight of stairs down where a heavy shell has penetrated and people, soldiers, women and children are literally plastered to the walls. At dusk a short pause in the fighting.[15]

The flooding, according to Rittmeister (Cavalry Captain) Gerhard Boldt, had been ordered by Hitler as a result of reports of the Russians using the tunnels to infiltrate the German lines. However, when Reichsleiter Martin Bormann had enquired of the Berlin Transport Authority (BVG) on the 24th as to the feasibility of such a measure, he had been advised that the water would not arise above a metre or so in the affected section and would soon drain away again because of the sandy nature of the subsoil, as appears to have happened. Nevertheless, this action had been taken despite the fact that the tunnels were of considerable value to the defence, providing shelter to thousands, stores and command posts, as well as accommodating the hospital trains that were parked in the S-Bahn section near the Brandenburg Gate.[16]

SS-Major-General Krukenberg moved his SS 'Nordland' Panzergrenadier Division back into this part of the city centre and was allocated a derelict railway carriage as his command post in the Stadtmitte U-Bahn Station beneath the junction of Mohenstrasse and Friedrichstrasse. There was no electric light or telephone, but food supplies were readily available from commandeered grocery shops in the Gendarmenmarkt nearby.[17]

There was an unusual development at the evening conference on 27 April. Hitler suddenly noticed the absence of SS-Lieutenant-General Hermann Fegelein, Himmler's liaison officer and Eva Braun's brother-in-law, who had not been seen around for the past three days. Hitler immediately issued orders for him to be found, suspecting desertion. Eventually Fegelein was traced to an apartment in Bleibtreustrasse, off the Kurfürstendamm. Telephoned instructions failed to bring him back and so an armed escort was sent to fetch him, although technically they could not arrest him as there were officers of senior enough rank available for the task. They found him drunk and unshaven, and returned with his promise to follow as soon as he had cleaned himself up. When he still failed to appear, a second escort was sent, and found him clean-shaven and properly dressed but no more sober than before. There was a young woman present, and they appeared to have been packing a suitcase together. On the pretext of getting fresh glasses, the woman left the room and was later discovered to have fled through a kitchen window. Fegelein and the suitcase were brought back to the Chancellery, where he was promptly stripped of his rank and handed over to SS-Major-General Mohnke for trial. However, he was found to be too drunk to stand trial at the time.[18]

In the meantime the SS colonel in charge of the escort had reported to Bormann, who, from the circumstances of the incident and contents of the suitcase, which included passports, valuables and money suitable for an escape attempt, immediately deduced they had at last uncovered the source of the leak of information from the Führer's headquarters that had been a cause of deep concern for the past few months. The missing woman was apparently a British agent, and Fegelein had been about to flee the city with her.

Bormann had Fegelein handed over for interrogation to the Gestapo chief, Heinrich Müller, who was in charge of the security investigation, and eventually Fegelein was shot in the Chancellery garden half an hour before Hitler's wedding in the early hours of 30 April. The fate of the woman remains a mystery.[19]

In the early hours of 28 April, Lieutenant-Colonel Hans Rudel, the Luftwaffe's highly-decorated, tank-busting, 'Stuka' pilot, flew to Berlin in a Heinkel III in response to Hitler's radioed instructions, with the intention of landing on the Brandenburg Gate airstrip. He reported:

> Upon arriving near Berlin we were picked up by the Russian detectors and anti-aircraft artillery opened fire on us. It was very difficult to recognise the features of the capital because of enormous clouds of smoke and a thin layer of mist. The fires were so fierce in some places that we were dazzled by them and prevented from seeing anything. I had to concentrate on the shadows in order to see anything, and was unable to pick out the East-West-Axis. There were flames and cannon-fire everywhere. The spectacle was fantastic.
>
> We then received a message that the landing was impossible as the East-West-Axis was under heavy artillery fire and the Russians had already taken Potsdamer Platz.[20]

When Keitel visited Steiner at 0400 hours on the 28th, he was unaware of the latest developments on the 3rd Panzer Army's front, and Steiner could give him no information on the 7th Panzer Division. Steiner assured him that, despite the diversion of his expected reinforcements, he was still preparing his remaining forces for an attack that night. Keitel promised to give him the 'Schlageter' RAD Division to make up his numbers, but this division, part of the 12th Army's ill-fated XXXIX Panzer Corps, had been virtually wiped out in operations west of the Elbe the week before. In any case, Steiner was bluffing, having no intention of committing his men to an enterprise with such little chance of success. Meanwhile, unknown to them, Hitler had already despaired of Steiner's procrastination and issued orders the previous evening for his replacement by Lieutenant-General Holste of the XXXXI Panzer Corps. Holste had promptly asked for 48 hours in which to prepare his attack, as his troops were some distance from the bridgehead and would need time to get into position; he also had the Soviet 47th Army to contend with.[21]

It was on his way back to Jodl's headquarters that Keitel discovered what had happened to the 7th Panzer and 25th Panzergrenadier Divisions, and that the 3rd Panzer Army was actually in full retreat, not only without the permission of the OKW but in direct contravention of Hitler's orders. Mad with anger, he hastened to inform Jodl and then summoned Heinrici and von Manteuffel to a rendezvous at a crossroads west of Neubrandenburg that afternoon. Von Manuteuffel's Chief-of-Staff, Major-General Müller-Hillebrand, was suspicious of Keitel's intentions towards his chief, and organised his staff officers to lay a precautionary ambush at the rendezvous. It was a bitter encounter, a show-down among the military hierarchy, with Keitel accusing the generals of cowardice and treason, and Heinrici countering that he could not obey orders issued by an OKW when it was so obviously out of touch with events. Keitel shouted that if they had had the guts to shoot a few thousand deserters as an example, there would have been no retreat, whereupon Heinrici invited Keitel to start the executions with the exhausted columns staggering past them. Stared down, Keitel left without another word.[22]

The only realistic hope for the city's defenders now lay with Wenck's 12th Army opening an escape corridor to the west. Wenck's attack continued to make progress on the 27th and by the evening his leading elements had reached the village of Ferch at the southern tip of the Schwielowsee lake, some six miles south of Potsdam.[23]

The Russians rallied, but they were in a predicament. The attack had isolated the 6th Guards Mechanised Corps from the rest of the 4th Guards Tank Army at a time when this corps was extended over a distance of 18 miles. The 5th Guards Mechanised Corps and the 13th Army were having to form a double front, expecting the 9th Army to try and break out to the west at any moment from behind them, while the rest of the 4th Guards Tank Army was still heavily engaged in the containment of the Potsdam and Wannsee 'islands'. Koniev had located the 13th Army's reserve corps at Jüterbog, but it would appear that it had already been deployed to form screens across the 9th Army's anticipated route.[24]

By the evening of 28 April, General Busse was all set to break his 9th Army out of its 'pocket'. Now incorporating the survivors of the Frankfurt-an-der-Oder Garrison, his formations were all concentrated ready for the move in a small area roughly between Halbe and Märkisch Buchholz, west of the Dahme River.[25]

Busse's intention was to save as many people as he could from the Russians' clutches. Although he had lately received approval for his move from Hitler in the guise of the order instructing him the 9th and 12th Armies to link up near Jüterbog to strike jointly towards Berlin, Busse, in his own words, 'neither acknowledged, nor answered.' He was in direct radio contact with General Wenck, who had advised him of his secret line of march towards Beelitz, where the Russian lines were considered weakest (in fact the 5th Guards Mechanised Corps's lines ended there), and as far as both generals were concerned this was strictly a salvage operation.

The point of breakout suggested by reconnaissance was at Halbe, roughly on the Soviet inter-front boundary, where coordination would be the least effective, particularly once the 9th Army had crossed the territory of one front, thus automatically checking the fire of the other. From there the proposed escape route ran some thirty-seven miles through a wide belt of woodland running westwards past Luckenwalde. They would have to move day and night to keep ahead of the inevitable countermeasures, but the trees would serve to hamper the effectiveness of the Soviet tanks and aircraft.

The 9th Army's preparations were both thorough and drastic. Anything not essential for the breakout was destroyed or discarded. Motor vehicles were wrecked and their tanks drained to provide fuel for the fighting vehicles. Artillery pieces lacking ammunition were rendered unserviceable, and every soldier with a firearm, whatever his trade or employment, was organised into a combat unit. It was planned to move in a tight wedge, for which the formations had been deployed as follows:

- XI SS-Panzer Corps: Facing the breakout line near and north of Halbe with all the available armoured vehicles, and tasked with effecting the initial breach and then taking over the northern flank of the breakthrough.
- V Corps: Covering the southern flank of the breakout position, then responsible for following the XI SS-Panzer Corps through the breach and taking over the point for the breakthrough while covering the southern flank.
- V SS-Mountain Corps: Covering the breakout from the east and northeast, thereafter covering the rear of the breakthrough.
- 21st Panzer Division: Covering the breakout from the northwest with orders to fall back on Halbe as soon as the V SS-Mountain Corps was through the breach, and to follow on as the rearguard under command of that corps.

The artillery was massed near Halbe with the few rounds remaining for a covering barrage.

Between the military units swarmed tens of thousands of refugees opting to break out with the troops, although they must have realised how slim the chances of survival were. Having spotted some of the preliminary moves from the air, the Russians knew where to concentrate their artillery and air resources, including bombing the crossings over the Dahme River, and inevitably the toll exacted from these wretched refugees was high. For most of them the conditions and prospects were now so bad that the breakout, however slender a chance it offered of getting safely over the Elbe, presented a worthwhile gamble.

As soon as dusk began to fall, the operation began with a brief artillery barrage on the area selected for the breach, and the XI SS-Panzer Corps started a night-long battle to clear the way.

Directly opposing them was the extreme left wing of the 3rd Guards Army, with the 21st Rifle Corps deployed in the woods between the front boundary on the Halbe–Teupitz road and the village of Teurow, where the Dahme River became the frontline as far as Märkisch Buchholz and was manned by the 120th Rifle Corps of the same army. The Dahme valley south of Teurow, where the forest had been cleared for cultivation, was crammed with Russian artillery. In addition to the integral formation artillery, the whole of the 1st Guards Artillery Division had been assigned to this operation with the sole object of eliminating the German 9th Army. Some of this artillery was sited in the woods immediately opposite Halbe. The Soviet deployment was facilitated by the proximity of the Berlin–Dresden autobahn, which served as their main supply route.[26]

After a night of desperate fighting, a breach was opened by first light. Before it became full light, the commanders had to get their people flooding through the breach. It was a hectic scramble, but the bulk of the XI SS-Panzer Corps and the V Corps managed to get through and away under the most chaotic and horrific conditions, making it even more difficult for those following. It seems that the Russians managed to close the breach before the V SS-Mountain Corps could get through, and it then had to bear the brunt of the Soviet artillery fire in an area already strewn with the casualties and debris of the leading corps. Meanwhile the main body worked its way westwards through the woods to reach the Soviet cordon on the Zossen–Baruth road by midday, breaking through that evening.[27]

On the morning of 28 April, with Gatow Airfield now secured, the 175th Rifle Division of the 47th Army's 125th Rifle Corps attacked Potsdam from the north with the assistance of the 50th Guards Tank and 23rd Guards Mechanised Brigades. General Reymann's 20,000-strong garrison, which had meanwhile established contact with the 12th Army on the far side of the Schwielowsee, pulled back before them, abandoning the town. The same night the troops made good their escape along the lakeside and by using inflatable boats.[28]

The same day Spandau Citadel, the ancient moated fortress standing at the junction of the Spree and Havel Rivers, surrendered to the 1st Mechanised Corps of the 2nd Guards Tank Army. The citadel commandant and his deputy had previously been killed in sorties in which three Soviet tanks had been knocked out with Panzerfausts. The Russians had refrained from shelling or attacking the fortress when they learned from local inhabitants that it contained a poison gas installation. (They were not to know that there were only very small quantities of gas remaining in the laboratories for testing military equipment, most of the stock having been evacuated previously.) In view of the dangers presumed to be present, they sent forward a negotiator, who was admitted by means of a rope ladder leading to a window in the commandant's quarters over the main entrance, which had been securely blocked by an old French tank. He readily obtained the surrender of the garrison, which consisted of a field hospital, some Volkssturm and the civilian laboratory staff. From then on the massive ramparts and the Juliusturm watchtower provided a useful vantage point overlooking the Charlotten Bridge between Spandau Altstadt (town centre) and Stresow, and a potential German escape route.[29]

However, this was but a sideshow to the 2nd Guards Tank Army's main efforts of that day. Having abandoned the Ruhleben scene to the 1st Ukrainian Front, General Bogdanov redeployed his forces during the night for three attacks commencing at dawn. The 1st Mechanised Corps concentrated its efforts on the bend in the Spree due north of the Schloss Charlottenburg gardens, where the Spree Locks provided a potential crossing point for its infantry. Meanwhile the 219th Tank Brigade conducted an assault on the adjacent Jungfernheide S-Bahn Station strongpoint, where the underpasses provided the only gaps in the railway embankment screening the approaches to Charlottenburg District. Despite all their efforts the Soviet troops were unable to break through here that day. Meanwhile the 12th Guards Tank Corps crossed by the 79th Rifle Corps's route over the Westhafen Canal into Moabit and began fighting its way down the tongue of land between the Spree and the mouth of the Landwehr Canal.[30]

On the afternoon of 28 April, the leading elements of the 79th Rifle Corps advancing along the street known as Alt Moabit first caught sight of the Reichstag building through the swirling clouds of smoke and dust that obscured the central districts of the city. The fixation of the Soviets on the Reichstag as their goal was to highlight this particular part of the battle to heroic proportions. Heroic as it undoubtedly was in its execution, this episode also emphasises the ruthless exploitation of the troops involved and the fundamental military errors made by the commanders in their haste to meet a politically dictated deadline. The pressure from Stalin downwards to get the Red Flag flying from the top of the Reichstag in time for the May Day celebrations was such that no one in the chain of command wanted to be in a position where he could be accused of sabotaging the project. The cost was of no consequence.[31]

The news created great excitement and the corps commander, Major-General Pervertkin, hastened forward to see for himself. He decided to set up his command post in the tall Customs building at the end of the street overlooking the Moltke Bridge and the approaches to the Reichstag. The 150th Rifle Division was already beginning to assemble in the vicinity of the Customs building, and he called forward the 171st Rifle Division to assemble in the ruins of the Lehrter Railway Station (now *Hauptbahnhof*) on the other side of the street.

Immediately to his left was the Schiffahrts Canal denoting the corps boundary, behind which the Germans were still holding out as far north as Invalidenstrasse against the 12th Guards Rifle Corps. There were also some German troops remaining in the goods station to his right, which was not on his corps's line of advance, and so had not been cleared. Across his front the river was about 50 yards wide, the stone quay of the Customs Yard dropping ten feet to water level in full view of the enemy ensconced opposite. The only ready means available for crossing was the massive, stone-built Moltke Bridge, which was strongly barricaded at either end, ready mined for demolition, strewn with barbed wire and other obstacles, and swept by artillery and machine-gun fire from positions concealed in the ruined buildings on the far bank. Across the bridge on either side of Moltkestrasse were the badly damaged but still standing and fortified buildings of the Diplomatic Quarter on the left and the Prussian Ministry of the Interior on the right. Behind them aerial reconnaissance had revealed a vast flooded pit, from which a flooded anti-tank ditch extended across the front of the Reichstag with a series of trenches and strongpoints extending up to the building. Further artillery and mortars were entrenched in the Tiergarten park and the whole area was expected to be mined. The doors and windows of the Reichstag had been bricked up, leaving ventilation slots like gunports, and its ruined dome crowned with a machine-gun nest. Street-level cellar windows in the surrounding buildings provided ready-made gun embrasures.[32]

Direct air support had been withdrawn due to the narrowness of the battlefield, but the massed Soviet heavy artillery were now concentrating their efforts on this area between the Spree and the Landwehr Canal, which Chuikov's troops were preparing to cross from the south, and there was no shortage of ammunition.

It was decided to attempt a surprise infantry attack across the Moltke Bridge with a view to establishing a foothold in the near corner of the Diplomatic Quarter on the left, using one battalion from each of the two leading divisions. This could then be expanded into a bridgehead to enable the 150th Rifle Division to attack across Moltkestrasse into the Ministry of the Interior building dominating the crossing point, while the 171st Rifle Division cleared the remainder of the Diplomatic Quarter. Once secured, these buildings would provide a firm base for the attack on the Reichstag itself.

Casualties sustained in the fierce fighting through Moabit had been replaced by released prisoners-of-war and the leading Russian battalions were now back up to full strength. A battalion had an establishment of 500 men and consisted of three rifle companies, a support weapons company and a battery of 45mm field guns, but for this operation the battalions were split into two assault groups each, to which were added detachments of armoured self-propelled artillery. Also under command of the 79th Rifle Corps were the 10th Independent Flame-Thrower Battalion and the 23rd Tank Brigade.

Opposing them in this sector were estimated to be over 5,000 troops, most of them SS, although not all Waffen-SS, with the 'Grossadmiral Dönitz' Naval Battalion of radar technicians, two battalions of Volkssturm and some minor elements of the 9th Parachute Division. These were supported by light and field artillery, including some 88mm guns, and several mortars.[33]

The exact time of the attack is not known, but is presumed to have been at about midnight.[34]

Throughout the 5th Shock Army's sector the fighting remained extremely confused, especially around Alexanderplatz and the Stock Exchange, although steady progress was being maintained. Around the Friedrichshain Flak-tower, Landsberger Chaussee and Frankfurter Allee area, fighting continued between bombardments. The flak-tower held out until the end of the battle, the civilians sheltering there being evicted on the night of the 23rd. Before leaving, the garrison blew up the magazine, causing the whole structure to crack open and tumble inwards. Fortunately the museum art treasures stored in the adjacent control tower were not affected.[35]

On 28 April, with the Schlesischer Railway Station and other positions still holding out in its rear, the 32nd Rifle Corps launched an attack across the Spree on Fischerinsel (Fishermen's Island), the southern part of the island on which stood the former royal palace, Schloss Berlin, and the Dom (cathedral). Little is known about this operation, although Marshal Zhukov regarded it as one of the 5th Shock Army's most difficult tasks. With all the bridges blown, the sheer granite-lined banks of the waterways must have presented considerable difficulties. However, both banks of the river upstream being in Soviet hands, it can be assumed the Dnieper Flotilla contingent took part and that some commercial barges would have been brought downstream from the Osthafen to assist with the crossing and for making pontoon bridges.

As part of the same operation, the 9th Rifle Corps on the west bank of the river seized the Spittelmarkt area, which had been pulverised by artillery bombardment beforehand and its defenders obliterated in the ruins. Thus the end of the day saw the leading elements of the 5th Shock Army at the eastern end of the broad expanse of Leipziger Strasse and less than 1,500 yards from their goal, the Reich Chancellery.[36]

Chuikov's preparations for his assault across the Landwehr Canal provided for the maximum possible deployment of heavy artillery and rocket-launchers in the direct fire support role. These were brought up and positioned during the day under cover of smokescreens. Ammunition was plentiful and orders went out not to spare it. However, the artillery and mortar fire plans had to be carefully coordinated with those of the other converging armies to avoid overshooting and inflicting casualties on their own troops, for now only 2,000 yards separated them on the north-south line through the Tiergarten.[37]

The area of assault extended between a point opposite the OKW in Bendlerstrasse in the west to Belle-Alliance-Platz in the east, an area about 2,700 yards long, and it was decided that individual units should determine their own means of getting across in small groups, as the circumstances varied so considerably. The large hump-backed Potsdamer Bridge was the only bridge still intact along this stretch of canal, and Chuikov reserved for himself direct control of the operation there. Two large aerial mines were suspended from the structure ready for detonation, and the whole area was swept by heavy enfilade fire from artillery, tanks and Panzerfausts, but it offered the only means of getting armour across during the initial assault, and was therefore vital for the operation. From there the broad expanse of Potsdamer Strasse led directly into the heart of the defence around Potsdamer Platz and the entrance to Leipziger Strasse, only a block from the Reich Chancellery.[38]

Reconnaissance activity continued throughout the day, and the scouts investigating the tunnels leading under the canal (i.e., the S-Bahn tunnel from the Yorckstrasse marshalling yards and the U-Bahn leading from Belle-Alliance-Strasse (now *Mehringdamm*) into Friedrichstrasse) reported them being impracticable as a means of approach, being blocked by barricades at regular intervals and very narrow. However, reinforced reconnaissance patrols were sent by these routes to try and harass the Germans from the rear.[39]

In his preparations for this final battle, Chuikov paid particular attention to the political reinforcement of his units. In the confined and confusing conditions of street-fighting it was impossible for the commanders to see exactly what was going on. It was therefore important to have reliable cadres of Communist Party and Komsomol members throughout his deployed units to ensure that the orders passed down from above were duly executed, especially in these closing phases of the war when the troops were naturally reluctant to take unnecessary risks.[40]

On the morning of the 28th, in accordance with orders issued the night before, the 3rd Guards Tank Army launched a concerted attack on the extreme right wing of its area of operations, the start line being Badensche Strasse between Kaiserallee (now *Bundesallee*) and Potsdamer Strasse, with the aim of crossing the Landwehr Canal by nightfall.[41] In support of this operation, Colonel Dragunsky's 55th Guards Tank Brigade was ordered out of its blocking role in the Westend and directed down the axis of Kantstrasse towards Charlottenburg Station, Savignyplatz and the Zoo.[42]

The main attack got under way as planned and it was not until sometime later that morning that it was suddenly realised that virtually the whole of the eastern half of the proposed line of advance was already occupied by Chuikov's troops, on whom the weight of Koniev's artillery preparations could hardly have been welcome. As a result of this discovery, the 3rd Guards Tank Army's 9th Mechanised Corps and its supporting 61st Guards Rifle Division had to be switched from the right to the left flank and given fresh instructions to head for Savignyplatz. The emotions that this event raised can well be imagined. However, it came as a welcome relief to the 56th Guards Tank Brigade on the exposed left flank of the 7th Guards Tank Corps's two-brigade front, which had been attracting the full attention of the German tank-hunting units based on Fehrbelliner Platz and suffering accordingly.[43]

With his Berlin ambitions thus thwarted, Koniev left Colonel-General Rybalko to complete the 1st Ukrainian Front's role in the city as best he might. Koniev had taken a tremendous gamble in concentrating all his available resources in a single powerful thrust on the Reichstag, leaving only one reinforced brigade to cope with all the enemy forces between the Havel and Wilmersdorf, but he had in fact been defeated by factors arising out of the rivalry between Zhukov and himself, which had then been skilfully exploited by Stalin without regard for the military implications. At midnight Moscow Time (2200 hours in Berlin) GHQ issued orders for a new inter-front boundary that was to run along the line Mariendorf–Tempelhof Station–Viktoria-Luise-Platz–Savigny Station and thence along the railway line via Charlottenburg, Westkreuz and Witzleben Stations.[44]

Meanwhile those elements of the 55th Guards Tank Brigade still remaining in the Westend area launched a triple-pronged attack on Ruhleben to keep the defence occupied. They overran the mixed flak and field artillery in the grounds of the Reich Sport Academy sharing the same hilltop as the Olympic Stadium, and pushed down the back of the hill over the Ruhleben ranges towards the Alexander Barracks, where the headquarters of Defence Sector 'F' were located. The defence had about 1,000 troops in this area, survivors of the fighting in Spandau and Siemensstadt, who concentrated on the line of the barracks and Ruhleben U-Bahn Station on its high embankment. Then, reinforced by about 2,000 local Hitlerjugend boys taken from their homes, most of whom were unarmed and relying upon picking up arms from the battlefield, part of the defending forces counterattacked and drove the Soviets all the way back over the hill to the Heerstrasse. On their way they suffered severe casualties when caught in enfilade fire from other Soviet troops ensconced in the Academy buildings, before the latter could be evicted by another group of the defence taking them from the rear. The third prong of the Soviet attack, with tanks advancing down the Charlottenburger Chaussee as far as the barrack gates, was also defeated by the defence and several tanks were destroyed. However, this action had achieved its purpose in tying down the defence in the area.[45]

The 'Müncheberg' Panzer Division diarist wrote:

Continuous attacks throughout the night. The Russians are trying to break through in Leipziger Strasse. Prinz-Albrecht-Strasse [now *Niederkirchener Strasse*] has been retaken, as has Köthener Strasse [then running along the eastern side of the Potsdamer Railway Station].

Increasing signs of disintegration and despair, but it makes no sense surrendering at the last moment and then spending the rest of your life regretting not having held on to the end.

'K' brings news that the American armoured divisions are on their way to Berlin, which makes them in the Reich Chancellery more certain of ultimate victory than ever before.

Hardly any communications among the battle groups, in as much as none of the active battalions have radio communications any more. Telephone cables are shot through in no time at all. Physical conditions are indescribable. No relief or respite, no regular food and hardly any bread. Nervous breakdowns from the continuous artillery fire. Water has to be obtained from the tunnels and the Spree, and then filtered. The not too seriously wounded are hardly taken in anywhere, the civilians being afraid to accept wounded soldiers and officers into their cellars when so many are being hanged as real or presumed deserters, and the occupants of the cellars concerned turfed out as accomplices by the members of the flying courts martial.

These flying courts martial appear particularly often in our sector today. Most of them are very young SS officers with hardly a decoration between them, blind and fanatical. Hope of relief and fear of these courts martial keep our men going. General Mummert had requested that no further courts martial visit our sector. A division that contains the most highly decorated personnel does not deserve to be persecuted by such youngsters. He has made up his mind to shoot any court martial team that he comes across in person.

Potsdamer Platz is a ruined waste. Masses of wrecked vehicles and shot-up ambulances with the wounded still inside them. Dead everywhere, many of them frightfully mangled by tanks and trucks.

In the evening we try to get news from the Propaganda Ministry of Wenck and the American divisions. There are rumours that the 9th Army is also on its way to Berlin, and that peace treaties are being signed in the west.

Violent shelling of the city centre at dusk with simultaneous attacks on our positions. We cannot hold on to Potsdamer Platz any longer, and at about 0400 hours make for Nollendorfplatz as Russians heading for Potsdamer Platz pass us in the parallel tunnel.[46]

At about 2100 hours on 28 April news of Himmler's peace talks with Count Bernadotte of Sweden was intercepted by the Propaganda Ministry from a Reuters broadcast in German on Radio Stockholm. This news profoundly shocked Hitler; that 'der treue Heinrich' could do this to him was absolutely unthinkable; it was treachery of the worst kind and must be avenged at all costs.[47]

The intrepid warrant officer who had flown Speer to Berlin and back, and then von Greim and Hanna Reitsch to Gatow, had managed to fly in an Arado 96 that night to fly them out again. Hitler instructed von Greim to use all remaining Luftwaffe resources in assisting the defence of Berlin and, above all, to find Himmler and bring him to justice. Von Greim was in pain and on crutches, but he was helped out of the bunker into an armoured vehicle that took them up Hermann-Göring-Strasse (now *Ebertstrasse*) to the airstrip. Dodging small-arms fire, flak and searchlights, the warrant officer pilot took off and found safety in a cloudbank at 4,500 feet above the city, and then followed a trail of burning villages marking the extent of the Soviet advance back to Rechlin Air Base.[48]

At this stage one sees that Hitler's personal influence on the conduct of the battle as a commander had ceased to have any meaning. He could of course have brought about an immediate end to the conflict, but that was not his intention. Direction was now in the hands of the field commanders who, although still bound by oaths of loyalty to the Führer, saw these as less important than the loyalty they owed their own troops in this predicament.

Weidling's forces were now confined to a sausage-shaped area extending from Alexanderplatz in the east some eight and a half miles to the banks of the Havel in the west, but barely a mile wide in places. He still had some 30,000 combatants and a handful of tanks and guns, but food and ammunition were running out fast, and he estimated that they could not hold out longer than another 48 hours. If surrender was out of the question, there was still chance of breaking out to the west to link up with Wenck's 12th Army. He therefore presented a plan on these lines to Hitler at the evening conference of the 28th but, after some debate, Hitler turned it down. He had decided that they should all hold out to the end, and that he could not take the risk of falling alive into enemy hands.[49]

General Weidling himself could have little influence on events. He had been given command of the defence too late to inject any idea of his own and, although he had substituted proper military commanders for the Defence Sectors, each had to fight his own battle with the existing resources, for Weidling had nothing extra to give them. SS-Major-General Krukenberg later complained that he had not received any orders or instructions from Weidling during the battle, but there were none to give. Weidling was not even in a position to take unilateral action as Wenck, Busse, Heinrici and von Manteuffel were now doing, for his forces contained too many hard-core Nazis to permit either a breakout or surrender without Hitler's sanction. Indeed, there are many recorded instances of these fanatics shooting down their own countrymen when they did attempt to surrender.[50]

At about 2230 hours von Manteuffel telephoned Heinrici to report that half his divisions and all his supporting Flak were in full retreat. He said that he had not seen anything like it since 1918; 100,000 men trekking westwards. He suggested that Jodl be invited to see the situation for himself. Shortly afterwards Heinrici passed on the news of the debacle to Keitel and asked permission to abandon Swinemünde, where the garrison of naval cadets was in imminent danger of being cut off. The scandalised Keitel accused him of flagrant disobedience of the Führer's orders. Heinrici rejoined that he could not accept the responsibility for continuing to command troops under the impossible conditions expected of him by the OKW, whereupon Keitel promptly relieved him of his command and would have had him court martialled if he had had the chance.[51]

There was a surprise in the Führerbunker that night when Hitler announced his intention of marrying his mistress, Eva Braun. Goebbels sent out for a suitably qualified official to perform the ceremony, and at about 0130 hours a bewildered man wearing a Volkssturm armband, Gauamtsleiter Walter Wagner, was brought in briefly from the street-fighting to legalise their union. Shortly afterwards Hitler began dictating his personal and political testaments to one of his secretaries, naming Grand Admiral Dönitz as his successor in the role of President and Goebbels as Chancellor. Clearly he was preparing himself for the end, having lost all hope in the future.[52]

During the course of the night of the 28th, commencing at 2100 hours, the 10th Guards Tank Corps, supported by the 350th Rifle Division, launched an attack across the Teltow Canal on the south-western tip of Wannsee 'island'. Within an hour a bridgehead had been established and work had begun on connecting a pontoon bridge to it. The few remaining men of the 20th Panzergrenadier Division and the other units there resisted fiercely and seem to have been able to contain this incursion for the time being. From Koniev's account it is clear that he did not approve of this operation, which to him must have appeared as an unnecessary distraction from his more pressing issues with the German 9th and 12th Armies.[53]

This action followed the taking of Potsdam 'island' by elements of the 47th Army and the 9th Guards Tank Corps earlier in the day. That same night the 9th Guards Tank Corps was returned to the command of the 2nd Guards Tank Army, which was now heavily engaged in the Charlottenburg and Moabit districts of Berlin, taking over the reserve position in the Siemensstadt area from the 1st Mechanised Corps.[54]

12

The Last Round

Throughout 29 April General Wenck's troops held on to their extended positions against increasing Soviet pressure all along the line as they waited the arrival of the 9th Army. It was clear that they would not be able to advance any further and Wenck signalled General Weidling in Berlin:

> Counterattacks by 12th Army stalled south of Potsdam. Troops engaged in very heavy defensive fighting. Suggest you break out to us.

This signal was not acknowledged, and it is doubtful if Weidling even received it.[1]

That same evening Wenck's position was further imperilled by a sudden attack towards Wittenberg by American troops bursting out of their bridgeheads in his rear. Fortunately this attack was not pursued, presumably because of the policy imposed from above of not intervening in the Soviet area of operations.[2]

As already mentioned, General Busse's spearhead broke through the Soviet lines on the Zossen–Baruth road that day and the survivors then rested in the woods west of the road prior to undertaking the next desperate stage of the breakout. The number of refugees managing to keep up with the wedge was diminishing rapidly. Contact had been lost with the V SS-Mountain Corps and one assumes that the whole of the rearguard with the majority of the refugees caught in the Russian trap were in the course of being liquidated. In the obscurity of the woods the Russians may well have been misled, at least temporarily, into thinking that they had caught the bulk of the 9th Army, and later, having realised their error, were happy to prolong the myth.[3]

The V SS-Mountain Corps and the 21st Panzer Division fought desperately to break out of the reinforced Soviet cordon, and in so doing not only inflicted heavy casualties on the enemy, but also served to distract attention from the remainder of the 9th Army. Although they managed to break out of the Halbe position, they were unable to break through the Soviet cordon and remained under a hail of shell and mortar fire. This bitter struggle continued for two days. The Soviets then claimed to have killed 60,000 and captured 120,000 prisoners,

300 tanks and self-propelled guns, and 1,500 pieces of artillery. Shortly afterwards a Soviet writer driving north along the autobahn found it littered for miles with wrecked vehicles and equipment mingled with dead and wounded German soldiers, whom the Russians had not yet had time to remove.[4]

However, the state of the troops in the breakout party was now such that General Busse signalled General Wenck:

> The physical state and morale of the officers and men, as well as the states of ammunition and supplies, permit neither a new attack nor long resistance. The misery of the civilians that fled the pocket is particularly bad. Only the measures taken by all the generals have enabled the troops to stick together. The fighting capacity of the 9th Army is obviously at an end.[5]

Wenck immediately passed this discouraging information on to the OKW, who in the meantime had themselves put an end to any chances of relief from this direction by disclosing the 12th Army's disposition and intentions in their afternoon radio communiqué. This made it even more difficult for the 12th Army to hold on to its positions in a situation already precarious enough, with the 5th Guards Mechanised Corps and 13th Army trying to cut off its line of retreat to the Elbe.

Wenck signalled the OKW again that evening:

> The Army, and in particular the XX Corps, which has momentarily succeeded in establishing contact with the Potsdam Garrison, is obliged to turn to the defensive along the whole front. This means that an attack on Berlin is now impossible, having ascertained that we can no longer rely on the fighting capacity of the 9th Army.[6]

During the night Wenck received the following reluctant acknowledgement of the situation by signal from Field Marshal Keitel:

> If the Commanding General 12th Army, in full knowledge of his present situation at the XX Corps, and despite the high historical and moral responsibility that he carries, considers continuing the attack on Berlin impossible…

Wenck now had a free hand to pursue his own plans.[7]

General von Manteuffel was ordered to take over Army Group 'Weichsel' but, loyal to his own troops and Heinrici, he refused with the words, 'Beg not at this time of crisis to be charged with the mission that the present commanding general, who has the full confidence of all commanders, is alleged not to have fulfilled.' Keitel and Jodl then decided to fly back Luftwaffe Colonel-General Kurt Student, the famous parachute commander, from Holland to take over the

Army Group. In the interim, General von Tippelskirch of the new 21st Army was to stand in. He too refused the appointment, but Keitel and Jodl went to see him and persuaded him to accept the post on the grounds that it was imperative for the Army Group to hold on to as much territory as possible, not with the intention of relieving Berlin, but in order to give the politicians something to bargain with.[8]

However, the 2nd Byelorussian Front was pressing hard and that day overran Anklam in the north, Neubrandenburg and Neustrelitz in the centre, and crossed the Havel in the Zehdenick–Liebenwalde sector on the southern flank. From the other side of the Elbe, the British 21st Army Group established a bridgehead at Lauenburg, where Field Marshal Ernst Busch was struggling to keep open the Elbe-Lübeck gap as an escape route to the northwest.[9]

Rain during the night caused the balloon supporting the OKW aerial to sink, but the weather was bright and warm on the morning of the 29th and communications were soon re-established with the Führerbunker. Unfortunately, the weather also brought the Russian aircraft out in swarms and, in the middle of a conversation between Hitler and Jodl, the balloon was shot down. This being the last one available, communications from then on were reduced to normal field radio transmissions. The Russian ground forces were now very close to their location, and at midday the OKW started moving out. Keitel and Jodl waited for dusk before taking the road to Waren, barely an hour before the camp was over-run.[10]

With the 3rd Panzer Army in full retreat, there was no longer any question of relieving Berlin from the north, or indeed of providing any further support for the city from that quarter.

It was decided that two copies of Hitler's personal and political testaments should be sent to Grand Admiral Dönitz by separate couriers to ensure delivery. Bormann selected his personal adviser, SS-Standartenführer (Colonel) Wilhelm Zander, and Heinz Lorenz of the Propaganda Ministry for this task. A third set of copies was to go to Field Marshal Schörner in the care of Hitler's Army Aide-de-Camp, Major Will Johannmeier, who, with his orderly, would escort the others through the Russian lines. They set off at noon on the 29th, making their way slowly through the Tiergarten to the Zoo position and along Kantstrasse to the Olympic Stadium, then down to the Hitlerjugend Regiment's position astride the Heerstrasse, where they rested until nightfall before setting off in two boats down the Havel.[11]

Inspired by this departure, three young and now redundant aides, Lieutenant-Colonel Weiss, Major Bernt Freiherr Freytag von Loringhoven and Rittmeister Gerhard Boldt, obtained permission to try and join up with Wenck's army. They left between 1400 and 1500 hours, taking the same route as the previous party. Boldt later recorded that they passed a position for twelve to fifteen artillery pieces in the Tiergarten, all abandoned for lack of ammunition.[12]

Then at midnight, Colonel von Below and his adjutant, escorted by their orderlies, also left the Führerbunker, taking with them a letter from Hitler to Field Marshal Keitel concerning the appointment of Grand Admiral Dönitz as his successor. This letter contained praise for the work of the Navy and the Luftwaffe, and also praised the common soldiers, but denounced the generals for betraying his trust in them. Just before dawn this group caught up with Lieutenant-Colonel Weiss's party at the Olympic Stadium, from where they continued their journey with a Hitlerjugend patrol to the Hitlerjugend Regiment's position on the Havel. There they had to wait until nightfall before they could continue downriver by boat.[13]

In the meantime, Johannmeier's party had reached the Wannsee 'island' before dawn on 30 April. There they found the remains of the 20th Panzergrenadier Division, with whose assistance they managed to radio a request to Grand Admiral Dönitz to send an aircraft to collect them. Then they moved to Pfaueninsel (Peacock Island) to await its arrival and were joined by Weiss's party early the next morning. However, von Below landed on the other side of the river near Gatow Airfield and struck off west for the Elbe, later burning the papers he was carrying when he realised the futility of his mission.[14]

The morning of the 29th saw a breakthrough in the 2nd Guards Tank Army's sector. The 1st Mechanised Corps's motorised infantry crossed the Spree and fought their way through the Schloss Charlottenburg gardens. Meanwhile the German resistance at the Jungfernheide S-Bahn Station had been overcome and, by using rubble to make a ramp up to the railway line, the Soviet engineers managed to get some tanks up to the railway line and across the still intact railway bridge across the Spree to join them. The 12th Guards Tank Corps, using massive artillery support, continued to make steady progress through the western part of Moabit, heading for the tongue of land between the Spree and the western end of the Landwehr Canal.[15]

The 79th Rifle Corps's attack across the Moltke Bridge was a daring and bloody affair. The exact time it was launched is not known, but by 0200 hours on the 29th the first objective, the building on the corner of the embankment and Moltkestrasse had been secured. The attack began with a fierce barrage from the supporting artillery firing over open sights that were massed in the Customs Yard and on Washingtonplatz. The first barricade having been bulldozed aside, the first wave of infantry had still to negotiate the far one and other obstacles while under machine-gun and artillery fire directed at them from concealed enfilade positions concealed in the buildings opposite and from further back along the line of the two streets converging on the bridge.[16]

In their haste to launch this attack, the Russians had not had time to clear the Germans out of the Lehrter Goods Station on their right flank. Consequently they now found themselves subjected to counterattacks on both sides of the river.

The Germans even succeeded in blowing the bridge, but the charges proved inadequate for the massive structure and only half of one span fell into the river, leaving sufficient room for vehicles to pass.

Having established a foothold in the corner house, the infantry began expanding their bridgehead by the usual method of mouseholing into the adjacent buildings. The 150th Rifle Division worked its way along the line of buildings fronting Moltkestrasse, while the 171st Rifle Division cleared the remainder of the block with the 525th Rifle Regiment working the Kronprinzenufer side on the left, and the 380th Rifle Regiment in the middle. By dawn the whole of the first echelons of both divisions and the flame-thrower battalion were across the river, and engineers were clearing a passage for the armour to follow. That so many units were able to cram into such a small space is indicative of the number of casualties they must have sustained in crossing the bridge, and the determination of the Soviet command.

By 0700 hours the next stage of the operation began with a ten-minute barrage, as the 150th Rifle Division prepared to cross Moltkestrasse into the entrance of the Prussian Ministry of the Interior building opposite, 'Himmler's House' as they called it. The two middle buildings on the Russian side of the street had their carriage entrances directly opposite, so one can assume this was the route taken. The Russians dashed across the street and flattened themselves against the walls of the Ministry, threw grenades into the doorway, and then charged up the steps into the hall beyond. Fighting rapidly spread up the main staircase and along the various floors, and was to last all day amid the choking smoke of fires started among the carpets and furniture littered about. The SS defenders resisted fiercely, and eventually the division's second echelon, the 674th Rifle Regiment had to be called in to help clear the southwest corner of the building.

Between 0830 and 1000 hours there was a massive artillery bombardment of the Reichstag itself in an attempt to weaken the defences there for the forthcoming attack, but it was to take a full 24 hours to secure the Ministry of the Interior building.

Fighting in the north-eastern arc occupied by the 12th Guards and 7th Rifle Corps of the 3rd Shock Army and 26th Guards Rifle Corps of the 5th Shock Army continued in the same manner as before with little outward progress made in the confusion. Strong resistance was encountered at the Stettiner Railway Station (now *Nordbahnhof*) strongpoint where the northern end of the S-Bahn tunnel emerged above ground.

In the 26th Guards Rifle Corps's sector, which was now astride the Spree in the city centre, the 1008th and 1010th Rifle Regiments of the 266th Rifle Division attacked the Rotes Rathaus, the massive red brick city hall, which had been turned into a strongpoint. The attack was supported by tanks and self-propelled guns against formidable opposition, but no progress was made until some holes had been blasted through the walls of the building to obtain access. The Russians were then obliged to fight for every room in turn through the clouds of dense smoke that filled the building.[17]

Meanwhile the 32nd and 9th Rifle Corps were having a hard fight against the SS 'Nordland' Panzergrenadier Division and other Waffen-SS elements in their progress towards the Reich Chancellery.

An hour before General Chuikov's artillery preparation was due to begin, the infantry took up their positions for the assault in the 29th Guards Rifle Division's sector opposite the Potsdamer Bridge, making their way either singly or in small groups. Some would be swimming or using improvised rafts and floating devices to get across the Landwehr Canal, and others were to try and rush the bridge under cover of a smokescreen. Among the latter was the standard bearer of the 220th Guards Rifle Regiment, Guards-Sergeant Nikolai Masalov, with his standard and two assistants. As the story goes, in the intense quiet that preceded the storm, they suddenly heard the sound of a young child crying for its mother coming from the other side of the bridge. Masalov handed over the standard to one of his assistants and approached his commanding officer for permission to try and rescue the child before the barrage began. He then managed to crawl across under covering fire from his comrades and found a 3-year-old German child lying in the rubble next to her dead mother. As soon as the artillery opened up, he dashed back with her in his arms.[18]

By this stage of the battle the Soviet armour had developed some ingenious methods of countering the prolific German anti-tank weapons. Their tanks were now festooned with sandbags, bed-springs, sheet metal and other devices to cause the projectiles to explode harmlessly outside the hull, and it was an inspired adaptation of one of these devices that finally enabled them to get their tanks across the Potsdamer Bridge.[19] Sappers had first to remove the mine planted on the bridge as well as neutralise the two large aerial mines suspended from it, all the while working under heavy machine-gun fire. Initial attempts to rush the infantry across the bridge met with costly failure, and the Soviet tanks found themselves helpless against the fire of a dug-in 'Tiger' tank covering the crossing from an enfilade position. More artillery fire and smoke were called for and eventually some infantry managed to get safely across, but the tanks were still being knocked out one by one as they approached. Then someone had the bright idea of steeping the protective covering of one of the tanks in inflammable oil and adding some smoke canisters. Thinking that the tank was merely careering forward out of control, the Germans ignored it until it was too late, and the Russian tank was across the bridge and firing into their flanks at point-blank range.[20]

Meanwhile other attempts to cross the canal along the assault line had met with varying degrees of success. In the 29th Guards Rifle Divisions' area towards the right flank, one successful unit used the sewers to obtain a concealed approach and exit route for swimming across, emerging in the middle of the German defences. Another unit of the same division, a company of the 120th Guards Rifle Regiment, used similar covered approaches to reach the wrecked footbridge leading across the canal to the elevated Möckern Bridge U-Bahn Station on the north bank, and was able to traverse the wreckage and seize the station, establishing a route for the rest of the battalion to follow. Further east at the Hallesches Tor, the engineers managed to get pontoons into the water so that tanks could reach Belle-Alliance-Platz, thereby giving Chuikov some powerful leverage on his right flank.[21]

Although several bridgeheads were established one way and another, the cost was appallingly high. The defence's artillery and machine guns had been cleverly concealed in enfilade positions behind the buildings and rubble on the northern bank. They could fire on these intrusions from the flank while remaining impervious to direct fire from the Russians on the other side of the canal. Chuikov eventually decided to bring his guns right up to the edge of the canal, from where they themselves could fire in enfilade across the convex curves of the waterway, thus using 'a wedge to knock out a wedge', as he put it. The artillery also had to cover the enemy rear areas, as the lines were now too close for air support.[22]

General Rybalko now redistributed his 3rd Guards Tank Army more evenly for the reduction of Wilmersdorf, and progress along the streets leading to the Kurfürstendamm was marked by the pounding of the guns. One consequence of the previous night's change of boundaries was that the 55th Guards Tank Brigade fighting its way down Kantstrasse had to be withdrawn from what had now become the 2nd Guards Tank Army's sector. However, the orders did not reach Colonel Dragunsky until after daylight, by which time fighting had resumed to such an extent that many of the units could not be extricated. Subsequently the arrival of some tanks of the 2nd Guards Tank Army and infantry of the 55th Guards Rifle Division all added to the confusion in this sector, and it was not until after nightfall that the brigade could effect its withdrawal and return to its blocking role in the Westend. Those elements of the 55th Guards Tank Brigade that had been driven off the Olympic Stadium the previous day resumed their attacks on that position and regained some ground, but the Westend area remained no-man's land all day.[23]

At Fehrbelliner Platz some 'Tiger' tanks of the 'Leibstandarte Adolf Hitler' Regiment made a strong counterattack during the day, but the defenders, which included elements of the 18th Panzergrenadier Division, were being slowly driven back. However, the Halensee–Westkreuz position continued to hold firm, presumably bypassed by the main tide of battle.[24]

The Hitlerjugend Regiment's position on the Heerstrasse also stood firm, being the other side of the inter-front boundary from the opposing 47th Army, but was under sporadic fire from across the Havel. Rittmeister Boldt described the situation as follows:

The Hitlerjugend lay alone or in pairs with their Panzerfausts at irregular intervals in the trenches on either side of the Heerstrasse in front of the Pichelsdorf bridges. The dawn was sufficiently advanced to distinguish the dark shapes of heavy Russian tanks against the even darker background, their guns pointing at the bridge. We found the leader of the combat group, who told us what had happened to his people: 'When the fighting started here five days ago, there were about 5,000 Hitlerjugend and a few soldiers available to take on this desperate struggle against overwhelming odds. Inadequately equipped with only rifles and Panzerfausts, the boys have suffered terribly from the effects of Russian shelling. Of the original 5,000 only 500 are still fit for combat.' [25]

At 2200 hours it was reported that the Russians had occupied all of Saarlandstrasse and the southern part of Wilhelmstrasse as far as the Air Ministry. From the north they had overrun Bismarckstrasse and were approaching Kantstrasse. General Weidling wrote of the 29th:

Catastrophe was inevitable if the Führer did not reverse his decision to defend Berlin to the last man, and if he sacrificed all who were still alive and fighting in the city for the sake of a crazy ideal. We racked our brains to see how we could avert this fate. Surely the Führer must realise that even the bravest soldier cannot fight without ammunition. The struggle was devoid of sense or purpose. The German soldier could see no way out of the situation. I set out for the next briefing with a heavy heart.

Once again I mentioned the possibility of a breakout and drew attention to the general situation. Like a man fully resigned to his fate, the Führer answered me, pointing to his map. Sarcastically he commented that the positions of our troops had been sketched in from reports on the foreign radio, as our own headquarters were no longer reporting them. Since his orders were not being carried out, it was pointless to expect anything – for instance from the 7th Panzer Division, which according to instructions should be approaching from the Nauen area.

As a gesture permitting me to leave, this completely broken man got up from his chair with a great effort, but I urged him to decide what should be done when the ammunition ran out, which would be by the evening of the next day at the latest. After a brief consultation with General Krebs, the Führer replied that in that case the only thing to do would be to break out of Berlin in small groups, since he still refused to surrender Berlin. I could go… [26]

On the evening of the 29th, in response to Hitler's query, SS-Major-General Mohnke reported that the Russians had almost reached the Weidendammer Bridge from the north, were in the Lustgarten to the east, in Potsdammer Strasse to the south and at the Air Ministry. In the west they were only 300 to 400 yards away in the Tiergarten. Hitler then asked how much longer they could hold out, and was told no more than 24 hours.[27]

Even Hitler could now see that the situation was truly desperate, and shortly before midnight he sent the following message to the OKW:

I am to be informed immediately:
    1. Where are Wenck's spearheads?
    2. When will they resume the attack?
    3. Where is the 9th Army?
    4. Where is it breaking through?
    5. Where are Holste's XXXXI Corps's spearheads?[28]

Field Marshal Keitel's surprisingly honest reply was received at 0100 hours on the 30th and read as follows:

1. Wenck's point is stopped south of the Schwielowsee. Strong Soviet attacks along the whole east flank.

2. Consequently the 12th Army cannot continue its attack towards Berlin.

3 & 4. The 9th Army is surrounded. An armoured group has broken out to the west; location unknown.

5. Corps Holste is forced on the defensive from Brandenburg via Rathenow to Kremmen.

The attack towards Berlin has not developed at any point since Army Group 'Weichsel' was also forced on the defensive on the whole front from north of Oranienburg via Neubrandenburg to Anklam.[29]

There was nothing further to be done; suicide was the only solution. Hitler spent a restless night, eventually summoning Mohnke at about 0600 hours on 30 April for a chat. Mohnke reported that the Russians were now in the famous Hotel Adlon at the junction of Wilhelmstrasse and the Unter den Linden. They were also in the U-Bahn tunnels in Friedrichstrasse and just outside the Chancellery beneath Voss-strasse.[30] His own troops were exhausted and could not possibly hold out much longer. In any event he expected a massive frontal attack on the Chancellery at dawn next day, being May Day. Hitler took all this calmly, reconciled to his fate. At the end of their talk Hitler gave Mohnke typed copies of his testaments for delivery to Grand Admiral Dönitz.[31]

Early on the 30th a young SS-Lieutenant delivered to General Weidling at his headquarters in Bendlerstrasse a letter from Hitler that read:

In the event that there should be a shortage of ammunition or supplies in the Reich capital, I hereby give my permission for our troops to attempt a breakout. This operation should be organised in combat teams as small as possible. Every effort should be made to link up with German units still carrying on the fight outside the city of Berlin. If such cannot be located, the Berlin forces must take to the woods and continue resistance from there.[32]

Mid-morning, General Weidling convened a conference of Defence Sector commanders at which he told them of the Führer-Order authorising a breakout attempt. He instructed them to plan a breakout at 2200 hours that night and that, if necessary, it would take place on his own authority.[33]

At the morning briefing in the Führerbunker, General Krebs reported that the Russians now controlled both sides of Leipziger Strasse and that the Anhalter Railway Station had just fallen. Everywhere the Russians were closing in.

Of the vicious fighting that was taking place in the streets near the Zoo, a civilian witness reported:

> The barricades built by the Volkssturm under the supervision of Party members were defended by the remnants of the Volkssturm units and some youngsters. The Russians had mounted some light guns outside our building to fire at these obstacles.
>
> The Russians pushed any men and women that appeared capable of work out of the cellars at gunpoint and made them clear the streets of the rubble, scrap metal and steel plates used as anti-tank obstacles, and that without any tools. Many were killed by the fire of German soldiers still holding out.[34]

By 0400 hours on the morning of the 30th, the 150th Rifle Division had finished clearing the Ministry of the Interior, and the 171st Rifle Division the western half of the Diplomatic Quarter. The latter's 525th Rifle Regiment was lining Alsenstrasse and its 380th Rifle Regiment occupying the Swiss Legation building[35] overlooking Königsplatz and their ultimate objective. Casualties on both sides had been very heavy, and it maybe significant that one hears no more of the 469th Rifle Regiment of the 150th Rifle Division from this point. However, there was to be no respite.[36]

The frantic urgency imposed from above can be seen in the way the Russians launched the next stage of their attack only half an hour later. The decision to push the exhausted soldiers forward without a break, involving a complete change of tactics as they emerged into the open from the building they had just taken, and without time for proper reconnaissance or preparation, was to prove a costly error. The constant long-range bombardment had failed to silence the defence, and the exposed infantry immediately came under a hail of fire, not only from the front and flank as expected, but also from the rear as they wheeled to face their objective. For the Germans had established a formidable strongpoint in the ruins of the Kroll Opera House with machine guns and artillery mounted high in the bombed-out structure. Under these circumstances, the attack quickly fizzled out.

It was now clear that the Kroll Opera House would have to be taken before the attack on the main objective could be developed further, and the 597th and 598th Rifle Regiments of the 207th Rifle Division were brought forward to deal with this problem. However, in order to get to the Kroll Opera House, they first had to clear the buildings standing on the Schlieffenufer, and this would take time. Meanwhile more support weapons were brought across the bridge to assist the main attack, all having to run a gauntlet of fire from the same Schlieffenufer buildings. Tanks, guns and rocket-launchers were brought forward, some 90 barrels in all, some of the guns and rocket-launchers being deployed in the upper floors and roof of the Ministry of the Interior building, and others around it.

The attack was resumed at 1130 hours with the usual heavy artillery preparation, and was reinforced by the 380th Rifle Regiment coming round the flooded pit from the Swiss Legation to join in the attack. This time the infantry got as far as the flooded U-Bahn cutting. The Germans mounted some local counterattacks, including one of battalion size across Alsenstrasse that the 525th Rifle Regiment managed to beat back.

At 1300 hours the Russians tried again with a massive barrage from their close-support artillery and tanks, plus more guns lined up across the river, and even some of the infantry joined in with captured Panzerfausts. After 30 minutes of this fire, the infantry started forward once more but were promptly pinned down again when the Zoo flak joined in. However, on the left flank, the 171st Rifle Division managed to clear the eastern half of the Diplomatic Quarter and secured the Kronprinzen Bridge against the possibility of a German counterattack from across the river. This progress also enabled the introduction of tanks and self-propelled guns forward of the line of the anti-tank ditch to provide enfilade fire for a frontal attack on the Reichstag.

The area which the infantry now had to cross was littered with the temporary structures and other debris of the abandoned works project, among which a series of trenches, barbed wire, mines and a determined enemy presented considerable obstacles for the attacking infantry to overcome, and it was now clear that they would need the cover of darkness for these last 200 yards.

It was therefore 1800 hours before the attack could be resumed, but this time, with the close support of the armour, some of the infantry were able to get right up the front steps of the Reichstag to the still intact bricked-up doorways. Fortunately, they had two light mortars with them and, by aligning these weapons horizontally, were able to blast a way through into the main entrance hall.

In these attacks across the open ground, the infantry had been led by their battalion and regimental standards, and the survivors of the leading battalion, which had in fact spearheaded the entire corps's operation through Berlin, took their standard in with them as they began to expand their holding within the building. By the time they had established telephone communication with their regimental headquarters, they had already fought their standard up to the second floor. However, the Military Council of the 3rd Shock Army had previously prepared a special 'Red Banner No. 5' for this historic occasion, and this was hastily despatched with a hand-picked escort of Party and Komsomol members with instructions to hoist it on the roof of the Reichstag without delay.

Meanwhile the vicious hand-to-hand fighting was spreading out on the various floors of the building as more and more Russians broke their way in. The Germans put up a very stubborn defence and the Russians experienced great difficulty trying to find their way in almost total darkness in unfamiliar surroundings. Eventually, by using small groups to distract attention from their main purpose, two sergeants of the special Banner party managed to find their way up to the roof and wedged the staff of the banner into a convenient crevice on an equestrian statue overlooking the rear of the building.

At 1530 hours on 30 April, Hitler and his bride committed suicide in their sitting room in the Führerbunker. Their bodies were then taken up into the Chancellery garden and placed in a ditch, petrol poured over them and set alight. Some time later the charred bodies were buried in a shell-hole nearby. The whole affair was kept a close secret among the very few in the know.[37]

This left Goebbels as Chancellor and anxious to establish the new government decreed by Hitler in his will, with a view to opening negotiations with the Russians and obtaining their recognition before the treacherous Himmler could do the same with the Western Allies. What neither Goebbels nor Himmler appreciated was that the Allies jointly regarded all the Nazi leaders as war criminals and had no intention of dealing with them in any other way. Their pretensions to continue in power were utterly ridiculous to all but themselves. Even Dönitz decided that he would have neither Goebbels nor Bormann in his cabinet.[38]

Bormann, who had achieved so much in his struggle for power during the past week, was still trying to dominate the scene. Instead of informing Dönitz of Hitler's death as was his duty, he merely sent the following signal at 1835 hours:

> The Führer has appointed you, Admiral, as his successor in place of Reichsmarschall Göring. Confirmation in writing follows. You are hereby authorised to take any measures the situation demands.

One wonders what Dönitz was meant to make of this message. Certainly he did not read from it that Hitler was dead and that he was now President of the Third Reich, for at 0122 hours that night he signalled back a further declaration of loyalty to Hitler.[39]

Meanwhile General Weidling, who had continued his preparations for a breakout on Hitler's authority, received a message from Krebs ordering him to report to the Führerbunker and cancelling permission for a breakout. Weidling received the message at about 1900 hours, and later recorded:

It took us nearly an hour to make our way to the Chancellery through the ruins of buildings and half-collapsed cellars. In the Chancellery I was taken to the Führer's room, where there were Reichsminister Goebbels, Reichsleiter Bormann and General Krebs. The latter informed us of the following:

The Führer had committed suicide at about 1515 hours today, 30 April.

His body had already been cremated in a shell-crater in the Chancellery garden.

The strictest silence must be maintained about the Führer's suicide. I was made personally responsible for keeping the secret pending subsequent developments.

Of the outside world only Marshal Stalin had been informed of the Führer's suicide by radio.

The Sector Commander, Lieutenant-Colonel Seifert, had received orders to make contact with the local Russian commanders to request safe passage for General Krebs to the Soviet High Command.

General Krebs was to give the Soviet High Command the following information: the Führer's suicide, the contents of his will, a request for an armistice, and the government's wishes to open negotiations with the Russians for the surrender of Germany.

I was deeply shocked. So this was the end.[40]

Thus the breakout was cancelled and General Krebs was to attempt to negotiate with the Russians. The troops would have to hang on and the population continue to suffer with them while Goebbels and Bormann played out their futile power game.[41]

The 30 April saw some particularly bitter fighting in the Charlottenburg and Wilmersdorf Districts as the 2nd and 3rd Guards Tank Armies converged on the S-Bahn tracks denoting the inter-front boundary, and German troops struggled to maintain a passage through the western parts of the city still in their hands. The 55th Guards Tank Brigade, which had returned to the Westend area, was heavily engaged all afternoon under increasing pressure from the surge westwards. The 1st Mechanised Corps sent the remains of the 19th and 35th Mechanised Brigades down Schloss-strasse to clear the areas north and south of Kantstrasse respectively, heading towards the Zoo, while the 219th Tank Brigade worked its way down Berliner Strasse (now *Otto-Suhr-Allee*) towards Am Knie.

However, the 2nd Guards Tank Army's infantry casualties now amounted to a staggering 90 percent, so it was decided to bring in the 1st Polish 'Tadiuscz Kosciuszko' Infantry Division from the 1st Polish Army as reinforcements that night. The 3rd Polish Infantry Regiment was then assigned to the 66th Guards Tank Brigade of the 12th Guards Tank Corps, which, through lack of infantry support, had already lost eighty-two tanks, mainly in Berlin. The 1st Polish Infantry

Regiment was split up into combat teams under the 19th and 35th Mechanised Brigades, and the 2nd Polish Infantry Regiment under the 219th Tank Brigade operating north of Bismarckstrasse.[42]

The territory still held by the defence in the city centre was now reduced to an area roughly defined by the Reichstag building, Friedrichstrasse Railway Station, the Gendarmenmarkt, the Air Ministry and the Reich Chancellery. In this area alone were about 10,000 troops, police and Volkssturm, many of the troops being foreign volunteers of the Waffen-SS, including the SS 'Nordland' Panzergrenadier Division and the 15th SS 'Latvian' Fusilier Battalion.[43]

Meanwhile the remains of General Busse's 9th Army, guided by General Wenck's radio, headed for the village of Wittbrietzen just four miles south of Beelitz. During the 30th they reached the village of Kummersdorf by noon, and then had a brief rest on the artillery ranges northwest of the village before going on to the next stage. This involved breaking though yet another Soviet cordon on the Berlin–Luckenwalde road and then fighting their way westwards through the night. The whole time they were being harassed by Soviet aircraft, artillery and mortar fire, attacks by infantry and tanks, as well as deception attempts and attacks by so-called 'Seydlitz-Troops' working for the Red Army. In the early morning darkness they had to make several detours in order to avoid pockets of Russian troops, and at dawn they came up against the 5th Guards Mechanised Corps's positions. They fought their way through this final obstacle with the last serviceable 'Tiger' tank in the lead, breaking through utterly exhausted into the 12th Army's lines on 1 May.[44]

Busse later estimated that some 40,000 men and several thousand refugees reached Wenck's lines. Other estimates are lower. Koniev says that only about 30,000 of the 200,000 that broke out of the Halbe 'pocket' reached the Beelitz area, but were then set upon again by his forces and that at most only 3,000–4,000 could have got through to the 12th Army. In any case, when one considers the odds ranged against them, the unification of the 12th and 9th Armies was a considerable feat for which both generals deserve full credit.[45]

13

Ultimate Victory

At midnight on 30 April the battle suddenly quietened down. It was May Day and, with victory just around the corner, the most joyous day in the history of the Soviet Union. The generals would have preferred to have completed their conquest of the city, and when Colonel-General Sokolovsky, Marshal Zhukov's deputy, visited Chuikov and asked him why his men were only crawling along when they had barely 300 yards to go and one last assault would finish the matter, Chuikov could only reply that his men were exhausted, they knew that the war was all but over, but none of them wanted to die in Berlin. Fighting and shelling continued in a desultory fashion, sometimes building up briefly and then dying down again, as was to occur in the late afternoon of 1 May, and the Soviet advance remained cautious. The Germans seized the opportunity to rest and ponder their fate, while the Russians celebrated as best they could.[1]

Shortly after midnight SS-Major-General Mohnke led General Krebs's party to Lieutenant-Colonel Seifert's Defence Sector Headquarters, from where the latter had arranged safe passage through to the Soviet lines. With Krebs as his aide was Colonel von Dufving, Weidling's Chief-of-Staff, and, as their interpreter, SS-Lieutenant Neilands of the 15th SS 'Latvian' Fusilier Battalion posing as an Army linguist, although in fact Krebs spoke perfect Russian. Krebs's party arrived safely at the command post of the 102nd Guards Rifle Regiment of the 35th Guards Rifle Division, 4th Guards Rifle Corps, and was taken on by jeep to Colonel-General Chuikov's headquarters at Tempelhof, where they arrived at 0350 hours.[2]

They were received by Chuikov accompanied by a bevy of officers, including what might loosely be described as some war correspondents, such as the writer Vishnevsky, the poet Dolmatovsky and the composer Blanter, but as all wore officer uniforms and no introductions were made it took Krebs quite a long time to discover Chuikov's identity.[3]

The discussion dragged on for hours. Krebs was out to obtain recognition of the new government and the opportunity to assemble it, but had no authority to negotiate unconditional surrender, which was all that the Soviets were interested in. The documents that Krebs had brought with him were immediately sent on to Marshal Zhukov at Strausberg, who then telephoned the contents through to Stalin in Moscow.

During the meeting it was agreed to establish telephone communication with Goebbels in the Führerbunker, and so Colonel von Dufving was sent back with a Soviet signals major to lay the field cable. However, they were fired on by German troops and the major was severely wounded, the cable proved too short, and Colonel von Dufving was arrested by Waffen-SS troops upon returning to the German lines, only being released when he insisted that Mohnke be consulted. He went on to report to Goebbels and Bormann in the Führerbunker, noting that although Goebbels appeared calm and composed, Bormann was definitely scared. When Goebbels discovered that Krebs was making no progress, and that the Russians were insisting on unconditional surrender jointly to all the Allies, Goebbels said that he could never agree to this and sent von Dufving to bring Krebs back.

Von Dufving set off again at 1100 hours and telephoned Krebs from the regimental command post. Krebs said that meanwhile they were still awaiting a call from Moscow, and that in the meantime von Dufving should make another attempt at establishing telephone communication with the Führerbunker. Von Dufving took another field cable and attached it to the first, but almost immediately the latter was cut by shellfire. He telephoned Krebs again and was told that the call had come through from Moscow, and that Krebs was on his way back. Once they had returned safely through the lines together, Krebs dismissed von Dufving saying that the German reply to the Russians would be sent in writing.

This, however, was not Goebbels's only attempt at negotiations with the Russians, for Colonel V.S. Antonov, commanding the 301st Rifle Division of the 9th Rifle Corps, 5th Shock Army, also received a delegation of four officers commanded by a colonel that morning. At this stage the 301st Rifle Division was on the corps's right flank as it approached Wilhemplatz from the east, with the 248th and 230th Rifle Divisions advancing respectively north and south of Leipziger Strasse. When Colonel Antonov reported the arrival of the mission, he was told not to negotiate with them, but to go ahead and storm the Chancellery instead. In the meantime the German colonel had contacted the Chancellery on the civilian telephone network and been instructed to return since he was making no progress. Colonel Antonov allowed him to leave with one officer but detained the other two. The whole business had lasted three to four hours, during which time fighting had been suspended in this sector.[4]

Goebbels and Bormann signalled Dönitz the news of Hitler's death only that afternoon, 29 hours after the event, together with details of the government listed in Hitler's will, which Dönitz chose to ignore. However, now officially President of the Third Reich, he had the news of Hitler's death announced by Radio Hamburg that evening without disclosing the cause of death as suicide, and then spoke to the German people. The news did not percolate through to the troops in Berlin until very much later, although rumours abounded.[5]

Both missions having failed, Goebbels prepared himself and his family for death, as they had previously decided. General Krebs, General Burgdorf and Colonel Franz Schaedl of Hitler's honour guards also opted for suicide.[6]

Between 1700 and 1800 hours that evening, Frau Magda Goebbels put her six children to bed in the bunker with drugged chocolates and then killed them all by forcing cyanide capsules into their mouths. Later it was discovered that the eldest child had struggled in the process. Then, after a chat over old times with some of their familiars in the Führerbunker, Goebbels and his wife put on their outer garments and climbed the stairs to commit suicide in the Chancellery garden. First Magda Goebbels bit into her cyanide capsule and slumped to the ground. Goebbels then shot her in the back of the head before simultaneously biting his own capsule and shooting himself in the head, just as Hitler had done. Their bodies were then burned in a ditch in similar manner.[7]

Colonel Antonov was just about to launch his attack on the Chancellery when the German colonel reappeared with a white flag, announcing that Goebbels and his family had committed suicide, and that Hitler's only successor was now Grand Admiral Dönitz. It is not clear what happened as a result of this second visit, but it seems as if the Russians used it as an excuse not to go ahead with their attack.[8]

Fighting in the Reichstag continued all day on 1 May. The German defence fought on desperately under the command of SS-Obersturmführer (Lieutenant) Babick, whose command post was located in a cellar across the street from the rear of the building, and connected to it by a tunnel. This day part of the Reichstag caught fire, adding to the misery of the contestants, for whom there was no water to quench the thirst aroused by the dust and smoke that choked them. Gradually the upper storeys were cleared, but the defence fought on from the cellars, and it was not until the general instructions for the surrender were received from the garrison commander that the 1,500 survivors laid down their arms at 1300 hours on 2 May.[9]

It seems that both the 674th and 756th Rifle Regiments of the 150th Rifle Division actually fought inside the Reichstag building, and that the 380th Rifle Regiment of the 171st Rifle Division that had assisted in the frontal attack had secured the exterior, in particular the corner of the Tiergarten next to the Brandenburg Gate, penetrating as far as Pariser Platz and the Hotel Adlon. The other two rifle regiments of the 171st Rifle Division had secured the river bank and Siegesallee approaches to the battlefield, while the 207th Rifle Division secured the western flank, while remaining north of the line of the Charlottenburger Chaussee (now *Strasse des 17. Juni*), their boundary with the 8th Guards Army approaching from the south.

In accomplishing this particular mission, the 79th Rifle Corps took some 2,600 prisoners and claimed having counted 2,500 enemy dead. The corps's own casualties were not published separately but, significantly, the Soviet War Memorial which was erected across the top of the adjacent Siegesallee shortly afterwards has 2,200 buried in its grounds.

As General Krebs's negotiations had accomplished nothing, Stalin called for a renewed offensive in the city, in which both fronts participated at 1630 hours. As usual, Chuikov began with a heavy rocket and artillery bombardment. Soon the 29th Guards Rifle Corps was reporting having crossed Budapester Strasse, and having knocked gaps through the perimeter walls of the Zoo gardens, where the tanks and infantry were now exchanging fire with the defence. It had also taken the Kaiser-Wilhelm-Gedächtniskirche (Memorial Church) at the eastern end of the Kurfürstendamm, from where artillery observers and snipers had an excellent view over the Zoo area. With the racecourse on the west side of the railway embankment from the Zoo Station under attack from the 12th Guards Tank Corps, and the 28th Guards Rifle Corps's penetration of the Tiergarten residential area just north of the Landwehr Canal, the Zoo position was now almost completely surrounded, as well as being cut off from Weidling's headquarters and the rest of 'Zitadelle'. The 79th Guards Rifle Division reported having taken Potsdamer Railway Station and fighting for the U-Bahn station, while other Soviet troops had crossed Bellevuestrasse from Potsdamer Platz into the southern end of the Siegesallee. The junction of Wilhelmstrasse and Leipziger Strasse was also reported to be in Soviet hands, as were the notorious SS and Gestapo installations on Prinz-Albrecht-Strasse.[10]

With nightfall the fighting died down again, and the Russians resumed their festivities. In Pariser Platz a group of them roasted an ox where earlier the poet Dolmatovsky, in naval uniform and standing on a tank, had recited some of his popular works to an enthusiastic audience.[11]

Meanwhile the 2nd Guards Tank Army with its Polish infantry support had made rapid progress that day. The 66th Guards Tank Brigade cleared its area north of the Landwehr Canal and took the strongpoint at the Tiergarten S-Bahn Station, while the 219th Tank Brigade stormed the Technical University strongpoint at Am Knie in an action in which artillery pieces were dismantled and reassembled on the third storey of the building opposite to provide covering fire for the assault across the broad space where Hitler had taken the salute on his 50th birthday parade in 1939. The 19th and 35th Mechanised Brigades advanced steadily eastwards, despite encounters with heavy opposition from strongpoints around the church in Karl-Augustus-Platz and near Charlottenburg Station.[12]

The 3rd Guards Tank Army was across the Kurfürstendamm by evening and closing up to the railway embankment marking the inter-front boundary, filtering through the buildings lining the embankment, then meeting up with elements of the 2nd Guards Tank Army on Savignyplatz at 0830 hours on 2 May.[13]

The 'Müncheberg' Panzer Division diarist recorded:

> Our anti-aircraft guns on the Zoo Bunker fire without stopping. The division
> has now only five tanks and four guns left. One group is fighting in front of
> the Zoo Bunker, where thousands of people are on the point of asphyxia. The
> Memorial Church has been taken by the Russians. Late afternoon there are
> rumours that Hitler is dead, and that surrender talks are in progress. That is all.
> Civilians ask us if we are going to break out.
>
> At dusk a patrol managed to cross the Spandau bridges and discovered that
> the Russian forces in Spandau are quite weak. We are planning to break out to
> the west via Spandau.
>
> Russian pressure long Budapester Strasse cannot be contained much longer.
> We will have to withdraw again. Wounded are screaming in the cellars. There
> is nothing left to ease their pain. Here and there, despite the fire, women come
> up out of the half-demolished cellar entrances with their hands over their ears,
> unable to bear the screaming any longer.[14]

These developments had created a vast difference in the situation since Hitler
had given his formal approval for a breakout on the night of the 29th/30th and
now General Weidling saw no alternative to surrender. However, some of his
commanders at the Zoo still thought it worthwhile attempting a breakout to the
west, while SS-Major-General Mohnke changed his original plan for a breakout
in the direction that would take him to the Humboldthain Flak-tower before
swinging northwest out of the city. Thus a miscellany of breakout plans evolved,
with Weidling holding back the surrender negotiations until after midnight to
give the others a chance to get away under cover of darkness.[15]

In the meantime the main corridor to the west had been closed. That morning
Wenck's 12th Army began withdrawing to the Elbe near Tangermünde, having
held out as long as it dared. With his troops went the survivors of Busse's 9th
Army and Reymann's Army Detachment 'Spree', as well as thousands of refugees.
Wenck sent Lieutenant-General Maximilian Freisherr von Edelsheim to negotiate
their surrender to the American 9th Army. Although the commander of the latter,
General William H. Simpson, agreed to let as many soldiers as were able make their
way across the river and offered assistance with the wounded, he absolutely refused
to accept any of the civilian refugees. This extraordinary decision, which was presumably based on the problems of feeding, would have resulted in their involuntary
abandonment on the east bank of the Elbe, had not the Russians themselves intervened. Their attacks on the German crossings forced the Americans to withdraw
sufficiently to enable the Germans to control their own crossings, which began
on 4 May using the XX Corps as a covering screen, and were not completed
until midnight on 7 May, by which time General Wenck reckoned some 100,000
soldiers and 300,000 civilians had been successfully evacuated.[16]

General Weidling called a meeting of those sector commanders who could attend at Bendlerstrasse that evening. The field telephone had been reconnected with the Zoo command post, having been out of order most of the day, and Colonel Wöhlermann was thus summoned to attend. He set off with a small escort and, because of the progress made by the Russians, his route took him via the Tiergarten S-Bahn Station on the East-West-Axis, which he followed as far as the Siegessäule (Victory Column) but then came under heavy shellfire and was obliged to crawl and sprint the rest of the way. When he eventually arrived exhausted at the Bendlerstrasse headquarters he found all of Weilding's staff present for the conference. It was decided that there was no alternative to surrender and that they would enter into negotiations with the Soviets soon after midnight.[17]

When Colonel Wöhlermann eventually returned to his command post, he found that a considerable number of his troops had already left on breakout bids, but that there were still some 2,000 combatants as well as several tens of thousands of civilians in his care.[18]

As soon as it was light enough, Colonel Wöhlermann and his troops paraded outside the flak-towers in front of their Soviet captors. The scene was marred by a sudden burst of machine-gun fire from some recalcitrant Nazis, the bullets ricocheting off the concrete and killing several of his men. When they were marched off, he was surprised to see the number of Soviet tanks lining the streets. At one point, Russian tankmen suddenly offered them cigarettes in a gesture of friendship, and Wöhlermann took advantage of the situation to obtain permission for the Hitlerjugend boys included among them to fall out and make their way home.[19]

Another group of 300 soldiers from Jebenstrasse made their escape via the U-Bahn tunnels from the Zoo Station to Adolf-Hitler-Platz, which took them two hours, and then headed straight down Heerstrasse. All went well until someone carelessly struck a match, attracting a burst of machine-gun fire. However, this was not followed up, and so they turned off for Ruhleben, where they came across an Austrian tank unit with 15 'Tiger' tanks and went on with them to Stresowplatz, which was thronged with refugees waiting to cross the Charlotten Bridge into Spandau. Russian machine-gunners suddenly opened fire on them from the rooftops, but the tanks fired back and survivors scrambled across the bridge under this covering fire into the old town centre and headed for Döberitz. The Russians pursued them and they were finally obliged to surrender at about 0500 hours on the morning of 2 May, having expended all their ammunition.[20]

On the night of 1 May, Luftwaffe Major-General Otto Sydow of the 1st 'Berlin' Flak Division, organised the breakout attempt from the Zoo. The remaining tanks and armour personnel carriers of the 'Müncheberg' Panzer and 18th Panzergrenadier Divisions were sent up Kantstrasse to Adolf-Hitler-Platz and then via Reichsstrasse and the Olympic Stadium to Ruhleben, while several hundred infantry with walking wounded and some hundreds of civilians made their way through the five miles of U-Bahn tunnels to reach Ruhleben and another two and a half miles to the Spandau bridges. Miraculously, the plan worked. The trek through the tunnels had to be done in silence and without lights, for virtually the whole route lay under the Soviet lines and there were many holes in the tunnel roof to the streets above. Although the going was slow, they were out of the tunnels by midnight.[21]

There were still two bridges available across the Havel, the Frey Bridge having blown up at 1800 hours that evening when a chance shell hit the demolition chamber. There are no reports of a breakout over the Schulenburg bridge in the centre, so one can only presume that it was too strongly guarded to use but, fortunately, the Russian forces on the opposite bank at the Charlotten Bridge were relatively weak. While the troops fought their way across, the refugees assembled and waited under shellfire. Eventually the way was open and the crowds fought their way through, some being crushed by the armoured vehicles running the gauntlet of fire. The troops then made their way down Brunsbüttler Damm to Staaken Airfield, which was the dispersal point. Most units then headed for the Döberitz Training Area but, as each group tended to fend for itself in this '*sauve qui peut*' chaotic atmosphere, there was no concerted effort beyond this point and most of them were rounded up fairly quickly over the next few days. Very few managed to reach the Elbe and get away to the west.

Soon after dusk, General Kutzetsov of the 3rd Shock Army telephoned Marshal Zhukov to report that some 20 German tanks had broken through the lines of the 52nd Guards Rifle Division and had set off at high speed for the northwest. Zhukov alerted the 47th, 61st and 1st Polish Armies with instructions to seal off all routes to the west and north, and the 2nd Guards Tank and 3rd Shock Armies were ordered to organise a pursuit. At dawn on 2 May the German tanks were found abandoned for lack of fuel some ten miles northwest of Berlin and destroyed.

The story of this attempt was related in the *History of the Grossdeutschland Panzer Corps*, which gives the following account:

Major Lehnhoff gave orders to his combat teams of the 'Grossdeutschland' Guard Regiment to assemble at 2300 hours on 1 May in Kastanienallee to attempt a breakout to the west via Rathenow.

The remaining vehicles were tanked up, millions of Reichsmark coins shared out among the men, the last rations issued, and then away. The break through the Soviet lines was made at the Schönhauser Allee Station, where Stalin-Organs and tank-fire inflicted heavy casualties.

With five tanks and 68 men, Major Lehnhoff broke out of the city towards Oranienburg, where unfortunately the tanks had to be blown up because of breakdowns. Divided into four groups, the men then pushed towards the Elbe and Schleswig-Holstein.[22]

We have no details, but it would appear that during the night of 30 April/1 May, General Bärenfänger pulled out what forces he could from the confused fighting around the Alexanderplatz and the Spree, where his 'Ost' Bastion had held out so well, and directed them in a breakout attempt northwards, but the Russians had already blocked the route up Schönhauser Allee as a result of the previous incident, and Bärenfänger, his wife and brother-in-law committed suicide in a side-street.[23]

The breakout from the Reich Chancellery was delayed 24 hours by SS-Major-General Mohnke because of the cutting of the East-West-Axis by the Soviets on 30 April. While he was planning a new route, he advised his men to get some rest. As a courtesy, he checked over his plans with Generals Krebs and Burgdorf, both of whom had opted to commit suicide. He also telephoned General Weidling to inform him of his intentions, obtaining the latter's agreement not to sign any surrender articles before daybreak on 2 May.[24]

The breakout started at 2300 hours on 1 May and was conducted in ten groups of irregular size, with Mohnke leading the first. His plan was for all the groups, which would set off at ten-minute intervals, to follow the U-Bahn and S-Bahn tunnels as far as the Stettiner Railway Station, which would hopefully bring them out behind the Soviet lines. From there they would march to the Gesundbrunnen Station next to the Humboldhain Flak-tower before splitting up and each group making its own way via Neuruppin to find the main German forces. This plan took advantage of the Russian troops' reluctance to use the tunnels, but also showed Mohnke's ignorance of the situation north of the Spree.[25]

Mohnke's group sprinted the 120 yards across Wilhelmplatz to the entrance to the Kaiserhof U-Bahn Station, which was packed with sheltering civilians, and marched in complete darkness to the Stadtmitte Station, from where they took the northern line to Friedrichstrasse Station. While they were in this last section, heavy firing broke out overhead and lasted for about an hour. They changed to the S-Bahn tunnel at Friedrichstrasse Station, but when they came to pass under the Spree, they found a group of civilians being held back by two watchmen guarding a watertight bulkhead that they refused to unlock. The watchmen were acting in accordance with standing regulations, whereby the bulkhead was locked between the last train at night and the first in the morning and, although no trains had passed through for a week, they were sticking to the rules. Strangely enough, although Mohnke's party was armed and could easily have brought an end to this nonsense, they accepted the situation and returned to Friedrichstrasse station to seek another route out above ground. The Weidendammer Bridge was blocked by a German anti-tank barrier and was being shelled by the Russians, so they took the footbridge incorporated under the structure of the railway bridge leading across the Spree from the station and cut their way through the barbed wire blocking it.[26]

They then worked their way northwards through a wilderness of rubble until they came to the ruins of the Natural History Museum, by which they recognised that they had just crossed Invalidenstrasse. So far they had seen no Russians, but had been joined by a few German stragglers. The civilians they encountered told them that the odd Russian patrol had come through the area, although the Charité Hospital to their left was strongly occupied. The shelling, which had died down at 0130 hours, suddenly resumed at 0230 hours and, looking back, they could see that Friedrichstrasse and the Weidendammer Bridge area were under heavy artillery and rocket fire from the Tiergarten, the whole area being illuminated by searchlights operated by the Russians.[27]

This outburst of fire had been provoked by other groups from the Reich Chancellery making their way above ground and thereby attracting Soviet attention. The third group had lost its way at the Stadtmitte Station, where it split into two separate sections, and had then decided to travel above ground, while another party led by Axmann had come the whole way above ground, suffering many casualties. SS-Major-General Krukenberg, whose foreign volunteers were holding this sector, was extremely annoyed that Mohnke had left before he could even complete organising his own breakout and briefing his troops, and now that Russians had been alerted he was obliged to take the opportunity of breaking out with only those troops immediately to hand, abandoning the others to their fate. He used his last five 'Tiger' tanks to break across the Weidendammer Bridge, and almost immediately they became involved in a tank battle in which he lost all his tanks and his troops suffered heavy casualties. Only a few survivors broke through with their general.[28]

Mohnke took advantage of this distraction to take his party up Chausseestrasse, the northern continuation of Friedrichstrasse, but when they reached the gates of the old Maikäfer Barracks, they found it guarded by a Soviet tank and were obliged to turn back to Invalidenstrasse. Just then a shell intended for the battle dropped short and killed SS-Major-General Jürgen Ziegler, Krukenberg's predecessor. They then took shelter in a disused goods yard near Stettiner Railway Station, where they were eventually joined by Krukenberg and the survivors of his group, together with other parties of German soldiers hiding in the vicinity.[29]

Meanwhile the five Chancery survivors who had turned left after crossing the Spree – Bormann, Axmann, SS-Colonel Dr Ludwig Stumpfegger (Hitler's last physician), Major Weltzin (Axmann's aide) and Luftwaffe General Hans Bauer (Hitler's pilot) – took shelter on the Schiffbauerdamm until the firing abated. They then followed the S-Bahn tracks leading into Moabit. Opposite the Reichstag they came under sniper fire and General Bauer became separated from the rest and was left behind. The four men then crossed the Humboldthafen by the railway bridge and dropped down to the roadway beneath the Lehrter S-Bahn Station, only to find themselves in the middle of a bivouacking platoon of friendly Russian soldiers, who took them to be Volkssturm making their way home. Bormann and Stumpfegger edged away from the group and then started running, thereby arousing the Russians' suspicions, but the other two managed to get away unnoticed. However, when Baur appeared shortly afterwards, he was shot and seriously wounded by the same troops before being captured.[30]

Axmann and Weltzin went on into Moabit until they were turned back by tank-fire. In crossing the road bridge over the main tracks leading into Lehrter Railway Station, they came across the bodies of Bormann and Stumpfegger, who had apparently committed suicide.[31] They then decided to split up, Axmann taking shelter with an old girlfriend and later getting safely away to the west, but Weltzin was captured the same morning.[32]

At 0700 hours Mohnke's group, now between 150 and 200 strong, marched through the deserted streets up Bernauer Strasse and Brunnenstrasse to reach the Humboldhain Flak-tower at 0900 hours. News was then received of General Weidling's orders to surrender, and instructions issued for all arms and equipment to be rendered unserviceable prior to surrendering, but Mohnke's group decided to break away and marched on to the Schultheiss Brewery nearby in Prinzenallee.[33]

At the brewery they found other groups of soldiers and civilians sheltering there. While the men settled down to a final party with ample beer and willing female partners, the officers went down into the cellars to confer. Some people left to make their own escape attempts, including two of Hitler's female secretaries and Bormann's secretary, all three women eventually getting through safely to the west. Finally Mohnke sent Colonel Claussen, who was not Waffen-SS and therefore more acceptable to the Russians as a spokesman, to organise their surrender before the Russians should decide to attack. The surrender was completed by 2000 hours, but Ambassador Hewel and a fanatical young SS-Lieutenant both committed suicide beforehand rather than give themselves up.[34]

During a lull in the fighting on the night of 1 May, the 80 surviving men of SS-Lieutenant Neilands's 15th SS 'Latvian' Battalion had withdrawn to new positions in the vast, massively-constructed Air Ministry. Somehow they had been overlooked in the breakout plans, and in the morning found themselves abandoned with the nearby streets empty of both German and Russian troops. They then decided to make their way north through the ruins to escape from the Russians, for they knew what to expect from the people who had annexed their country in 1940. Eventually they came to a square in Pankow, where they found about 1,000 German soldiers waiting to be marched off into captivity, and there they split up, each man making his own bid for freedom.[35]

Also forgotten in the breakout were some of the French Waffen-SS volunteers that had fallen asleep exhausted in the cellars of Air Ministry, where they were later captured.[36]

At 2240 hours on 1 May, the 79th Guards Rifle Division picked up the following radio message in Russian:

> Hello, hello, This is the LVI German Panzer Corps. We ask you to cease fire. At 0500 hours Berlin Time we are sending envoys to parley at the Potsdamer Bridge. The recognition signal is a white square with a red light. We await your reply.

This message was repeated five times. The Russians then replied:

> Your message received, message received. Request passed to superior officer.

The Germans acknowledged this with:

> Russian station I am receiving you. You are reporting to a superior officer.[37]

Colonel-General Chuikov then called for a cessation of fighting in the area where the envoys were due to appear. Colonel Theodor von Dufving, however, went to the remains of the Bendler Bridge, where the Russians had a tiny bridgehead, and the message was passed on that General Weidling wished to surrender. Colonel Shemchevko, the acting divisional commander, asked how long the Germans would require to prepare themselves, and Colonel von Dufving replied three to four hours, but that the task would have to be accomplished in darkness, as Goebbels had issued instructions that anyone attempting to surrender should be shot in the back, and there were plenty of fanatical Nazis who might not comply with General Weidling's instructions to surrender. The message then came from General Chuikov that Colonel von Dufving was to return to General Weidling and inform him that his offer to surrender was accepted. Honourable terms were guaranteed; officers would be allowed to keep their side-arms, each could take as much hand luggage as he could carry, and the Soviet High Command would ensure the protection of the civilian population and care for the wounded.[38]

In the meantime, Dr Hans Fritzsche, Permanent Under-Secretary at the Propaganda Ministry, had discovered that he was the senior government official left after the death of Goebbels and the evacuation of the Führerbunker, and decided to act in the interests of the civilian population by asking the Russians to take them under their protection. His delegation arrived at Chuikov's head-quarters at 0530 hours bearing a letter from him with a request to be allowed to broadcast to the people and the garrison. Although the Russians were prima-rily interested in the military surrender and were expecting General Weidling to appear at any moment, they agreed to Dr Fritzsche's request and sent an escort to take him to a radio station to make the broadcast. While they were discussing this, a report arrived from the 47th Guards Rifle Division that the Germans were forming up in columns. Colonel-General Chuikov then ordered an immediate ceasefire in his area of operations.[39]

At 0400 hours General Weidling arrived, saying that he had decided not to consult with Goebbels about the surrender of the garrison, being unaware that Goebbels was already dead. Colonel-General Sokolovsky then appeared from Marshal Zhukov's headquarters at Strausberg and, after answering a few questions, General Weidling sat down to compose his formal order of surrender to the garrison, which read as follows:

On 30 April, the Führer, to whom we had all sworn an oath of allegiance, forsook us by committing suicide. Faithful to the Führer, you German soldiers were prepared to continue the battle for Berlin even though your ammunition was running out and the general situation made further resistance senseless.

I now order all resistance to cease immediately. Every hour you go on fighting adds to the terrible suffering of the Berlin population and the wounded. In agreement with the High Command of the Soviet Forces, I call on you to stop fighting forthwith.

> Weidling
> General of Artillery
> Former Commander
> Berlin Defence Area

This format was accepted by the Russians, and Weidling's staff, including two retired generals, was called in to produce and arrange the distribution of copies of this order. Weidling was then driven to a Political Department office in Johannisthal, where he recorded his order to surrender for broadcasting by Russian propaganda vehicles around the remaining areas of resistance.[40]

All hostilities were due to cease by 1300 hours, but it was nearer 1700 hours before the fighting finally came to an end throughout the city. Endless columns of prisoners began the long trek eastwards. The Russians claim to have taken 134,000 prisoners in Berlin that day, but this actually amounted to a big round-up of all able-bodied men, and sometimes even women, for the labour camps back in the Soviet Union.[41]

On the night of 1/2 May, the remains of the 20th Panzergrenadier Division, to which Lieutenant-Colonel Weiss's party had attached themselves, attempted to break out of the Wannsee 'island' position. Their plan was to force their way through the Soviet lines at Wannsee S-Bahn Station and then turn south through the dense woods to meet up with the 12th Army. However, when they charged across the bridge leading to the underpass beneath the railway, they found it blocked by an anti-tank barrier and were met by a hail of fire that mowed them down in vast numbers. Weiss was captured at Wannsee, but his two companions escaped by hiding in a fir thicket. Next morning they discarded their uniforms and donned civilian clothes before crawling through the lines of Russians still scouring the woods for survivors, eventually managing to escape to the west in the guise of returning foreign labourers.[42]

The heavy shelling that this escape attempt had attracted all over Wannsee 'island' also affected Major Johannmeier's courier party. During the fighting a three-engined Dornier flying boat landed on the Havel close to Pfaueninsel and contact was established with couriers, but the shelling forced the pilot to take off again without them. Although they eventually reached safety, none of these couriers accomplished their missions, and the documents they were carrying were all subsequently recovered by the Western Allies during the investigation into Hitler's death.[43]

According to Marshal Koniev, General Lelyushenko of the 4th Guards Tank Army had an unpleasant surprise that day when a large group of Germans, estimated at 2,000 strong, attacked his headquarters in the village of Schenkenhorst. The Russians took them to be part of the Potsdam Garrison, but they were more likely to have been survivors of the Wannsee breakout. It took two hours of hard fighting by the headquarters guards and staff eventually reinforced by the 7th Guards Motorcycle Regiment and other units from nearby, before the Germans were defeated, but a German account says that the survivors crossed the Autobahn ring and they were only rounded up when they burst unexpectedly out of the woods on to a Soviet air strip.[44]

That same day Marshal Koniev started withdrawing his forces from the Berlin area in preparation for another big operation in conjunction with the 2nd and 4th Ukrainian Fronts, which was due to start on 6 May against Army Group 'Mitte' in Czechoslovakia.[45]

The 1st Polish Division was also pulled out of Berlin at noon on 2 May to rejoin its parent formation at Nauen, but not before Polish soldiers had hoisted their red and white national flags on the Siegessäule and the Brandenburg Gate.[46]

The 2nd Byelorussian Front reached the line Wittenberge–Parchim–Bad Doberan on 2 May, pushing back the remains of the 3rd Panzer and 21st Armies. Meanwhile the British 21st Army Group had taken Lübeck and Wismar, and the American 9th Army had taken Ludwigslust and Schwerin, so that the German forces now themselves crushed into a narrow pocket barely fifteen to twenty miles wide. That night Generals von Manteuffel and von Tippelskirch surrendered their armies to the Americans.

The 1st Byelorussian Front still had to finish clearing up to the Elbe to complete its part of Operation 'Berlin'. So, during 1 May the flanking armies were moved forward so that progress could be maintained westwards next day. The 33rd Army started off from Kropstädt, the 69th Army from Niemegk, the 3rd Army from Brandenburg, the 47th Army from Rathenow, the 1st Polish Army from south and the 61st Army from north of Havelberg. By 6 May they had closed up to the river everywhere except in Wenck's army's sector, where the XX Corps held them at bay for yet another day to enable the evacuation to be completed.

So Operation 'Berlin' ended, and it was time to count the cost. The tally given by the Russians for the three fronts claims 480,000 prisoners, 1,500 tanks and self-propelled guns, 8,600 guns and mortars, and 4,500 aircraft taken. Their own casualties they gave as 304,887 killed, wounded and missing between 16 April and 8 May 1945, together with the loss of 2,165 tanks and self-propelled guns, 1,220 guns and mortars, and 527 aircraft. The Red Air Force claimed to have destroyed 1,132 German aircraft in combat, plus another 100 destroyed on the ground, and to have knocked out some 400 tanks and self-propelled guns.[47]

The Soviet medal for the capture of Berlin was awarded to 1,082,000 persons, which gives some indication of the numbers involved, including rear area personnel, in the actual taking of the city. The Soviet military cemeteries in the city at Treptow, Pankow and the Tiergarten hold the bodies of approximately 20,000 of their dead.[48]

Abbreviations

AA	Anti-aircraft	M/C	Motorcycle
Amb	Ambulance	Mech	Mechanised
APC	Armoured Personnel Carrier	Med	Medium; Medical
		MMG	Medium Machine Gun
Armd	Armoured		
Arty	Artillery	MO	Medical Officer
Aslt	Assault	Mor	Mortar
A/Tk	Anti-Tank	Mot	Motorised
B, Bde	Brigade	Mtd	Mounted
Bn	Battalion	Offr	Officer
Cav	Cavalry	OR	Other Rank
Coy	Company	Para	Parachute
D, Div	Division	Pl	Platoon
Def	Defence	Pol	Polish
Det	Detachment	Pol Sect	Political Section
Engr	Engineer	Pz	Panzer
Fd	Field	R, Regt	Regiment
Fmn	Formation	RAD	Reichsarbeitsdienst
Fus	Fusilier	Recce	Reconnaissance
GAD	Guards Artillery Division	RL	Rocket Launcher
		Sigs	Signals
GC	Guards Corps	SMG	Submachine Gun
GCC	Guards Cavalry Corps	SP	Self-propelled
Gds	Guards	Sy	Security
GMB	Guards Mechanised Brigade	TB	Tank Brigade
		TC	Tank Corps
GMC	Guards Mechanised Corps	Tk	Tank
		Tpt	Transport
Gr, Gren	Grenadier	V	Volks
How	Howitzer	Vet	Veterinary
Hy	Heavy	VGr	Volksgrenadier
Ind	Independent	Vol	Volunteer
Inf	Infantry	VS	Volkssturm
LMG	Light Machine Gun		
Lt	Light; Lieutenant		
MB	Mechanised Brigade		
MC	Mechanised Corps		

Appendices

ORGANISATION OF A RED ARMY
RIFLE DIVISION — 1945

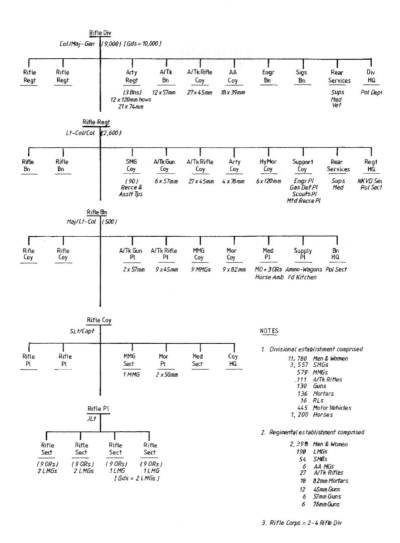

Rifle Div
Col/Maj-Gen (9,000) [Gds = 10,000]

Rifle Regt	Rifle Regt	Arty Regt	A/Tk Bn	A/Tk Rifle Coy	AA Coy	Engr Bn	Sigs Bn	Rear Services	Div HQ
		(3 Bns) 12 x 120mm hows 21 x 74mm	12 x 57mm	27 x 45mm	18 x 39mm			Sups Med Vet	Pol Dept

Rifle Regt
Lt-Col/Col (2,600)

Rifle Bn	Rifle Bn	SMG Coy	A/Tk Gun Coy	A/Tk Rifle Coy	Arty Coy	Hy Mor Coy	Support Coy	Rear Services	Regt HQ
		(90) Recce & Asslt Tps	6 x 57mm	27 x 45mm	4 x 76mm	6 x 120mm	Engr Pl Gas Def Pl Scouts Pl Mtd Recce Pl	Sups Med	NKVD Sec Pol Sect

Rifle Bn
Maj/Lt-Col (500)

Rifle Coy	Rifle Coy	A/Tk Gun Pl	A/Tk Rifle Pl	MMG Coy	Mor Coy	Med Pl	Supply Pl	Bn HQ
		2 x 57mm	9 x 45mm	9 MMGs	9 x 82mm	MO + 3 ORs Horse Amb	Ammo-Wagons Fd Kitchen	Pol Sect

Rifle Coy
SLt/Capt

Rifle Pl	Rifle Pl	MMG Sect	Mor Pl	Med Sect	Coy HQ
		1 MMG	2 x 50mm		

Rifle Pl
JLt

Rifle Sect	Rifle Sect	Rifle Sect	Rifle Sect
(9 ORs) 2 LMGs	(9 ORs) 2 LMGs	(9 ORs) 1 LMG	(9 ORs) 1 LMG [Gds = 2 LMGs]

NOTES

1. Divisional establishment comprised

11,780	Men & Women
3,557	SMGs
579	MMGs
111	A/Tk Rifles
130	Guns
136	Mortars
16	RLs
445	Motor Vehicles
1,200	Horses

2. Regimental establishment comprised

2,398	Men & Women
198	LMGs
54	SMGs
6	AA MGs
27	A/Tk Rifles
18	82mm Mortars
12	45mm Guns
6	57mm Guns
6	76mm Guns

3. Rifle Corps = 2-4 Rifle Div

ORGANISATION OF RED ARMY
TANK AND MECHANISED FORMATIONS — 1945

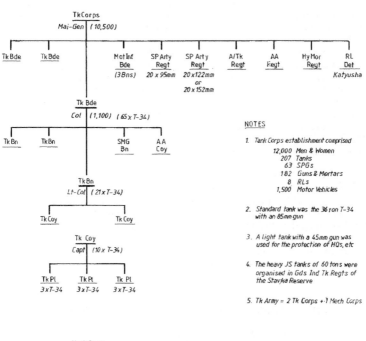

NOTES

1. Tank Corps establishment comprised

    12,000 Men & Women
       207 Tanks
        63 SPGs
       182 Guns & Mortars
         8 RLs
     1,500 Motor Vehicles

2. Standard tank was the 36 ton T-34 with an 85mm gun

3. A light tank with a 45mm gun was used for the protection of HQs, etc

4. The heavy JS tanks of 60 tons were organised in Gds Ind Tk Regts of the Stavka Reserve

5. Tk Army = 2 Tk Corps + 1 Mech Corps

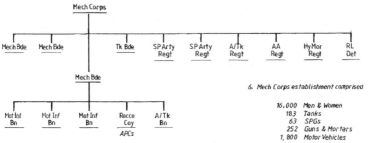

6. Mech Corps establishment comprised

    16,000 Men & Women
       183 Tanks
        63 SPGs
       252 Guns & Mortars
     1,800 Motor Vehicles

SOVIET STRENGTHS FOR 'OPERATION BERLIN'

(Front-line strengths, excluding reserves and Rear Area Troops)

	2nd Bye Front	1st Bye Front	1st Ukr Front	Total*
Men & Women	314,000	768,000	511,700	1,593,700
Tanks	644	1,795	1,388	3,827
Self-propelled guns	307	1,360	677	2,344
Anti-tank guns	770	2,306	1,444	4,520
Field guns (76mm +)	3,172	7,442	5,040	15,654
Mortars (88mm +)	2,770	7,186	5,225	15,181
Rocket launchers	807	1,531	917	3,255**
Anti-aircraft guns	801	1,665	945	3,411
Trucks	21,846	44,332	29,205	95,383
Aircraft (total)	1,360	3,188	2,148	6,696
Fighters	602	1,567	1,106	3,275
Ground attack	449	731***	529	1,709
Bombers	283	762	422	1,467
Reconnaissance	26	128	91	245

NOTES

*   The full total is given as: 2,500,000 men & women; 6,250 tanks &
self-propelled guns; 41,650 guns & mortars; 7,500 aircraft.

** Excluding the 4th, 5th and 10th Anti-Aircraft Artillery Corps defending
the Rear Areas.

***Excluding the 800 long-range bombers of the 18th Air Army operating
with the 1st Byelorussian Front.

SOVIET ORDER–OF–BATTLE FOR 'OPERATION BERLIN'

Drawn from F.D.Vorbeyev, I.V. Propotkin and A.N. Shimansky's *The Last Storm*
with additional information on units identified in the encirclement of the city.
The armies are listed in order of deployment from north to south.

2ND BYELORUSSIAN FRONT
(MARSHAL K.K. ROKOSSOVSKY)

19th Army
40th Gds Rifle Corps (only)

2nd Shock Army (Col-Gen I.I. Fedyurinsky)
107th & 116th Rifle Corps

65th Army (Col-Gen P.I. Batov)
18th, 46th & 105th Rifle Corps

70th Army (Col-Gen V.S. Popov)
47th, 96th & 114th Rifle Corps

49th Army (Col-Gen I.T. Grishin)
70th & 121st Rifle Corps
191st, 200th & 330th Rifle Divs

Air Forces

4th Air Army (Col-Gen K.A.Vershinin)
4th Air Aslt, 5th Air Bomber & 8th Air Fighter Corps

1ST BYELORUSSIAN FRONT
(MARSHAL G.K. ZHUKOV)

61st Army (Col-Gen P.A. Belov)
9th Gds Rifle Corps (Lt-Gen G.A. Halyuzin/Lt-Gen A.D. Shtemenko)
    12th & 75th Gds, 415th Rifle Divs
80th Rifle Corps (Maj-Gen V.A.Vyerzhbitsky)
    212th, 234th & 356th Rifle Divs
89th Rifle Corps (Maj-Gen M.A. Siyzov)
    23rd, 311th & 397th Rifle Divs
312th, 1811th & 1899th SP Aslt Arty Regts

7th Gds Cav Corps (Maj-Gen M.P. Konstantinov)
    14th, 15th & 16th Gds Cav Divs
    1816th Sp Aslt Arty Regt
    7th Gds R/L Bn

1st Polish Army (Lt-Gen S.G. Poplowski)
1st Pol Inf Div 'Tadiuscz Kosciusko' (Maj-Gen W. Bevziuk)
2nd, 3rd, 4th & 6th Pol Inf Divs
1st Pol Cav Bde
4th Pol Hy Tk Regt
13th Pol SP Aslt Arty Regt
7th Pol SP Aslt Arty Bn

47th Army (Lt-Gen F.I. Perkhorovitch)
77th Rifle Corps (Maj-Gen/Lt-Gen Y.s.Vorobyev)
    185th, 260th & 328th Rifle Divs
125th Rifle Corps (Maj-Gen/Lt-Gen A.M. Andreyev)
    60th, 76th & 175th Rifle Divs
129th Rifle Corps (Maj-Gen M.B. Anaskin)
    82nd, 132nd & 143rd Rifle Divs
70th Gds Ind Tk Regt
    334th, 1204th, 1416th, 1825th & 1892nd SP Aslt Arty Regts

3rd Shock Army (Col-Gen V.I. Kutznetsov)
7th Rifle Corps (Maj-Gen V.A. Christov)
    146th, 265th & 364th Rifle Divs
12th Gds Rifle Corps (Lt-Gen A.F. Kazanin/Maj-Gen A.A. Filatov)
    23rd Gds Rifle Div
        63rd Gds Rifle Regt
    52nd Gds & 33rd Rifle Divs

79th Rifle Corps (Maj-Gen S.I. Perevertkin)
    150th Rifle Div
        469th, 674th & 756 Rifle Regts
    171st Rifle Div
        380th, 525th & 713th Rifle Regts
    207th Rifle Div
        594th, 597th & 598th Rifle Regts
9th Tank Corps
    23rd, 95th & 108th Rifle Bdes
    8th Mot Rifle Bde
    1455th & 1508th SP Aslt Arty Regts
    286th Gds M/C Regt
88th Gds & 85th Ind Tk Regts
1049th, 1203rd, 1728th &1818th SP Aslt Arty Regts

5th Shock Army (Col-Gen N.E. Berzarin)
9th Rife Corps (Maj-Gen/Lt-Gen I.P. Rossly)
    230th Rifle Div (Col D.V. Shiskov)
    248th Rifle Div (Maj-Gen N.Z. Galai)
    301st Rifle Div (Col V.S. Antonov)
        1054th Rifle Regt (Col N.N. Raderiev)
26th Gds Rifle Corps (Maj-Gen P.A. Firsov)
    89th Gds Rifle Div (Maj-Gen M.P. Seryugin)
        286th Gds Rifle Regt (Lt-Col A.N. Kravchenko)
    94th Gds Rifle Div (Maj-Gen I.G. Gospoyan)
        228th Gds Rifle Regt
        283rd Gds Rifle Regt (Lt-Col A.A. Ignatiev)
        199th Gds Arty Regt (Lt-Col I.F. Zherebtsov)
    266th Rifle Div (Col/Maj-Gen Fomicheno)
        1006th Rifle Regt
        1008th Rifle Regt (Col Borisov)
        1010th Rifle Regt (Col Zagoredski)
32nd Rifle Corps (Lt-Gen D.S. Zherebin)
    60th Gds Rifle Div (Maj-Gen V.P. Sokolov)
    295th Rifle Div (Maj-Gen A.P. Dorofeyev)
    416th Rifle Div (Maj-Gen D.M. Syranov)
11th & 67th Gds, & 220th Tk Bdes
92nd Ind Tk Regt
396th Gds & 1504th SP Aslt Arty Regts

8th Gds Army (Col-Gen V.I. Chuikov)
4th Gds Rifle Corps (Lt-Gen V.A. Glazonov)
    35th Gds Rifle Div (Col Grigorye)
        102nd Gds Rifle Regt
    47th Gds Rifle Div (Lt-Gen V.M. Shugeyev)
        137th, 140th & 142nd Gds Rifle Regts
    57th Gds Rifle Div (Maj-Gen P.I. Zalizyuk)
        170th, 172nd & 174th Gds Rifle Regts
28th Gds Rifle Corps (Lt-Gen A.I. Ryzhov)
    39th Gds Rifle Div (Col E.T. Marchenko)
        117th & 120th Gds Rifle Regts

79th Gds Rifle Div
    22nd Gds Rifle Regt
    220th Gds Rifle Regt (Col Sheikin)
88th Gds Rifle Div (Maj-Gen G.I. Pankov)
    269th Gds Rifle Regt
29th Gds Rifle Corps (Lt-Gen A.D. Shememkov/Maj-Gen G.I. Hetariov)
    27th Gds Rifle Div (Maj-Gen V. S. Glebov)
    74th Gds Rifle Div (Maj-Gen D.E. Bakanov)
        236th Gds Rifle Regt
    82nd Gds Rifle Div (Maj-Gen M. Duka)
        242nd Gds Rfle Regt (Col I.F. Sukhorukov)
        271st Gds Rifle Regt
7th Gds Tk Bde
84th Gds, 65th & 259TH Ind Tk Regts
371st & 374th Gds, 694th, 1026th, 1061st, 1087th & 1200th SP Aslt Arty Regts
41st Ind Engr Bde

69th Army (Col-Gen V.Y. Kolpakchi)
25th Rifle Corps (Maj-Gen N.I. Trufanov)
    77th Gds & 4th & 134th Rifle Divs
61st Rifle Corps (Lt-Gen I.F. Grigoryevsky)
    41st, 246th & 274th Rifle Divs
91st Rifle Corps (Lt-Gen F.A. Volkov)
    134th, 312th & 370th Rifle Divs
117th & 283rd Rifle Divs
68th Tk Bde
12th SP Aslt Arty Bde
344th Gds, 1205th, 1206th & 1221st SP Aslt Arty Regts

33rd Army (Col-Gen V.D. Svotaev)
16th Rifle Corps (Maj-Gen/Lt-Gen E.V. Dobrovolvsky)
    323rd, 339th & 383rd Rifle Divs
38th Rifle Corps (Maj-Gen/Lt-Gen A.D. Tyereshkov)
    39th, 64th & 129th Rifle Divs
62nd Rifle Corps (Lt-Gen V.S. Vorobyev)
    49th, 222nd & 362nd Rifle Divs

2nd Gds Cav Corps (Lt-Gen V.V. Krukov)
    3rd, 4th & 17th Gds Cav Divs
    1459th SP Aslt Arty Regt
    10th Gds RL Bn
95th Rifle Div
257th Tk Regt
360th & 361st SP Arty Aslt Regts

Air Forces

16th Air Army (Col-Gen S.I. Rudenko)
3rd Air Bomber Corps
    241st & 301st Air Bomber Divs
6th Air Bomber Corps
    326th & 339th Air Bomber Divs

6th Air Aslt Corps
   197th & 198th Air Aslt Divs
9th Air Aslt Corps
   3rd Gds & 300th Air Aslt Divs
1st Gds Air Fighter Corps
   3rd & 4th Gds Air Fighter Divs
3rd Air Fighter Corps
   265th & 278th Air Fighter Divs
6th Air Fighter Corps
   234th & 273rd Air Fighter Divs
13th Air Fighter Corps
   193rd & 283rd Air Fighter Divs
1st Gds, 240th, 269th & 287th Air Fighter Divs
2nd & 11th Gds, 113th, 183rd, 188th & 221st Air Bomber Divs
9th Gds & 242nd Air Night Bomber Divs
16th, 72nd, 93rd & 98th Air Recce Regts
176th Gds Air Fighter Regt
226th Air Tpt Regt

18th Air Army (Col-Gen A.Y. Golovanov)
1st Gds Air Bomber Corps
   11th & 16th Gds, 36th & 48th Air Bomber Divs
2nd Gds Air Bomber Corps
   2nd, 7th, 13th & 18th Air Bomber Divs
3rd Gds Air Bomber Corps
   22nd Gds, 1st, 12th & 50th Air Bomber Divs
4th Gds Air Bomber Corps
   14th & 15th Gds, 53rd & 54th Air Bomber Divs
45th Air Bomber Div
56th Air Fighter Div
742nd Air Recce Regt

Front Reserves

1st Gds Tk Army (Col-Gen M.Y. Katukov)
8th Gds Mech Corps (Maj-Gen I.F. Dremov)
   19th, 20th & 21st Gds Mech Bdes
   1st Gds Tk Bde
   48th Gds Tk Regt
   353rd & 400th Gds SP Aslt Arty Regts
   8th Gds M/C Bn
11th Gds Tk Corps
   40th, 44th & 45th Gds Tk Bdes
   27th Gds Mech Bde (Col Fioderovich)
   362nd & 399th Gds, & 1454th SP Aslt Arty Regts
   9th Gds M/C Bn
11th Tk Corps (Maj-Gen I.I. Badadyanyan)
   20th, 36th & 65th Tk Bdes
   12th Mot Rifle Bde
   50th Gds Tk Regt
   1461st & 1493rd SP Aslt Arty Regts
   115th Gds RL Bn
   93rd M/C Bn

64th Gds Tk Bde
19th SP Aslt Arty Bde
11th Gds Ind Tk Regt
79th Gds Mech Regt
6th Gds RL Regt
12th Gds M/C Bn

2nd Gds Tk Army (Col-Gen S.I. Bogdanov)
1st Mech Corps (Lt-Gen S.M. Krivosheina)
    19th, 35th & 37th Mech Bdes
    219th Tk Bde
    347th Gds, 75th & 1822nd SP Aslt Arty Regts
    41st Gds RL Regt
    57th M/C Bn
9th Gds Tk Corps (Maj-Gen A.F. Popoc)
    47th, 50th & 65th Gds Tk Bdes
    33rd Gds Mech Bde
    341st, 369th & 386th Gds SP Aslt Arty Regts
    126th Gds RL Regt
    17th Gds M/C Bn
12th Gds Tk Corps (Maj-Gen N.M. Telyokov/Maj-Gen M.F. Salminov)
    48th, 49th & 66th Gds Tk Bdes
    34th Gds Mech Bde
    79 Gds Tk Regt
    387th & 393rd Gds SP Aslt Arty Regts
    89th Gds RL Regt
    86th Gds M/C Regt

3rd Army (Col-Gen A.V. Gorbatov)
35th Rifle Corps (Maj-Gen N.A. Nikitin)
    250th, 290th & 348th Rifle Divs
40th Rifle Corps (Lt-Gen V.S. Kuznyetsov)
    5th & 169th Rifle Divs
41st Rifle Corps (Lt-Gen V.K. Ubranovich)
    120th & 269th Rifle Divs
1812th, 1888th & 1901st SP Aslt Arty Regts

Front Troops

3rd Gds Cav Corps (Lt-Gen N.S. Oslikovsky)
    5th & 6th Gds, & 32nd Cav Divs
    1814th SP Aslt Arty Regt
    3rd Gds Mech Regt
1st Gds Tk Corps (Maj-Gen/Lt-Gen M.F. Panov)
    15th, 16th & 17th Gds Tk Bdes
    1st Gds Mot Rifle Bde
    397th, 1001st & 1226th SP Aslt Arty Regts
43rd Gds RL Regt
13th Gds M/C Bn
3rd Gds Tk Corps (Lt-Gen A.P. Panfilov)
    3rd, 18th & 19th Gds Tk Bdes
    2nd Gds Mot Rifle Bde
    375th Gds, 1436th & 1496th SP Aslt Arty Regts

10th Gds M/C Bn
8th Gds Tk Corps (Maj-Gen A.F.Popov)
    58th, 59th & 60th Gds Tk Bdes
    28th Gds Mot Rifle Bde
    62nd Gds Ind Tk Regt
    301st Gds & 1817th SP Aslt Arty Regts
    307th Gds RL Regt
    6th Gds M/C Bn
8th Mech Corps (Maj-Gen A.N. Firsovich)
    66th, 67th & 68th Gds Mech Bdes
    116th Tk Bde
    86th Gds Ind Tk Regt
    114th & 895th SP Aslt Arty Regts
    205th Gds RL Regt
    97th Gds M/C Bn
66th Gds SP Aslt Arty Bde
233rd Ind Tk Regt
1277th SP Aslt Arty Regt

Naval Forces

Dnieper Flotilla (Rear Adm V.V. Grigoryev)
1st, 2nd & 3rd River Boat Bdes
(8 Monitors, 34 Gunboats & 20 Anti-Aircraft Gunboats)

1ST UKRAINIAN FRONT
(MARSHAL I.S. KONIEV)

3rd Gds Army (Col-Gen V.N. Gordov)
21st Rifle Corps (Maj-Gen A.A. Yamanov)
    121st Gds & 395th Rifle Divs
76th Rifle Corps (Lt-Gen M.I. Gluhov)
    106th & 287th Rifle Divs
120th Rifle Corps (Maj-Gen S.I. Donskov)
    127th, 149th & 197th Rifle Divs
25th Tk Corps (Maj-Gen E.I. Fomonich)
    111th, 162nd & 175th Tk Bdes
    20th Mot Rifle Bde
    262nd Gds & 1451st SP Aslt Arty Regts
    2nd Gds RL Bn
389th Rifle Div
87th Gds Ind Tk Regt
938th SP Aslt Arty Regt

13th Army (Col-Gen N.P. Phukov)
24th Rifle Corps (Maj-Gen D.P. Onoprienko)
    121st Gds & 395th Rifle Divs
27th Rifle Corps (Maj-Gen F.M. Chyerokmanov)
    6th Gds, 280th & 350th Rifle Divs (350th Rifle Div later detached to 4th
    Gds Tk Army)
102nd Rifle Corps (Maj-Gen/Lt-Gen I.M. Puzikov)
    117th Gds, 147th & 172nd Rifle Divs

88th Ind Tk Regt
327th & 272nd Gds, 768th & 1228th SP Aslt Arty Regts

5th Gds Army (Col–Gen A.S. Zhadov)
32nd Gds Rifle Corps (Lt–Gen A.I. Rodimtsev)
 13th, 95th & 97th Gds Rifle Divs
33rd Gds Rifle Corps (Maj–Gen N.F. Lyebedyenko)
 9th Gds Airborne, 78th Gds & 118th Rifle Divs
34th Gds Rifle Corps (Maj–Gen E.V. Boklanov)
 14th, 15th & 58th Gds Rifle Divs
4th Gds Tk Corps (Lt–Gen P.P. Poluboyarov)
 12th, 13th & 14th Gds Tk Bdes
 3rd Gds Mot Rifle Bde
 293rd & 298th Gds SP Aslt Arty Regts
 240th Gds RL Regt
 76th Gds M/C Bn
39th & 226th Ind Tk Regts
1889th SP Aslt Arty Regt

2nd Polish Army (Lt–Gen K.K. Swiersczewski)
5th, 7th, 8th, 9th & 10th Pol Inf Divs
1st Pol Tk Corps
 2nd, 3rd & 5th Pol Tk Bdes
 1st Pol Mot Inf Bde
 24th, 25th & 26th Pol SP Aslt Arty Regts
 2nd Pol M/C Bn
16th Pol Tk Bde
5th Pol Ind Tk Regt
28th Pol SP Aslt Arty Regt
52nd Army (Col–Gen K.A. Koroteyyev)
48th Rifle Corps (Maj–Gen Z.Z. Roganzt/Lt–Gen A.A. Gryechkin)
 116th & 294th Rifle Divs
73rd Rifle Corps (Maj–Gen S.S. Martirosyan)
 50th, 111th & 254th Rifle Divs
78th Rifle Corps (Lt–Gen A.I. Akimov)
 31st, 214th & 373rd Rifle Divs
213th Rifle div
8th SP Aslt Arty Bde
124th Ind Tk Regt
1198th SP Aslt Arty Regt

Air Forces

2nd Air Army (Col–Gen S.A. Krasovsky)
1st Gds Air Aslt Corps
 8th & 9th Gds Air Asslt, & 12th Gds Air Fighter Divs
2nd Gds Air Aslt Corps
 5th & 6th Gds Air Aslt, & 11th Gds Air Fighter Divs
3rd Air Aslt Corps
 307th & 308th Air Aslt, & 181st Air Fighter Divs
4th Air Bomber Corps
 202nd & 219th Air Bomber Divs

6th Gds Air Bomber Corps
   1st & 8th Gds Air Bomber Divs
2nd Air Fighter Corps
   7th Gds & 322nd Air Fighter Divs
5th Air Fighter Corps
   8th Gds & 256th Air Fighter Divs
6th Gds Air Fighter Corps
   9th, 22nd & 23rd Gds Air Fighter Divs
208th Air Night Bomber Div
98th & 193rd Gds Air Recce Regts
222nd Air Tpt Regt

Front Reserves

3rd Gds Tk Army (Col-Gen P.S. Rybalko)
6th Gds Tk Corps (Maj-Gen V.A. Mytrofanov)
   51st, 52nd & 53rd Gds Tk Bdes
   22nd Gds Mot Rifle Bde
   385th Gds, 1893rd & 1894th SP Aslt Arty Regts
   439th Gds RL Regt
   3rd Gds M/C Bn
7th Gds Tk Corps (Maj-Gen V.V. Novikov)
   54th Gds Tk Bde
   55th Gds Tk Bde (Col D. Dragunsky)
   56th Gds Tk Bde (Col Z. Slyusarenko)
   23rd Gds Mot Rifle Bde
   384th Gds, 702nd & 1977th SP Aslt Arty Regts
   440th Gds RL Regt
   4th Gds M/C Bn
9th Mech Corps (Lt-Gen I.P. Suhov)
   69th, 70th & 71st Mech Bdes
   91st Tk Bde
   383rd Gds, 1507th & 1978th SP Aslt Arty Regts
   441st Gds RL Regt
   100th M/C Bn
16th SP Aslt Arty Bde
57th Gds & 90th Ind Tk Regts
50th M/C Bn

4th Gds Tk Army (Col-Gen D.D. Lelyushenko)
5th Gds Mech Corps (Maj-Gen I.P. Yermankov)
   10th, 11th & 12th Gds Mech Bdes
   24th Gds Tk Bde
   104th & 397th Gds, & 1447th SP Aslt Arty Regts
   11th Gds RL Regt
   2nd Gds M/C Bn
6th Gds Mech Corps (Col V.I. Koryetsky/Col S.F. Puthkaryev)
   16th, 17th & 35th Gds Mech Bdes
   28th, 117th & 188th Gds Tk Regts
   423rd & 424th Gds SP Aslt Arty Regts
   52nd Gds RL Regt

19th Gds M/C Bn
10th Gds Tk Corps (Lt-Gen Y.Y. Belov)
  61st, 62nd & 63rd Gds Tk Bdes
  29th Gds Mot Rifle Bde
  72nd Gds Tk Regt
  416th & 425th Gds SP Aslt Arty Regts
  248th Gds RL Regt
  7th Gds M/C Bn
68th Gds Tk Bde
70th Gds Sp Aslt Arty Regt
13th & 119th Gds Ind Tk Regts
7th Gds M/C Regt

28th Army (Lt-Gen A.A. Luchinsky w.e.f. 20 Apr 45)
3rd Gds Rifle Corps (Maj-Gen P.A. Alexandrov)
  50th, 54th & 96th Gds Rifle Divs
20th Rifle Corps (Maj-Gen N.A. Shvarev)
  48th, 55th Gds, & 20th Rifle Divs
128th Rifle Corps (Maj-Gen P.F. Batirsky)
  61st, 130th & 152nd Rifle Divs

Front Troops

1st Gds Cav Corps (Lt-Gen V.K. Baranov)
  1st, 2nd & 7th Gds Cav Divs
  1st Gds RL Regt
  1224th SP Aslt Arty Regt
7th Gds Mech Corps (Lt-Gen I.P. Korchagin) (attached 52nd Army)
  24th, 25th & 26th Gds Mech Bdes
  57th Gds Tk Bde
  291st & 355th Gds, & 1820th SP Aslt Arty Regts
  410th Gds RL Regt
  5th Gds M/C Bn
152nd Tk Bde
98th Ind Tk Regt
368th Gds, 416th & 1976th SP Aslt Arty Regts
21st, 45th, 49th & 58th Ind Armd Train Bns

ORDER–OF–BATTLE OF THE MAIN GERMAN FORCES ENGAGED IN 'OPERATION BERLIN'

ODER–NEISSE FRONT

Army Group 'Weichsel'
(Col-Gen Gotthard Heinrici)

3rd Panzer Army
(Gen Hasso von Manteuffel)

'Swinemünde' Corps (Lt-Gen Ansat)
    402nd Inf Div (Maj-Gen Wittkopf)
    3rd Naval Div (Cl von Witzleben)
XXXII Corps (Lt-Gen Schack)
    'Voigt' Inf Div (Maj-Gen Voigt)
    549th VGr Div (Maj-Gen Jank)
    Stettin Garrison (Maj-Gen Brühl)
    281st Inf Div (Lt-Gen Ortner/Col Schmidt)
'Oder' Corps (SS-Lt-Gen von dem Bach-Zelewski/Gen Hörnlein)
    610th Inf Div (Col Summer/Col Fullriede)
    'Klossek' Inf Div (Maj-Gen Klossek)
XXXXVI Panzer Corps (Gen Martin Gareis)
    547th VGr Div (Maj-Gen Fronhöfer)
    1st Naval Div (Maj-Gen Bleckwenn)

9th Army
(Gen Theodor Busse)

CI Corps (Gen Wilhelm Berlin/Lt-Gen Friedrich Sixt)
    5th Lt Inf Div (Lt-Gen Friedrich Sixt/Lt-Gen Edmund Blaurock)
        56th Lt Inf Regt [3 Bns] (Col Haiden)
        75th Lt Inf Regt (Col Sparrer)
    606th Inf Div (Maj-Gen Maximilian Rosskopf)
        3rd Pz Depot Bn
        'Potsdam' Emergency Bn
        'Brandenburg' Emergency Bn
        'Spandau' Emergency Bn
        'Bremen' Police Bn
    309th 'Berlin' Inf Div (Maj-Gen Heinrich Voigtsberger)
        'Grossdeutschland' Gd Regt [2 Bns]
        365th Gren Regt [2 Bns]
        652nd Gren Regt [2 Bns]
        4th Luftwaffe Trg Regt
        5th Luftwaffe Trg Regt
        309th Arty Regt [1 Bn]
Corps Reserve:
25th PzGr Div (Lt Gen Arnold Burmeister)
    35th PzGr Regt [3 Bns]
    119th PzGr Regt [3 Bns]
    5th Pz Bn
    25th Arty Regt
111th SPG Trg Bde (Capt Schmidt)
'1001 Nights' Combat Gp (Maj Blancblois)

LVI Pz Corps (Gen Helmuth Weidling)
    9th Para Div (Gen Bruno Bräuer/Col Harry Herrmann)
        25th Para Regt [3 Bns]
        26th Para Regt [3 Bns]
        27th Para Regt [3 Bns]
        9th Para Arty Regt [4 Bns]
    20th PzGr Div (Col/Maj-Gen Georg Scholze)
        76th PzGr Regt [3 Bns] (Col Rheinhold Stammerjohann)

90th PzGr Regt [3 Bns] (Cokl von Loisecke)
8th Pz Bn
20th Arty Regt [3 Bns]
'Müncheberg' Pz Div (Maj-Gen Werner Mummert)
    1st 'Müncheberg' PzGr Regt [2 Bns] (Col Goder)
    2nd 'Müncheberg' Pz Gr Regr [3 Bns] (Lt-Col Werenr Rodust)
'Müncheberg' Pz Regt (Lt-Col Kuno von Meyer)
    1st Bn 'Müncheberg' Pz Regt (Maj Marquardt)
    2nd Bn 'Müncheberg' Pz Regt (Capt/Maj Horst Zobel)
'Müncheberg'Arty Regt [2 Bns] (Lt-Col Martin Buhr)

XI SS Pz Corps (SS-Gen Mathias Kleinmeisterkamp)
    303rd 'Döberitz' Inf Div (Col Scheunemann/Col Albin)
        300th Gren Regt [2 Bns] (Lt-Col Helmut Weber)
        301st Gren Regt [2 Bns]
        302nd Gren Regt [2 Bns]
    169th Inf Div (Lt-Gen Georg Radziej)
        378th Gren Regt [3 Bns]
        379th Gren Regt [2 Bns]
        392nd Gren Regt [3 Bns]
        230th Arty Regt [4 Bns]
    712th Inf Div (Maj-Gen Joachim von Siegroth)
        732nd Gren Regt [2 Bns]
        745th Gren Regt [2 Bns]
        764th Gren Regt [2 Bns]
        1712th Arty Regt
    920th SPG Trg Bde [1 Bn] (Maj Wolfgang Kapp)
Corps Reserve:
'Kurmark' PzGr Div (Col/Maj-Gen Willi Langkeit)
    'Kurmark' PzFus Regt [2 Bns]
    1234th PzGr Regt [2 Bns]
    'Kurmark' Pz Regt [2 Bns]
502nd SS Hy Tk Bn (SS-Maj Hartrampf)

Frankfurt-an-der-Oder Garrison (Col/Maj-Gen Ernst Biehler)

V SS Mountain Corps (SS-Gen Friedrich Jackeln)
    286th Inf Div (Maj-Gen Emmo von Rohde)
        926th Gren Regt [2 Bns]
        927th Gren Regt [2 Bns]
        931st Gren Regt [2 Bns]
        286th Arty Regt [3 Bns]
    32nd SS '30. Januar'VolGr Div (SS-Col Kempin)
        86th SS Gren Regt [2 Bns] (SS-Lt-Col Eccer)
        87th SS Gren Regt [2 Bns] (SS-Col Voss)
        88th SS Gren Regt [2 Bns] (SS-Lt-Col Becker)
        32nd SS Arty Regt [3 Bns] (SSlt-Col Lorenz)
    391st Sy Div (Lt-Gen Rudolf Sickenius)
        95th Gren Regt
        1233rd Gren Regt
        391st Arty Regt

Corps Reserve:
561st SS Tk-Hunting Bn (SS-Capt Jakob Lobmeyer)

Army Troops:
156th Inf Div (Gen Siegfried von Rekowsky)
    1313th Gren Regt [3 Bns]
    1314th Gren Regt [3 Bns]
    1315th Gren Regt [3 Bns]
541st VGr Div
    'Dorn' Tk-Hunting Bde
    'Pirat' Tk-Hunting Bde
    'F' Tk-Hunting Bde
    'R' Tk-Hunting Bde
404th Volks Arty Corps (Col Bartels)
406th Volks Arty Corps (Lt-Col Adams)
408th Volks Arty Corps (Col Vogt)

Army Group Reserve:
III SS 'Germanic' Pz Corps (SS-Lt-Gen Felix Steiner)

Reinforcements later allocated to the 9th Army:
11th SS 'Nordland' PzGr Div (SS-Maj-Gen Jügen Ziegler/SS-Maj-Gen Dr
    Gustav Krukenberg)
    23rd SS 'Norge' PzGr Regt (1st Norwegian)
    24th SS 'Danmark' PzGr Regt (1st Danish) (SS-Lt-ColKlotz/SS-Maj
    Sörensen)
    11th SS 'Hermann von Salza' Pz Bn [4 Coys] (SS-Lt-Col Paul Kausch)
    503rd SS Hy Tk Bn (SS-Maj Friedrich Herzig)
    11th SS 'Nordland' Armd Reccen Bn [4 Coys] (SS-Maj Saalbach)
23rd SS 'Nederland' PzGr Div (SS-Maj-Gen Wagner)
    48th SS 'Gen Seyffarth' PzGr Regt (1st Dutch) (SS-Lt-Col Scheibe)
    49th SS 'de Ruiter' PzGr Regt (2nd Dutch) (SS-Lt-Col Lohmanns)

Reinforcements later allocated to the 3rd Panzer Army:
27th SS 'Langemarck' PzGr Div (Col Müller)
28th SS 'Wallonien' Gren Div

OKW Reserve later transferred to the 9th Army:
18th PzGr Div (Maj-Gen Josef Rauch)
    30th PzGr Regt [2 Bns]
    51st PzGr Regt [2 Bns]
    118th Pz Regt [part only]
    18th Arty Regt [3 Bns]

Army Group 'Mitte'
(FM Ferdinand Schörner)

4th Pz Army
(Gen Fritz-Herbert Glaser)

V Corps (later transferred to the 9th Army) (Lt-Gen Wagner)

35th SS Police Gren Div (SS-Col Rüdiger Pipkorn)
    89th SS Police Gren Regt [2 Bns]
    90th SS Police Gren Regt [2 Bns]
    91st SS Police Gren Regt [2 Bns]
36th SS Gren Div (SS-Maj-Gen Dirlwanger)
    72nd SS Gren Regt [2 Bns]
    73rd SS Gren Regt [2 Bns]
275th Inf Div
    983rd Gren Regt [2 Bns]
    984th Gren Regt [2 Bns]
    985th Gren Regt [2 Bns]
    275th Fus Bn
    275th Arty Regt
342nd Inf Div
    554th Gren Regt [2 Bns]
    697th Gren Regt [2 Bns]
    699th Gren Regt [2 Bns]
Corps Reserve:
21st Pz Div (Maj-Gen Marcks)
    125th PzGr Regt [2 Bns] Col Hans von Luck)
    192nd PzGr Regt [2 Bns]
    22nd Pz Regt
    155th Pz Arty Regt [3 Bns]
    305th Army Flak Bn

ELBE FRONT

12th Army
(Gen Walter Wenck)

XX Corps (Gen Carl-Erik Koehler)
    'Theodor Körner' RAD Div (3rd RAD) (Lt-Gen Bruno Frankewitz)
        1st 'TK' RAD Gren Regt [2 Bns] (Maj Bieg)
        2nd 'TK' RAD Gren Regt [2 Bns] (Maj Becker)
        3rd 'TK' RAD Gren Regt [2 Bns] (Maj Menzel)
    'Ulrich von Hutten' Inf Div (Lt-Gen Gerhard Engel)
        1st 'UvH' Gren Regt [2 Bns] (Maj Wesemann)
        2nd 'UvH' Gren Regt [2 Bns] (Maj Anton Siebert)
        3rd 'UvH' Gren Regt [2 Bns] (Maj Hobra)
    'Ferdinand von Schill' Inf Div (Lt-Col Alfred Müller)
        1st 'FvS' Gren Regt [2 Bns] (Maj Carstens)
        2nd 'FvS' Gren Regt [2 Bns] (Maj Kley)
        3rd 'FvS' Gren Regt [2 Bns] (Maj Müller)
    'Scharnhorst' Inf Div (Lt-Gen Heinrich Götz)
        1st 'S' Gren Regt [2 Bns] (Maj Mathias Langmaier)
        2nd 'S' Gren Regt [2 Bns] (Maj Mahlow)
        3rd 'S' Gren Regt [2 Bns] (Lt-Col Gerhard Pick)

XXXIX Pz Corps (Lt-Gen Karl Arndt)
12–21 Apr 45 under command OKW with following structure:

'Clausewitz' Pz Div (Lt-Gen Unrein)
'Schlageter' RAD Div (1st RAD) (Lt-Gen Hein)
  1st, 2nd & 3rd 'Schlageter' Gren Regts [each 2 Bns]
84th Inf Div
21–26 Apr 45 under command 12th Army with the following structure:
  'Clausewitz' Pz Div [3 Bns only] (Lt-Gen Unrein)
  'Schlageter' RAD Div (1st RAD) (Lt-Gen Hein)
    1st, 2nd & 3rd 'Schlageter' Gren Regts [each 2 Bns]
  84th Inf Div [3 Bns only]
    'Hamburg' Res Inf Div [2 Regts]
    'Meyer' Inf Div [2 Regts]

XXXXI Pz Corps (Lt-Gen Holste)
  'von Hake' Inf Div (Col Friedrich von Hake)
    1st 'vH' Gren Regt (Lt-Col Joachim Bahr)
    2nd 'vH' Gren Regt (Lt-Col von dem Bottlemberg)
  199th Inf Div [1 Regt only]
  'V-Weapons' Inf Div
  1st HJ Tk-Destroyer Bde
  'Hermann Göring' Tk-Hunting Bde

XXXXVIII Pz Corps (Gen Maximilian Reichsherr von Edelsheim)
  14th Flak Div
  'Leipzig' Battle Gp [8 Bns] (Lt-Gen Rathke)
  'Halle' Battle Gp [8 Bns] (Col von Poncet)

Ungrouped formations:
'Friedrich Ludwig Jahn' RAD Div (2nd RAD) (Col Gerhard Klein/Col Franz
  Weller)
  1st 'FLJ' RAD Gren Regt [2 Bns] (RAD-Lt-Col Gerhard Konopka)
  2nd 'FLJ' RAD Gren Regt [2 Bns] (Maj Berhard Schulze-Hagen)
  3rd ' FLJ' RAD Gren Regt [2 Bns] (Maj Dahms)
'Potsdam' Inf Div (Col Erich Lorenz)
  1st, 2nd & 3rd 'Potsdam' Gren Regts [each 2 Bns]

FÜHRER–ORDER

21 January 1945

I order as follows:
  1. Commanders-in-Chief, Commanding Generals and Divisional
  Commanders are personally responsible to me for reporting in good time:
  a. Every decision to carry out an operational movement.
  b. Every attack planned in divisional strength and upwards which does not
    conform with the general directives laid down by the High Command.
  c. Every offensive action in quiet sectors of the front, over and above normal
    shock-troop activities, which is calculated to draw the enemy's attention to
    the sector.
  d. Every plan for disengaging or withdrawing forces.

e. Every plan for surrendering a position, a local strongpoint or a fortress. They must ensure that I have time to intervene in this decision if I think fit, and that my counter-orders can reach the front-line in time.

2. Commanders-in-Chief, Commanding Generals and Divisional Commanders, the Chiefs of the General Staffs, and each individual officer of the General Staff, or officers employed with the General Staffs, are responsible to me that every report made to me either directly or through normal channels, should contain nothing but the unvarnished truth. In future I shall impose draconian punishment on any attempt at concealment, whether deliberate or arising from carelessness or oversight.

3. I must point out that maintenance of signals communications, particularly in heavy fighting and critical situations, is a prerequisite for the conduct of the battle. All officers commanding troops are responsible to me for ensuing that these communications both to higher formations and to subordinate commanders are not broken, and for seeing that, by exhausting every means and engaging themselves personally, permanent communications are ensured with commanders above and below whatever the situation.

Adolf Hitler

Notes on Sources

GENERAL

I have drawn heavily on Gosztony's excellent 1970 collection of pertinent extracts of source material, which otherwise would have been difficult to come by in original form.

No Soviet source material was published before 1952, and what appeared during Stalin's reign was designed to show that he alone was responsible for the victory over Fascist Germany. Zhukov was progressively humiliated during the remainder of Stalin's lifetime and reappeared to public view only after Khrushchev's denunciation of the dictator. Then he was quickly promoted to Deputy Minister of Defence, only to be deposed again later for seven further years of rustication. While he worked on his memoirs, his political enemies eliminated him from the histories then being published. Subsequent rewriting of Soviet history to meet changes in the political climate did not alter the original bland presentation of all having gone to plan, whoever was in charge. Little has emerged to indicate what really went on behind the scenes or to give colour to the principal players. However, Chuikov's book, having been published as an attack on Zhukov, inevitably pointed to some cracks in the façade, and some of the articles published on the activities of individual formations have proved useful in revealing certain important aspects of the overall operation not properly covered in the major works. Also the order-of-battle in Appendix IV reveals a surprising amount of upheaval among the commanders of formations during the course of this 'Operation Berlin' – well beyond what would be attributable to battle casualties.

The German source material has proved more generous in scope and some recently published titles, such as Tieke's *Das Ende zwischen Oder und Elbe* on certain aspects of the battle, and O'Donnell's *The Berlin Bunker*, have added much useful detail to the overall picture.

The recent increase in Soviet and German sources has given me the advantage on earlier writers on this subject, such as Kuby, Ryan, Toland and Tully, who were obliged to work within much narrower parameters in describing the military aspects of the battle.

Details of all the books cited in the notes will be found in the bibliography. Where I have quoted from more than one title by the same author I have used initials to identify the title in question.

Throughout I have placed considerable emphasis on the detailed examination and appreciation of maps in the study of this operation. Apart from the obstacle presented by the Seelow Heights, the water courses provided the most significant factor, both as obstacles and in channelling the lines of attack. One aspect that became particularly significant once fighting began within the devastated city was the establishment of formation boundaries readily identifiable to the troops on the ground, and here water courses and railway lines had far greater value than named but rubble-choked streets. At this stage too, the changes of scale in the maps having to be used, and the narrowing of formation and unit frontages as they gradually converged on the city centre, all added to the difficulties of command.

The motivation of those involved in this gigantic and cataclysmic conflict and the soldier's general idolatry of their leaders is difficult to understand several decades later. I have therefore tried to set the scene by means of four introductory chapters.

I. THE PLAN

As the Soviets held the initiative as the attackers in this battle, the first chapter is designed to present the line of attack, the personalities responsible and the means at their disposal. The main sources are the *Great Patriotic War of the Soviet Union* [GPW], Vorbeyev, Propotkin and Shimansky's *The Last Storm*, Marshal G.K. Zhukov's *The Memoirs of Marshal Zhukov*, Marshal I.S. Koniev's *Year of Victory* and Marshal V.I. Chuikov's *The End of the Third Reich*. (I quote from a translation of Chuikov's book produced by Progress Publishers, Moscow, in 1978, which varies considerably from the first edition, being far less critical of Zhukov.)

It is significant that neither Zhukov nor Koniev admits to the rivalry between them in their accounts as published, but this is presumably due to Party censorship.

The biographical notes on Zhukov are mainly drawn from his own memoirs, from Harrison E. Salisbury's introduction to *Marshal Zhukov's Greatest Battles* and Otto P. Chaney Jnr's *Zhukov*.

Interestingly, but inaccurately, Earl F. Ziemke's *Battle for Berlin – End of the Third Reich*, Battle Book No. 6 in Purnell's *History of the Second World War* series (Macdonald, London, 1968) places Zhukov as the overall commander of 'Operation Berlin', citing Colonel-General Vasili D. Sokolovsky, Zhukov's actual Deputy, as the commander of the 1st Byelorussian Front. This presumably was a result of Zhukov having been written out of his true role at this stage by the Soviets but being known to the West as having played a prominent role in the battle – see Ziemke, p. 73, in particular.

The first two maps serve to illustrate the content of this chapter by showing respectively the approaches to Berlin and the original Soviet outline plan of action for 'Operation Berlin'.

1   Zhukov, p. 602.
2   Tieke, p. 93.
3   Zhukov, pp. 602–3.
4   Shtemenko [SGSW], p. 305.
5   Montgomery-Hyde, pp. 447–8.
6   Busse article, p. 160. The claim to have taken Küstrin was passed on by Front HQ and duly celebrated with a victory salute in Moscow. It was not until 29 March that Zhukov was relieved of this dilemma, when the citadel fell to a combined assault by the 8th Guards and 5th Shock Armies.

7   Montgomery-Hyde, pp. 521–2; Shtemenko [SGSW], pp. 307–17; Chuikov, pp. 115, 166. The formations remaining on the Oder were the 5th Shock Army, 33rd Army, 69th Army (less one corps) and half of 8th Guards Army.

8   Shtemenko [SGSW], p. 319.

9   Chaney, p. 307.

10 Rokossovsky's position was not unique, for Stalin's great purge of the 1930s was still fresh in people's minds and the NKVD were at hand to remove to forced-labour camps or execute anyone who displeased him. Fear of Stalin ruled everyone – see Tolstoy, pp. 1–68. As late as November 1986 the people of the Soviet Union were reminded of some of the horrors of life under Stalin's rule through the authorities' release of films.

11 Shtemenko [SGSW], pp. 304–5. The Stavka 'modus operandi' and the description of events in Moscow are drawn from Shtemenko as well as the memoirs of Koniev and Zhukov.

12 From the details given by Koniev, this was Field Marshal Montgomery's plan, and was presumably reported by the Soviet Mission at General Eisenhower's Headquarters, who may not have known that this plan had been rejected.

13 Koniev, p. 79; Zhukov, pp. 587–9.

14 Zhukov, pp. 588–92; *The Great Patriotic War of the Soviet Union* [GPW], pp. 376–8; Erickson, pp. 531–5.

15 GPW, pp 376–7; Erickson, pp. 535–7.

16 Koniev, pp. 81–2 – '250 guns per kilometre'; GPW, p. 377.

17 Novikov article, p. 89.

18 Novikov, pp. 88–9; Wagener, p. 353.

19 GPW, p. 377.

20 Shtemenko [SGSW], p. 320; Koniev, p. 83; Erickson, pp. 532–3.

21 Koniev, p. 89.

22 Eisenhower, pp. 397–403; Montgomery-Hyde, p. 525; Ziemke, p. 142; Seaton [RGW], pp. 562–5

23 John Ehrmann's *Grand Strategy, October 1944–August 1945*, p. 142, as quoted in Gosztony, p. 122.

24 Seaton [RGW], pp. 588–90; Ziemke, p. 71; Wagener, Appx 2. Lease-lend supplies delivered included 1,900 locomotives and 11,000 railway flats, 427,000 trucks and jeeps, 35,000 motorcycles, 13,000 armoured fighting vehicles (including 10,000 tanks) and nearly 19,000 aircraft.

25 Zhukov, pp. 598–9; Novikov, p. 89.

26 Zhukov, pp. 598–9.

27 Air transportation from Ryan, p. 237. The scraping of the manpower barrel did not of course involve the estimated over a quarter of a million NKVD troops guarding the Gulag camps containing over ten million prisoners back in the Soviet Union. See Tolstoy, pp. 64, 248.

28 Zhukov, p. 598.

29 Zhukov, p. 604.

30 Zhukov, p. 599; Chuikov, p. 140; Erickson, pp. 538–9.

31 Zhukov, p. 593; Novikov, p. 89. The table model is now on display in the Karlshorst Museum.

32 Chuikov, pp. 126–7, 32

33 GPW, p. 378. The build-up of Communist Party and Komsomol membership comes from the official histories, as does the information on the carrying of standards in action and oath-taking ceremonies beforehand.

Ryan, p. 347, gives another reason for joining the Party, which was to ensure that soldiers' families would be informed should they be killed in action, a privilege denied the ordinary soldier. The 1st Byelorussian Front claimed 5,807 granted full and 5,890 granted probationary membership of the Communist party in March 1945, the figures being 6,849 and 6,413 for the following month.

34 Chuikov, pp. 140–41.
35 Alexander Werth's *Russland im Krieg 1941–1945* (Munich and Zurich, 1965), p. 644, as quoted in Gosztony, p. 58; Klimov, p. 59. The role of Ehrenburg is also covered by Ryan and Tolstoy.
36 Tolstoy, pp. 282–4.
37 Ziemke, p. 74; Zhukov, p. 600; GPW, p. 383.
38 Red Army atrocities on German soil are well covered in Gosztony, Ryan and Tolstoy. The latter, pp. 265–71, suggests that the Red Army was encouraged to behave in this fashion in order to destroy or loot as much of the evidence of capitalist comfort as possible and to create an irredeemable rift between the conquerors and their victims. See also Toland [LHD], p. 9.
39 Mackintosh, p. 222. Comments on alcoholism from Colonel Harry Herrmann (see Note 17 to Chapter 6).
40 Mackintosh, p. 226. The 2nd Guards Tank Army was said to be particularly well supplied with American equipment, including Sherman tanks.
41 Mackintosh, pp. 224–5.
42 Mackintosh, pp. 222–4.
43 Tolstoy, pp. 281–2.
44 Mackintosh, pp. 226–7.
45 Mackintosh, pp. 228–9.
46 Mackintosh, p. 226.
47 Source untraced.
48 Komornicki, p. 79.
49 Tieke, pp. 76–9; Tully, p. 102. See also Altner and Plievier, and the author's article in *Militärgeschichte*, Heft 4, 1995. However, no mention is found in official East German publications such as *An der Seite der Roten Armee* (Militärverlag der DDR, 1982), which limits support to the Red Army to propaganda only.
50 Tolstoy, pp. 143, 255.
51 GPW, pp. 375, 378; Tully, p. 79. Soviet estimates of German strengths were summarised as: 3rd PzArmy – 105,000 men, 1,150 guns, 700 RLs, 223 tanks; 9th Army – 235,000 men, 2,500 guns, 1,500 RLs, 833 tanks; 4th PzArmy – 110,000 men, 1,300 guns, 780 RLs, 285 tanks. But see Kuby, p. 93, for comment on Soviet exaggeration of figures and general boastfulness about this operation.
52 Zhukov, pp. 601–2; Chuikov, pp. 138–9; Tieke, pp. 82–91.

2. THE OBJECTIVE

Much of the basic material for this chapter comes from *Götterdämmerung – La Prise de Berlin* by Colonel Pierre Rocolle, who conducted his own investigations while stationed in Berlin shortly after the war, and Willemer's report on *The German Defense of Berlin* for HQ USAREUR.

General Reymann's defence plans for Berlin will be found incorporated on the applicable maps. However, the implementation of these plans and the manning of the positions do not necessarily follow.

1   This is evident from all Soviet publications on the subject of the battle for Berlin.

2   Ziemke, p. 75; Ryan, pp. 13–16; O'Donnell, p. 18; Tully, p. 111. Since September 1944 the British had dropped 42,825 tons of bombs on Berlin and the Americans 28,268 tons.

3   The boundaries of Greater Berlin encompass 341 square miles, being about twenty-three miles from north to south and twenty-eight miles from east to west, but over half of this area consists of woods, parks, fields and lakes.

4   Rocolle, pp. 5, 10–11; Ryan, pp. 26–7.

5   Rocolle, pp. 7–8.

6   Rocolle, pp. 8–9; Ryan, pp. 137–8; Willemer, p. 33. See also Borkowski for descriptions of conditions in the big flak towers, and Altner, pp. 170–74. The Berlin-based Stiftung Preussischer Kulturbesitz published a report by Irene Kühne-Kunze in a special supplement to its 1984 annual review on the subject of the art treasures stored in these towers.

7   Of these three the Humboldthain is the only one to have partially survived demolition, the rear having been covered with rubble to make an artificial hill. The destroyed Friedrichshain tower is concealed in this manner and that at the Zoo completely removed.

8   See Harry Schweizer's account in the author's *With Our Backs to Berlin,* pp. 123–130.

9   Willemer, p. 15; Clark, pp. 388–9. Detailed information on the basic German Army organisation in the city comes from Zippel.

10   Willemer, p. 8; Tieke, pp. 58–9.

11   Tieke, p. 50.

12   General Reymann's plan is taken from an article entitled 'Die Zerstörung Berlins war von der Werhmachtführung einkalkuliert' in the East German magazine *Zeitschrift für Militärgeschichte* No. 2/1965, the accompanying orders being quoted in Gosztony, pp. 144–6.

13   Rocolle, p. 6; Willemer, pp. 26–7.

14   Willemer, p. 28.

15   Willemer, p. 27.

16   Willemer, pp. 28–31.

17   Willemer, pp. 31–3.

18   Willemer, pp. 33–4; Jacob Kronika's *Der Untergang Berlins* (Flensburg/Hamburg, 1946), p. 114, as quoted in Burkert, p. 41.

19   Willemer, p. 22.

20. Rocolle, p. 16.

21   Willemer, p. 38; Trevor-Roper [LDH], p. 96.

3. THE OPPOSITION

This third introductory chapter describes the Nazi leadership and the Nazi Party organisations available to them for the defence of the city.

The description of Adolf Hitler is taken from Joachim C. Fest's *Hitler,* Alan

Bullock's *Hitler – A Study in Tyranny*, John Toland's *Adolf Hitler* and David Irving's *Hitler's War*; that of the Führerbunker from Trevor-Roper's *Last Days of Adolf Hitler* and James P. O'Donnell's *The Berlin Bunker*.

1   Tieke, p. 22; Ziemke, p. 65; Erich Kempa's *Ich habe Adolf Hitler verbrannt* (Munich, undated), p. 76, and Hans Schwarz's *Brennpunkt HQ – Menschen und Massstäbe in Führerhauptquartier* (Buenos Aires, 1950), p. 25, as quoted in Gosztony, pp. 91–3.
2   Rocolle, p. 13; Trevor-Roper [LDH], pp. 104–16.
3   Tieke, p. 62; Trevor-Roper [LDH], p. 135; Tully, p. 40.
4   Trevor-Roper [LDH], pp. 65, 101. Hitler's fascination for others is described by Dönitz, pp. 476–7.
5   Rocolle, p. 14.
6   Toland, pp. 1118–19
7   Kuby, p. 86; Toland, p. 955.
8   O'Donnell, pp. 40–43.
9   Trevor-Roper [LDH], pp. 65–6.
10 General Reymann in Tieke, pp. 55–6; Willemer, pp. 20–21. The Sturmabteilung (SA) was the Nazi Party Brownshirt activist organisation that had once rivalled the Wehrmacht, but had declined in influence after the murder of its leaders on Hitler's instructions in 1934.
11 Kuby, pp. 87–8; O'Donnell, pp. 197–8.
12 Willemer, pp. 40–42.
13 From Milton Schumann's *Defeat in the West* (Secker & Warburg, 1947) as quoted in Flower and Reeve, p. 1004.
14 Dr Stumm's statement comes from his denazification questionnaire.
15 From Dr Gustav Pourroy's account in the author's *Death Was Our Companion* (Sutton, 2003), pp. 117–49.
16 Letter to author.
17 Rocolle, p. 16. See also Koch and an extract from Axmann's article in *Stern* magazine, 'Mit Hitler im Führerbunker' of 25 April 1965, as quoted in Gosztony, pp. 202–20. Such a hanging is quoted in Altner, pp. 123–4.
18 Colonel Wöhlermann in Tieke, p. 139.
19 Tieke, p. 192, says that girls of the BDM served as 'Kampfhelferinnen' with the HJ Regiment 'Frankfurt/Oder', which formed part of the Frankfurt Garrison and later took part in the 9th Army's breakout to the west.
20 The information on the Waffen SS Regiment 'Anhalt' comes from Willy Rogmann's account in the author's *With Our Backs to Berlin*, pp. 140–208; Tieke, p. 233. Mohnke's forces are also described in Tully, further information coming from Mohnke in O'Donnell, Tully again being the source of the Allgemeine SS, the police, fire brigade, etc.
21 Willmer, pp. 42–3.
22 Trevor-Roper [HWD], pp. 207–8; Tully, p. 83.
23 Trevor-Roper [LDH], pp. 119–22.
24 Trevor-Roper [HWD], pp. 207–8; Trevor-Roper [LDH], pp. 123–4; O'Donnell, pp. 51–75.
25 Speer, pp. 575–7; O'Donnell, pp. 56–62; Trevor-Roper [LDH], pp. 124–6. There is no supporting evidence for Speer's claim about poison gas, although it was brought up at his trial at Nuremburg.
26 Thorwald, pp. 67–8; Reymann in Tieke, pp. 57–8.
27 Speer, pp. 624–5. Speer says only eighty-eight out of 950 bridges were

blown, but it is difficult to define exactly what constitutes a bridge in this context, or what was the actual cause of damage to those found wrecked after the battle.

28 Toland, p. 10.
29 Trevor-Roper [HWD], pp. 209–12.
30 Trevor-Roper [LDH], pp. 135–8.
31 Vienna had fallen the day before.
32 President Franklin D. Roosevelt of the United States had died on 12 April.
33 Trevor-Roper [HWD], pp. 212–13.

4. THE MAIN GERMAN FORCES

Georg Tessin's *Verbände und Truppen der deutschen Wehrmacht und Waffen-SS im zweiten Weltkrieg 1939–1945* in its numerous volumes provides a brilliant analysis of the German Armed Forces based on a study of the Field Post Office records. However, it is the accounts of Generals Heinrici and Busse on the situation on the Oder Front, and that of Gellermann and General Wenck on the Elbe, that have provided most of the detail given here.

Tieke's sketch maps provided much valuable information on the deployment and boundaries of the German formations, which I have incorporated into my own drawings in conjunction with information gleaned from other sources.

1 Houston, p. 417.
2 Tessin, with additional information on the Volksarmee from Tully. Note that the Germans used Roman numerals for their corps formation titles (including the unusual XXXX for 40) but not for their artillery corps. The Russians did not use Roman numerals at all.
3 Clark, p. 354; see also Strik-Strikfeld. Tieke, p. 47, says that the 600th Division made its way down to Czechoslovakia, where it took part in the defence of Prague.
4 Felix Steiner's *Die Armee der Geächteten* (Göttingen, 1965), pp. 224–5, as quoted in Gosztony, p. 190. Additional material on the Waffen-SS is taken from Burn, Quarrie, and Clark, p. 386. In Manvell and Fraenkel's *Heinrich Himmler* it is said that some senior SS offices were entertaining doubts about a successful conclusion to the war some two years earlier.
5 Marshall Cavendish's *Illustrated Encyclopedia of World War II* (Marshall Cavendish, New York, 1981), Vol. 11, p. 195.
6 GPW, pp. 374–5.
7 Wenck's article, p. 62; Gellermann, pp. 29–49.
8 Gellermann, p. 97.
9 Heinrici's letters to Gosztony, p. 94.
10 Thorwald, pp. 1–16; Erickson, p. 554; Tully, p. 58, Strawson, pp. 120–21.
11 Schwarz, pp. 23ff, as quoted in Gosztony, pp. 91–3.
12 Thorwald, p. 31.
13 General Gotthardt Heinrici's 'Die Abwehrvorbereitungen an der Oder' (1947 MS), pp. 43, 47, as quoted in Gosztony, pp. 91–3.
14 Ziemke, pp. 66–7; Shtemenko [SGSW], pp. 300–302.
15 Heinrici's MS, pp. 36ff, as quoted in Gosztony, pp. 156–9.
16 Busse, p. 162. Busse's serialised article, written in Soviet captivity and obviously subjected to censorship, remains the principal source on the 9th

Army, despite errors in chronology. Tully, p. 59 – Busse had 850 tanks.

17 Thorwald, p. 32; Rocolle, p. 19.

18 Heinrici's MS, p. 47, as quoted in Gosztony, p. 159. According to Heinrici, the dam whose waters were used to inundate the Oderbruch was at Ottmachau.

19 Ziemke, p. 76; Rocolle, pp. 19–20.

20 Thorwald, pp. 40–41.

21 Busse, p. 163. The two brigades referred to were the remains of the SS 'Nordland' and 'Nederland' Panzergrenadier Divisions.

22 Ryan, pp. 345, 351; Erickson, p. 555.

5. AN EARLY DAWN

This chapter describes the first two days of the decisive opening battles on the Oder/Neisse line, where the last of the available forces for the defence of the capital were committed. Of the lines of attack the most difficult proved to be the direct route to Berlin, where Marshal Zhukov blundered and foundered in uncharacteristic form. Although Pykathov on the 3rd Shock Army and Komornicki on the 1st Polish Army provide more detail on these respective formations, I have concentrated on the 8th Guards Army's area of operations on the critical main axis of advance where the focus of attention lay.

How much wider Zhukov's attack front was in comparison to Koniev's can be seen from Maps 3a and 3b. Once Koniev had secured his crossing of the Neisse, despite the unexpected problems from extensive forest fires, he could then concentrate his armoured thrusts to push through the opposition, leaving the infantry to mop up. Zhukov was far more handicapped by the nature of the Oderbruch terrain, which prevented him from adopting such a concentration of force and obliged him to use the expensive 'human wave' technique to swamp the Seelow Heights defences. The premature introduction of his armour, discussed in this chapter, only added to his difficulties.

1   0300 hours local German time, but the Soviets were operating to Moscow Time, which is 0500 hours in their accounts.

2   Novikov, p. 90; Zhukov, p. 603; Chuikov, p. 142; Ryan, pp. 348–9.

3   Zhukov, pp. 593–4, 603; Chuikov, pp. 138–9, 142–3; Ryan, pp. 347–8.

4   Seaton [RGW], p. 568; Chuikov, p. 143; Ryan, pp. 360–61.

5   Novikov, p. 91; Wagener, pp. 349–50.

6   Zhukov, p. 603; Chuikov, p. 143.

7   Chuikov, pp. 145–6; Wagener, pp. 350–51.

8   Zhukov, pp. 604–5.

9   Chuikov, p. 146.

10 Zhukov, p. 605; Chuikov, p. 146; Erickson, p. 565 – this added 1,377 tanks and self-propelled guns to the battle area.

11 Zhukov, p. 594.

12 The description of the chaos caused by the introduction of the tank armies to the battle on the first day comes from Chuikov, p. 146. That the situation was similar where the 2nd Guards Tank Army intervened can be seen from the maps illustrating the even more limited progress of the 3rd Shock Army in Pykathov, and as shown in Sergeyev's article, which describes how even on the third day of battle the Kunersdorf position had

still to be taken by the infantry before the tanks could be brought forward for the breakthrough. Von Hopffgarten; Tieke, pp. 104–6.

13   Chuikov, pp. 146–7; Erickson, p. 566; Zobel to author.

14   Chuikov, p. 147.

15   Zhukov, pp. 607–8; Chuikov, pp. 147–9.

16   Chuikov, p. 138.

17   Discussion with Professor Donnelly.

18   Novikov, pp. 91–2.

19   This was the equivalent of roughly a complete tank corps and two air divisions respectively. The tank figures are probably reasonably accurate, but the problems of aircraft claims are too well known for comment here.

20   Busse, p. 164; Tieke, p. 111; *Aktenbestände der Heeresgruppe Weichsel vom 1. März bis 28. April 1945* (National Archives, Washington DC) as quoted in Gosztony, pp. 176–8.

21   Wagener, p. 352.

22   Koniev, p. 90.

23   Koniev, pp. 90–91; Wagener, p. 352.

24   Koniev, pp. 92.

25   Novikov, p. 91; Wagener, p. 352.

26   Seaton [RGW], p. 574.

27   Novikov, pp. 91–2.

28   Novikov, p. 92; Wagener, p. 353.

29   Koniev, p. 93.

30   Koniev, p. 95.

31   Koniev, p. 97.

32   Koniev, p. 93.

33   Ziemke, p. 83.

34   Busse, p. 164; Tieke, pp. 120–1, 124–7.

35   Chuikov, pp. 1144–5.

36   Novikov, p. 92.

37   Koniev, pp. 101–2.

38   Koniev, pp 105–6. I am presuming that Stalin deliberately did not inform Zhukov of his decision to permit Koniev to intervene directly in the battle for Berlin. I have based this assumption on Chuikov's account of Zhukov's reactions to the discovery of some of Koniev's troops on what he presumed to be his own preserve on the morning of the 24th, which will be discussed later. But Ryan, p. 393, says otherwise.

39   Koniev, pp. 107–8.

40   Ziemke, p. 84.

41   Ziemke, p. 84

42   Rocolle, p. 23. According to Rocolle, p. 3, the French POW camp in Berlin, Stalag III/D, comprised 197 detachments (Kommandos) scattered in and around the city, accommodating some 20,000 prisoners, of whom 200 died of illness, 220 were killed in air raids, and 40 were killed in this battle.

6. BREAKTHROUGH

I have deliberately kept accounts of the 2nd Byelorussian's Front's battle to a minimum, as it was not directly concerned in the taking of the city, nor, apart from the initial phase, did the battle contain any unusual characteristics. However, its progress is reflected in the accompanying maps and the German staff reactions to this are in the text.

The punishment taken by the 1st Byelorussian Front in the battle for the Seelow Heights is evident from the casualties, the time taken to achieve the breakthrough and then follow-up against a broken enemy offering negligible opposition and, above all, the evidence of the change of plan for the encirclement of the city. Instead of the two tank armies converging in a classic pincer movement, we find the 2nd Guards Tank Army split up between three combined-arms armies, and the 1st Guards Tank Army tasked with integrating with the 8th Guards Army.

Meanwhile the 1st Ukrainian Front's tank armies were speeding towards Berlin in a desperate gamble to get there first from the south.

1   GPW p. 381. Rokossovsky's attack was ahead of schedule, but took so long to develop that it could not directly assist Zhukov's encirclement of Berlin, as it had been mooted at one stage. Its emphasis was now to the northwest instead of towards Berlin, as it was appreciated that by the time his troops secured a foothold on the west bank Zhukov would no longer require their assistance with the encirclement of the city.

2   Novikov, p. 90.

3   Chuikov, p. 151.

4   Sergeyev (see note 12 to Chapter 5).

5   Chuikov pp. 149–51; Zhukov, p. 607; Novikov, p. 92 – 'With the help of the 16th Air Army, Soviet troops not only held their positions but even advance a little.' According to Tieke, pp. 136–7, the Luftwaffe claimed to have destroyed 43 tanks, plus another possible 19 tanks, and 59 enemy aircraft.

6   This was the formation commander's council of war, the Political Adviser being known simply as 'Member of the Military Council'.

7   Chuikov, pp. 158–9.

8   Chuikov, who quotes Zhukov's orders of 18 April, is severely critical, and some of his reasons read oddly. The belatedness of these coordination instructions, issued at a critical period in the development of the battle, he regards as an abdication of responsibility by Zhukov, and of the exchange of liaison officers he says it 'could not improve the organisation of coordination; on the contrary, it evoked suspicion and mistrust.'

9   Ziemke, p. 84.

10   Lt Wilfred von Oven's *Mit Goebbels bis zum Ende* (Buenos Aires, 1950), p. 305, as quoted in Gosztony, p. 186.

11   Chuikov, p. 151.

12   Koniev, p. 103

13   Koniev, pp. 104–8; Wagener, p. 351.

14   Koniev, map on pp. 142–3; Komornicki, pp. 127–9.

15   *Neue Zürcher Zeitung* of 18 April 1945, as quoted in Gosztony, pp. 217–20; Ryan, p. 27.

16   Von Oven, pp. 305ff, as quoted in Gosztony, pp. 187–8.

17   Chuikov, pp. 152–3; Tieke, pp. 137 (quoting Göring), 138.

18   Pykathov, Komornicki, pp. 111–13.

19   *Die Geheimen Tagesberichte der deutschen Wehrmachtsführung im zweiten Weltkrieg 1939–1945* (Biblioverlag, Osnabrück, 1984), Vol 12, p. 396. The calumnies then heaped on the 9th Parachute Division and its commander

survived the war but were totally unjustified. The division had been reformed at the beginning of 1945 and had served on the Eastern Front since the beginning of January. It had just sustained the heaviest artillery barrage of the war before taking on the full weight of the 5th Shock Army and had been virtually annihilated in the process, while itself inflicting heavy casualties on the enemy. In a letter to the author, Colonel Harry Herrmann says that he spent hours during that night talking with General Bräuer, whom he had known well and served with frequently since the early 1930s, and that Bräuer had shown no signs of physical or nervous disability. Bräuer, a revered leader of parachutists, was later executed by the Greeks for alleged war crimes during his governorship of Crete. Hermann, who had been awarded the Ritterkreuz for bravery as a company commander in the invasion of Crete, survived over ten years of Soviet prison camps before returning to serve with distinction in the Bundeswehr until his retirement in 1967. (Wagener, pp. 57–62.)

20 The change of plan involving the 2nd Guards Tank Army is drawn mainly from Pykathov and from Skorodumov's article, whose accompanying map shows exactly how these formations were split and functioned in the advance on the city after the breakthrough at the Seelow Heights. The chronology of this phase emphasises the exhaustion of the combatants, the infantry in particular.

21 Wagener, p. 348.

22 Busse, p. 165; Tieke, pp. 169, 278.

23 Busse, pp. 165–6; Tieke, p. 160.

24 Tieke, p. 135.

25 Tieke, pp. 168–9.

26 Von Oven, p. 307, as quoted in Gosztony, p. 201.

27 Novikov, p. 93.

28 Koniev, p. 111.

29 Koniev, pp. 112–13.

30 Tieke, PP. 144, 171; Steiner, p. 228, as quoted in Gosztony, p. 207.

31 Tieke, p. 295. Seaton [RGW], p. 575; Willemer, pp. 14, 18.

32 Gosztony, pp. 228–9, including quotation from *Der grundlegende Befehl des Führers vom 21. April 1945* (National Archives, Washington DC).

33 Kuby, p. 105 (quoting Col Refior); Tieke, p. 214.

34 *Neue Zürcher Zeitung* of 20 April 1945, quoted in Gosztony, pp. 196–8; Thorwald, pp. 152–3.

35 Novikov, p. 93 – 'We did not know that the enemy had so few troops to defend this boundary and expected strong opposition.'

36 Zhukov, p. 609 – but not mentioned in Koniev!

37 Koniev, pp. 116, 121–2, 128–9.

38 Koniev, p. 115.

39 In discussion at Spandau Allied Prison some 40 years later with Soviet Army officers, who regarded the matter as common knowledge.

40 Gerhard Boldt's *Die letzten Tage der Reichskanzlei* (Zurich, New York, Vienna, 1947), p. 49, as quoted in Gosztony, pp. 193–5; Tieke, p. 147, says originally 12 tanks had set off from the Kummersdorf Training Area nearby.

41 Kuby, p. 105 (quoting Col Refior); Koniev, p. 122; Tieke, pp. 183; Gellermann, p. 35.

42 Kuby, p. 97; Koniev, p. 115.

43 Chuikov, pp. 153–4.
44 Tieke, pp. 159–71.
45 Skorodumov, pp. 90–93.
46 Komornicki, p. 116 and map on p. 112; but Erickson, p. 577 – Bernau taken by the 125th Rifle Corps of the 47th Army.
47 Zhukov, pp. 609, 612.
48 Ryan, pp. 414–15; Tieke, p. 283; Klaus Scheel's *Die Befreiung Berlins* (VEB Deutscher Verlag der Wisssenschaft, East Berlin, 1975), pp. 73ff, as quoted in Buckert, pp. 58–60. Footnote on Müller's Brigade from Gellermann, p. 39.
49 Seaton [RGW], p. 578; Novikov, p. 94.
50 Axmann, p. 66, as quoted in Gosztony, pp. 202–3.
51 Gorlitz, pp. 196–7.
52 Gorlitz, p. 199.
53 Trevor-Roper [LDH], p. 151; Thorwald, pp. 91–2.
54 Trevor Roper [LDH], p. 148.
55 Tieke, p. 159.
56 Trevor-Roper [LDH], pp. 151–2; Thorwald, p. 93.
57 Dönitz, p. 435; Trevor-Roper [LDH], pp. 152–3.
58 Trevor-Roper [LDH], pp. 130, 155–6; Borkowski, pp. 126–7.
59 Dönitz, pp. 436–7; Speer, p. 634; Trevor-Roper, [LDH], pp. 153–5.
60 O'Donnell, p. 101; Ryan, p. 403.
61 Koller, pp. 38–42; Trevor-Roper [LDH], p. 153.
62 Novikov, pp. 93–4; Wagener, p. 357.
63 *Geschichte des Großen Vaterländischen Krieges der Sowjet-Union*, Vol. 5 (East Berlin, 1967), p. 309, as quoted in Gosztony, p. 186.
64 Zhukov, p. 610 – 'In order to speed up to the utmost the smashing of the enemy defences inside Berlin itself it was decided to…'
65 Altner was with the 156th Infantry Division at Lietzen – pp. 38–44.
66 Tieke, pp. 129–80.

7. ENCIRCLEMENT

In this chapter the Soviet forces close in on the city, the pattern of their revised plan emerging, but Zhukov remains apparently unaware of Koniev's participation.

1 Ryan, p. 324. The location of the Luftwaffe Academy given in Ryan has been corrected to Gatow by Col Hermann. It seems that as the location of the Gatow was a state secret, it was commonly referred to as being in Potsdam, that being the nearest communications centre.
2 Skorodumov, p. 93.
3 Rocolle, p. 44.
4 Skorodumov, p. 93.
5 Ryan, pp. 27, 484–94; O'Donnell, p. 143 – Governing Mayor Ernst Reuter once quoted the figure of 90,000 Berlin rape victims.
6 Chuikov, pp. 156–7.
7 Trevor-Roper [LDH], pp. 203–4.
8 These rumours were the result of false orders passed on by Seydlitz-Troops to the retreating German forces, telling them to reassemble west of Berlin.
9 Willemer, p. 19; Tieke, pp. 240–43 – *Fall Ziegler und Hintegrund*. Ziegler's motives were no doubt honourable but from a disciplinary and command

point of view clearly unacceptable. General Weidling's own account only
covers the period 23 April–5 May 1945.

10 Gorlitz, p. 201.
11 Kuby, p. 111; GPW, p. 382.
12 Koller, pp. 43–4.
13 Koller, pp. 44–5.
14 Seaton [RGW], p. 576; Gorlitz, p. 199 – Keitel says that Schörner was
    promoted that day, but Ziemke, p. 78, gives his date of promotion as 5
    April 1945; Koniev, p. 119; Erickson, p. 591.
15 Seaton [RGW], p. 576; Gorlitz, pp. 199–200.
16 Thorwald, pp. 94–6; K.G. Klietmann's *Die Waffen-SS – Ein Dokumentation*
    (Osnabrück, 1965), p. 56, as quoted in Gosztony, p. 206; GPW, p. 382.
17 Tieke, pp. 144–5, quoting from General Felix Steiner's *Die Freiwilligen*
    (Göttingen, 1958), p. 233; Tully, p. 138.
18 Ryan, pp. 375, 475; Thorwald, p. 87.
19 GPW, p. 381.
20 Koniev, pp. 120–21.
21 GPW, p. 381.
22 Novikov, p. 95; Wagener, pp. 355–6.
23 Novikov, p. 93.
24 Thorwald, pp. 88–9.
25 Koller, p. 45; Speer, p. 571 – the division had been at Karinhall when he
    visited in February 1945.
26 Koller, pp. 46–7.
27 Koller, p. 47.
28 Koller, pp. 48–9.
29 Koller, p. 50.
30 Trevor-Roper [LDH], p. 157.
31 Busse, p. 166; Ryan, p. 325.
32 Busse, p. 166; Tieke, p. 193.
33 Busse, pp. 166–7.
34 Busse, pp. 166–7.
35 Komornicki, p. 116.
36 Seaton [RGW], p. 578.
37 Ziemke, pp. 92, 95.
38 Altner, pp 123–4. 'Stalin-Organs', otherwise known as 'Katyushas', were
    multiple rocket-launchers mounted on standard truck-beds.
39 Skorodumov, p. 93.
40 Chuikov, pp. 156, 160–61.
41 Willemer, pp. 29–30.
42 Kuby, p. 108; Tieke, pp. 216–17. However, in a letter to the author, Col.
    Hermann, then commanding the 9th Parachute Division, says he was not
    at this meeting.
43 Koniev, pp. 126–8.
44 These were most likely T-34s.
45 Rocolle, p. 30.
46 Rocolle, p. 31.
47 Koniev, pp. 131–2.
48 Koniev, pp. 128–9, 132.
49 Trevor-Roper [LDH], pp. 158–9; O'Donnell, pp. 93–5; Koller, p. 54;
    Thorwald, pp. 109–13.

50 Trevor-Roper [LDH], pp. 159–60, O'Donnell, pp. 94–7; Koller, p. 55.
51 O'Donnell, pp. 81, 97–9; Koller, p. 63; *Stern* magazine no. 18, 28 April 1963
    – abortive authentication of 'The Hitler Diaries'.
52 Trevor-Roper [LDH], pp. 160–61; Gorlitz, p. 202; Thorwald, pp. 116–17.
53 Trevor-Roper [LDH], pp. 161–2; Gorlitz, pp. 202–3; Thorwald, pp. 118–19.
54 Trevor-Roper [LDH], pp. 163–5; O'Donnell, p. 126.
55 Kuby, p. 109; Willemer, pp. 16–17; Tieke, p. 215.
56 Kuby, p. 118; Tieke, pp. 184, 214, 223.
57 From a photocopy of a memo from Beate Rotemund-Uhse quoting an
    extract from her pilot's logbook, together with a cutting of an article on
    her flight in *Neue Revue*, date unknown. Beate Uhse later became famous
    throughout Germany for founding a chain of sex shops with that name.

8. SIEGE PREPARATIONS

This chapter reviews the preparations of both sides for the forthcoming fighting
in a densely built-up area.

General Helmuth Weidling's account covering the period 23 April–5 May
1945 was written in Soviet captivity, where he later died, and was translated from
Russian and introduced in German by Wilhelm Ahrens in the *Wehrwissenschaftliche
Rundschau,* no. 1/1962, as 'Der Todeskampf der faschistischen Clique in Berlin aus
der Erinnerung des Generals Weidling'. It was therefore subjected to censorship,
but appears authentic in content (Kuby, p. 79).

1   Gosztony, pp. 232–4; Tieke, p. 214.
2   Rocolle, pp. 34–5; Tieke, p. 141.
3   Trevor-Roper [LDH], p. 197; Rocolle, p. 35; Wenck, pp. 64–5; Thorwald, pp.
    133–4; Kuby, p. 113; Strawson, p. 132.
4   Schwarz, p. 108, as quoted in Gosztony, pp. 262–3; Thorwald, p. 145.
5   Wenck, p. 64; Gorlitz, pp. 203–4; Tieke, pp. 196–7.
6   Wenck, p. 64; Gellermann, pp. 80–83; Ryan, p. 351.
7   Gellermann, p. 48; Ryan, p. 443.
8   Gorlitz, pp. 204–5.
9   Gorlitz, p. 205.
10 Gorlitz, pp. 206–8; Thorwald, p. 163.
11 Gorlitz, pp. 207–9.
12 Kuby, p. 137; Tieke, p. 346.
13 Thorwald, p. 142.
14 Thorwald, pp. 138–9.
15 Thorwald, pp. 125–6. The underground shelter at Alexanderplatz still exists.
    Danziger Strasse has since been renamed Dimitroffstrasse.
16 Letter to the author.
17 Weidling article, p. 42; Gorlitz, p. 221; Tieke, pp. 216–18; Wagner, p. 67 –
    the 9th Parachute Division's route to the city was via Friedrichshagen,
    Köpenick and Alt Glienicke to Hermannplatz in Neukölln.
18 Weilding, pp. 42–5; Willemer, p. 10; Tieke, p. 224.
19 Weidling, pp. 45–6. However, although Weidling may have intended the
    9th Parachute Division to occupy Lichtenbeg, it seems that the Russians
    arrived there first. Wagner, p. 67, makes no mention of Lichtenberg (see

Note 17 above) but says that the 9th parachute Division was ordered to Sector 'H'. Colonel Hermann, in a letter to the author, denies having been to Lichtenberg, the division having passed through Neukölln, which he had known well as a policeman before joining the Luftwaffe.

20 Weidling, p. 46; Tieke, p. 227.
21 Weidling, pp. 46–7; Tieke, p. 224.
22 Weidling, pp. 47–8; Tieke, pp. 227–8.
23 Weidling, p. 4; Willemer, p. 17.
24 Wilmer, p. 46; Kuby, pp. 83–4; Tieke, p. 226. *Der Spiegel* magazine in an article dated 10 January 1966, quoted in Gosztony, p. 228, gives 44,630 soldiers, 42,531 Volkssturm and 3,532 Hitlerjugend, RAD and Organisation Todt members as constituting the Berlin Garrison on 23 April.
25 Tieke, p. 34 – Major-General Scholze's wife and children had been killed in an air raid on Potsdam.
26 Tieke, p. 55.
27 Tieke, pp. 231–2 – quoting from Wöhlermann's MS *Notizen über der letzten Einsatz ostwarts und in Berlin im April/Mai 1945*.
28 The Wehrtechnischen Facultät was never completed and is now buried under the rubble of the Teufelsberg.
29 Willemer, pp. 48–9.
30 Trevor-Roper [LDH], p. 204.
31 Ryan, p. 479.
32 Chuikov, p. 156.
33 Wagner, p. 356; Novikov, p. 95 – 'The smoke of countless fires and the dust hindered our pilots in seeking their objectives. It demanded exceptionally accurate bombing not to hit our own troops. In these tasks only the best of bomber pilots were sent, real virtuosos of the strike assault.'
34 Kuby, p. 60.
35 Thorwald, p. 176; Kuby, pp. 153–4.
36 Rocolle, p. 43.

9. ENCIRCLEMENT COMPLETED

Inevitably Koniev's and Zhukov's forces meet up. I can only presume that Stalin had briefed Novikov to keep Zhukov in the dark about the 3rd Guards Tanks Army's advance beyond the boundary laid down by the Stavka at Easter into the southern suburbs, but that Zhukov would have been aware of their rapid progress northwards from the news bulletins and that his suspicions would have been aroused.

This appears to have been part of Stalin's plot to humiliate Zhukov by throwing his plans off balance by introducing Koniev into the race for the Reichstag.

1 Thorwald, pp. 166–7.
2 GPW, p. 381; Ziemke, p. 94.
3 Chuikov, p. 177.
4 Willemer, p. 30.
5 Rocolle, p. 31.
6 Rocolle, p. 45.

7 Chuikov, p. 163 and map on p. 161.
8 Chernyayev article, p. 105.
9 Chuikov, pp. 162–3.
10 GPW, p. 383.
11 Willemer, p. 29.
12 Koniev, p. 132.
13 Koniev, pp. 134–5. Koniev estimated that he was paced by 15,000 enemy (p. 132) at a density of 1,200 per kilometre, against which he placed 650 guns per kilometre along his attack front!
14 Koniev, p. 135.
15 Koniev, p. 135.
16 Koniev, p. 137.
17 Koniev, pp. 137–41; Komornicki, pp. 128–34.
18 Koniev, p. 124.
19 Trevor-Roper [LDH], pp. 168–9; Koller, pp. 64–73; Emmy Göring's *An der Seite meines Mannes: Begebenheiten und Bekenntnisse* (Göttingen, 1967), pp. 240ff, as quoted in Gosztony, pp. 294–6.
20 Trevor-Roper [LDH], pp. 176–9: O'Donnell, p. 110; Boldt, p. 72, as quoted in Gosztony, pp. 297–8.
21 Trevor-Roper [LDH], pp. 173–5; O'Donnell, pp. 102–5; 108–9; Speer, pp. 638, 643–5.
22 Trevor-Roper [LDH], pp. 175–6; O'Donnell, p. 104; Speer, pp. 639–40.
23 Trevor-Roper [LDH], p. 179; O'Donnell, pp. 115–16; Speer, pp. 647–8.
24 Willemer, pp. 57, 61; Tieke, p. 288; Komornicki, p. 117.
25 Rocolle, pp. 37–8.
26 Altner, pp. 94–9.
27 Willemer, p. 31.
28 Tieke, pp. 234–8 – quoting Kurkenberg's MS *Kampftage in Berlin: 24.4–2.5.1945,*
   p. 4.
29 The heath on which Tegel Airport now stands, and where Professor Wernher von Braun conducted his early rocket experiments, which later led to the 'V' series of rocket weapons and ultimately took man into space.
30 Tully, p. 163.
31 Tully, p. 201.
32 Rocolle, p. 44.
33 Pykathov. The northern face with its two corner gun platforms still stands and an artificial hill of rubble stacked behind it has been created, the rear of the tower having been blown up. Access to the interior is now possible on tours conducted by 'Berliner Unterwelt' from offices in the adjacent Gesundbrunnen U-Bahn station.
34 Wolfgang Karow's article 'Bei der Verteidigung von Berlin' in *Alte Kameraden* magazine No. 5/1965 (Karlsruhe), p. 14, as quoted in Gosztony, pp. 267–8.
35 Pykathov.
36 They were opposed here by the Siemensstadt Volkssturm Battalion 3/115, by then down to 150 rifles. (See the author's *Death Was Our Companion,* pp. 135–8.)
37 Ryan, p. 45. Treptower Park now contains the main Soviet cemetery where commemorative parades were held until the Soviet troops left in 1994.
38 Chernyayev, p. 105; Zhukov, p. 615.

39 Zhukov, pp. 614–15.
40 Rocolle, p. 46. According to Koniev this was 23 April, but it is quite clear from the accounts of both Zhukov and Chuikov that it must have occurred on the 24th.
41 Chuikov, p. 164; Kuby, pp. 52–3; Tieke, p. 201 – gives the time of encounter as 0900 hours. Zhukov does not even mention it!
42 Koniev, p. 131. The new inter-front boundary followed the main railway line into Berlin, being clearly discernable to the troops on the ground, however badly damaged the environment, then crossed the Landwehr Canal into the Anhalter Railway Station. Any extension of this line left the Reichstag clearly to the west of it and in Koniev's path. (Here I disagree with Both Ryan, p. 354, and Erickson, p. 586, for the reasons stated.) North of the canal, Zhukov could only approach the Reichstag from the east, south or west. Chuikov's group, originally intended to cover the whole southern arc of the city, could now, however, concentrate a disproportionately powerful punch on the eastern flank of that arc in competition with Koniev's 3rd Guards Tank Army. From then on one suspects that Zhukov must have pushed Chuikov deliberately across Koniev's route to the Reichstag, thus causing the forthcoming changes in the inter-front boundary with a 'fait accompli'. Koniev, p. 90, writing of the opening battle of 16 April, says: 'The fighting at both fronts was coordinated by GHQ and the fronts, as usual, exchanged information and reconnaissance summaries'!
43 Chuikov, p. 163.
44 Chuikov, pp. 159–60.
45 Dragunsky, pp. 68–9.
46 Koniev, pp. 68–9.
47 Tieke, p. 244.
48 Source untraced.
49 Koniev, pp. 158, 161; Wagener, p. 350; Erickson, p. 592.
50 Chernyayev, p. 105.
51 Koniev, pp. 161–2; Zhukov, p. 610.
52 Koniev, p. 120.
53 Weilding, p. 49.
54 Thorwald, p. 179.
55 Koller, pp. 88–9; Tieke, p. 301.
56 Trevor-Roper [LDH], p. 183; Koller, pp. 81–2.
57 Gellermann, p. 101; Ziemke, p. 105.
58 Tieke, p. 245.
59 Zhukov, p. 616.

IO. THE NOOSE TIGHTENS

Dragunsky's *A Soldier's Life* not only provides a most interesting account of his 55th Guards Tank Brigade's role as Koniev's flank guard, but also neatly dovetails with Helmut Altner's account of his experiences based on Ruhleben at this time.

1 Friedrich Husemann's *Die guten Glaubens waren* (Osnabrück, 1973), p. 558, as quoted in Tieke, p. 297.
2 Thorwald, pp. 374–5.

3   Ryan, pp. 374–5.

4   Tieke, pp. 204–13.

5   GPW, p. 382; Koniev, p. 172; Toland, p. 451.

6   Weidling, pp. 48–9.

7   Weidling, p. 112.

8   O'Donnell, pp. 143–4.

9   GPW, p. 382; Zhukov, p. 610.

10 Weidling, p. 49.

11 Novikov, p. 94; Wagener, pp. 357–8.

12 Komornicki, p. 146.

13 The area has changed here considerably since the battle. The T- shaped canal has been extended at either end to connect the Westhafen with the Spree north of Schloss Charlottenburg, and the original canal closer to Moabit has been filled in.

14 Tully, p. 203.

15 Rocolle, p. 53.

16 Rocolle, p. 53

17 Chuikov, pp. 183–4; Plievier, p. 151; Tully, pp. 182, 189–90; Peter de Mendelssohnn's *Zeitungsstadt Berlin* (Ullstein Verlag, Berlin, 1959), pp. 416–22, as quoted in Burkett, pp. 117–22.

18 Thorwald, pp. 178–9.

19 Rocolle, p. 53.

20 Krukenberg, p. 14, as quoted in Tieke, p. 246; Kuby, pp. 125–7.

21 Rocolle, p. 53.

22 Koniev, pp. 167–8. Luftgau III Headquarters was later taken over as the American Sector Headquarters and still accommodates the US Consul General's offices.

23 Dragunsky, pp. 61–2, 93.

24 Novikov, p. 95; Koniev, p. 171. This change of inter-front boundary still kept the Reichstag within Koniev's reach for the same reason as before, that is, the boundary projected beyond Potsdamer Station would pass well to the east of the building.

25 Koniev, p. 171.

26 Rocolle, p. 53.

27 This truly extraordinary person, holder of the Iron Cross First and Second Class, was the first woman to hold an airline pilot's licence, the first to become a test pilot, the first to fly a helicopter and the first to fly a jet. She continued flying until her death in 1979 at the age of 67, having established a new women's world long-distance gliding record of 805 km only four months previously.

28 Trevor-Roper [LDH], pp. 183–5; O'Donnell, p. 127; Koller, pp. 83–5, 94.

29 Tieke, p. 355; Kuby, pp. 136–7.

30 Tieke, p. 304.

31 Seaton [RGW], p. 574.

32 Tieke, pp. 301–2; Ziemke, pp. 99, 104.

33 Altner, pp. 128–35; Weidling, p. 51.

34 Wenck, pp. 65–6; Gellermann, pp. 83–7; Tieke, p. 331.

35 Novikov, p. 94.

36 Tully, pp. 203–4; Borkowski, p. 131; Rocolle, p. 51 – Beusselstrasse Station held out until the 27th. Research into Bärenfänger's background reveals that he had been a member of the SA since 1933 and was promoted

to Sturmbannführer (Major) in 1944, nine months after his equivalent promotion in the Army. He had gained rapid promotion to Lieutenant-Colonel by the age of 30 in his brief military career, winning many decorations for bravery, including the Knight's Cross of the Iron Cross with Oak Leaves and Swords, and was exactly the kind of soldier that appealed to Hitler.

37 Weidling, p. 52.
38 Rocolle, p. 53
39 The area between the Spree and Alexanderplatz opposite Museum Island.
40 Thorwald, pp. 179–80.
41 Weidling, p. 111.
42 Rocolle, pp. 53–4.
43 Rocolle, p. 42.
44 Chuikov, pp. 196–7.
45 Chuikov, pp. 184–5.
46 Dragunsky, pp. 93–104; Rocolle, p. 51 – Grunewald flak battery destroyed by 33 'Stormovik' ground-attack aircraft.
47 Koniev, pp. 179–80.
48 Tieke, p. 350.
49 Weidling, p. 52.
50 Boldt, p. 71, as quoted in Goszton, p. 311. The telephone conversation with Goebbels is taken from Kuby, pp. 57–9.
51 Trevor-Roper [LDH], pp. 185–7; O'Donnell, pp. 127–8; Tully, p. 193; Koller, pp. 94, 103; Hanna Reitsch's *Fliegen, mein Leben* (Stuttgart, 1951), as quoted in Gosztony, pp. 298–300, describes the flight, while General Hans Baur's *Ich flog Mächtige der Erde* (Kempten, 1956), p. 269, as quoted in Gosztony, p. 299, describes how he was engaged in having the East-West-Axis landing strip widened to 120 yards by having the bordering trees chopped down when von Greim's aircraft landed.
52 Ziemke, p. 98.

11. NO RELIEF

The precariousness of the 1st Ukrainian Front's deployment is shown up by the success of Wenck's advance to Ferch and the break-out of the 9th Army. Koniev's last bid for the Reichstag turns out to be a disastrous fiasco, and he leaves the city humiliated, as Stalin had intended.

Meanwhile the 79th Rifle Corps prepares for the battle for the Reichstag from the north, a distinctly separate episode in the overall conflict. Although generally well documented, it has only been through a detailed study of photographs taken before, during and after the event that I have been able to produce a plan (Map 12) showing the actual course of action and the nature of the 'water-filled anti-tank ditch' (hitherto depicted by the Soviets as being a straight line cutting across Königsplatz) to assist in my analysis of this operation.

1 Thorwald, pp. 180–81.
2 Tieke, p. 303.
3 Tieke, p. 346; Weidling, p. 112.
4 The same communications problems were to plague the Western Allied troops in Berlin during the Cold War.

5   Dragunsky, pp. 104–20.
6   Tully, pp. 203–4.
7   Karow, p. 15, as quoted in Gosztony, pp. 386–7.
8   Zhukov, p. 211.
9   Zhukov, pp. 211–12; Kuby, pp. 60, 154.
10 Borkowski, pp. 132–7.
11 Chuikov, p 188; Kuby, pp. 139.
12 Chuikov, pp. 188–9. In the accounts of the 8th Guards Army's activities,
    I have kept to Chuikov's chronology, which does not always tally with
    German accounts but seems more reliable in this respect.
13 'Hitlers Lagesbesprechungen' article in *Der Spiegel* magazine of 10 January
    1966, as quoted in Gosztony, p. 307.
14 Tully, p. 221. Koniev later said that the 1st Ukrainian Front lost a total of
    800 tanks and self-propelled guns in the Berlin operation.
15 Thorwald, pp. 181–2.
16 Kuby, pp. 141–2; O'Donnell, p. 226. In fact very few bodies were found
    here after the fighting, but the Russians later made a film depicting the
    water coming up to chest height.
17 Kuby, p. 141; Tieke, p. 352.
18 O'Donnell, pp. 151–60.
19 Bauer, p, 272, as quoted in Gosztony, pp. 327–8; Loringhoven, p. 123;
    Trevor-Roper [LDH], pp. 277–8.
20 Rocolle, pp. 49–50.
21 Tieke, pp. 354–5; Thorwald, pp. 169–70; Gorlitz, pp. 216–17.
22 Thorwald, pp. 197–9; Gorlitz, pp. 217–19.
23 Wenck, p. 66.
24 Tieke, p. 328.
25 Busse, pp. 167–8; Tieke, pp. 195, 204.
26 Domank article and map; Koniev, p. 153.
27 Tieke, pp. 304–13.
28 Tieke, pp. 332–3.
29 Private letters to author.
30 Komornicki, pp. 146–8.
31 Tully, pp. 200, 204–6; Tieke, pp. 361–2, 369.
32 This obstacle was in fact the remains of excavations in connection with
    the proposed development of this area as the focal point of 'Germania',
    the new Third Reich capital planned by Hitler and Albert Speer. The
    big pit was to be for an underground diversion of the Spree to enable
    the construction of the Great Hall of the People to the north of it, and
    the 'anti-tank ditch' was in fact the cutting for a U-Bahn tunnel to serve
    the area. Work on the site had been abandoned two years previously and
    the area was still littered with temporary structures. These items had all
    been incorporated into the defence system, and the size and shape of the
    flooded area were clearly to influence the line of attack. Curiously enough,
    Soviet maps of the battlefield were based on the pre-war layout of formal
    gardens, omitted the pit and showed the 'anti-tank ditch' as a straight line.
33 Tully and Tieke as above, together with numerous Soviet sources; Wagener,
    p. 69.
34 Erickson, p. 601.
35 Borkowski, pp. 136–7.
36 Tieke, pp. 361–2, 369.

37 Chuikov, p. 189.
38 Chuikov, p. 193.
39 Chuikov, p. 201.
40 Chuikov, pp. 190–92.
41 Koniev, p. 184; Erickson, p. 600 – Koniev was still aiming for the Reichstag.
42 Dragunsky, p. 120.
43 Koniev, p. 185.
44 Koniev, p. 187. Some texts quote Ruhleben instead of Witzleben Station, but this does not tally with either the final deployment of the 55th Guards Tank Brigade, nor the geographical factors.
45 Altner, pp. 155–62.
46 Thorwald, pp. 182–3.
47 Trevor-Roper [LDH], p. 202; O'Donnell, pp. 171–2; Axmann's article 'Mit Hitler im Führerbunker' in *Stern* magazine of 25 April 1965, p. 70, as quoted in Gosztony, p. 313.
48 Trevor-Roper [LDH], pp. 205–6; O'Donnell, pp. 128–9; Thorwald, pp. 208–9; Reitsch, p. 302, as quoted in Gosztony, p. 311.
49 Weidling, p. 115; Tieke, p. 357; O'Donnell, pp. 175–6.
50 Kuby, p. 133; Ziemke, p. 105.
51 Thorwald, pp. 201–5; Gorlitz, p. 220; Percy Ernst Schramm's edition of the *Kriegstagebuch des Oberkommandos der Wehrmacht (Wehrmachtführungsstab)* (Frankfurt, 1961, Vol. 4, p. 1466), as quoted in Gosztony, pp. 325–6.
52 Trevor-Roper [LDH], pp. 207–13; O'Donnell, pp. 132–5; Nerin E. Gun's *Eva Braun – Hitler, Leben und Schicksal* (Stuttgart, 1968), p. 199, as quoted in Gosztony, pp. 325–6.
53 Koniev, pp. 186, 188.
54 Koniev, p. 188.

12. THE LAST ROUND

1   Wenck, pp. 66–7; Strawson, p. 146.
2   Wenck, p. 68.
3   Busse, p. 168.
4   GPW, p. 383; Kuby, p. 211; Ziemke, p. 110 – the writer was Konstantin Simonov; Stawson, pp. 125–6.
5   Thorwald, p. 190.
6   Wenck, p. 66; Gellermann, pp. 93–4.
7   Gellermann, p. 176.
8   Thorwald, p. 205; Ziemke, pp. 119–20; Tieke, p. 306; Gorlitz, p. 22.
9   Thorwald, pp. 193–4.
10 Gorlitz, pp. 220–22.
11 Trevor-Roper [LDH], pp. 218–21; Tieke, p. 358.
12 Trevor-Roper [LDH], pp. 221–5; Boldt, p. 83, as quoted in Gosztony, p. 329.
13 Trevor-Roper [LDH], pp. 221–5.
14 Trevor-Roper [LDH], pp. 221–5, 248–9.
15 Komornicki, pp. 148–57.
16 Tully, pp. 206–7.
17 Zhukov, p. 616–17.
18 Chuikov, pp. 197–9. Like most Soviet military writers, Chuikov interlarded his work with reminiscences about individuals and tales of heroism.

Unfortunately the presentation and style are so blatantly dictated by
political considerations that it is often difficult to give them full credence.
This particular incident has been immortalised with a statue of Masalov
holding a child in his arms while symbolically smashing a swastika with a
sword, which dominates the Soviet War Cemetery in Treptow Park.

19 Chuikov, p. 196; Koniev, p. 177.
20 Chuikov, p. 202.
21 Chuikov, p. 202.
22 Chuikov, p. 200.
23 Dragunsky, pp. 124–33.
24 Tieke, pp. 359, 362; Tully, p. 222.
25 Boldt.
26 Weidling, pp. 117, 169.
27 Trevor-Roper [LDH]. p. 229; Artur Axmann's article 'Das Ende im
    Führerbunker' [Ende] in *Stern* magazine of 2 May 1965, p. 82, as quoted in
    Gosztony, p. 330.
28 Gellermann, p. 177
29 Gellermann, pp. 97–8; Gorlitz, p. 223.
30 These were probably just rumours, for the Russians showed a marked
    reluctance to use the tunnels, and the Stadtmitte and Kaiserhof U-Bahn
    stations were still in German hands at midnight on 1 May.
31 Trevor-Roper [LDH], p. 229; O'Donnell, pp. 147–50.
32 Weidling, p. 170.
33 Weidling, p. 169.
34 Rocolle, p. 59.
35 This, now the Swiss Embassy, apart from the Reichstag, is the only
    building to have survived in this area south of the Spree.
36 Tully, pp. 248–58.
37 Trevor-Roper [LDH], pp. 230–33; O'Donnell, pp. 179–93; Axmann [Ende],
    p. 82, as quoted in Gosztony, pp. 332–3; Erick Kempka's *Ich habe Adolf Hitler
    verbrannt* (Munich, undated), p. 108, as quoted in Gosztony, pp. 333–4.
38 Gorlitz, p. 226; Dönitz, pp. 443–4.
39 Trevor-Roper [LDH], pp. 236–7; Dönitz, p. 441.
40 Weidling, pp. 169–71.
41 Trevor-Roper [LDH], p. 238.
42 Dragunsky, p. 134; Komornicki, pp. 166–75.
43 Hildegard Springer's *Es sprach Hans Fritzsche, Nach Gesprächen, Briefen und
    Dokumenten* (Stuttgart, 1949), pp. 51–2, as quoted in Gosztony, pp. 365, 369.
44 Busse, p. 168; Tieke, pp. 309–45.
45 Busse, p. 168 – describes the breakout as having taken place on the night
    of the 26/27 April and the union with the 12th Army on the morning of
    the 29th, but this is in conflict with Wenck's chronology and that of other
    witnesses, and allowance should be made for the fact that Busse's article
    was apparently written some ten years after the event; Wenck, pp. 68–9;
    Koniev, pp. 180–82 – denies that the breakout was effective.

13. ULTIMATE VICTORY

1 Chuikov, pp 228–32.
2 Weidling, 172; Kuby, pp. 184–6.

3   Chuikov, pp. 205–37; Tully, pp. 261–70.
4   Kuby, pp. 61, 198–9.
5   Trevor-Roper [LDH], pp. 239–40; Dönitz, pp. 444–5.
6   Axamnn [Ende], p. 86, as quoted in Gosztony, pp. 363–4; Tieke, p. 378.
7   Trevor-Roper [LDH], pp. 241–2; Tieke, p. 378.
8   Kuby, pp. 61, 198–9.
9   GPW, p. 384; Kuby, pp. 66–9; Strawson, pp. 153–5.
10 Zhukov, pp. 622–3; Chuikov, pp. 238–9; Tully, p. 218.
11 O'Donnell, p. 247; Kuby, p. 186.
12 Komornicki, pp. 178–229; Edward Kmiecik's *Berliner Victoria 24.4.–2.5.1945.
    Polnische Soldaten am Brandenburger Tor* (Ruch Verlag, Warsaw, 1972), pp.
    52–6, as quoted in Burkert, pp. 100–102.
13 Koniev, p. 191.
14 Thorwald, pp. 248–9.
15 Weidling, pp. 173–4.
16 Gellermann, pp. 105–19.
17 Weidling, p. 173; Kuby, pp. 201–2.
18 Before the breakout attempts began it was estimated that there were some
    29,000 civilians sheltering in the Zoo Flak-towers, apart from the wounded
    and fighting troops.
19 Kuby, pp. 214–15; Toland, p. 551.
20 Tully, pp. 277–80.
21 Tieke, pp. 415, 419 – possibly more than 10,000 took part in this breakout
    to the west; Altner, pp. 210–45; Zhukov, p. 606; Plievier, pp. 291–2; Tully, pp.
    274–5.
22 Tieke, p. 386; Zhukov, p. 623.
23 Horst Denkinger in a letter to the author.
24 Helmut Später's *Die Geschichte des Panzerkorps Grossdeutschland* (Duisburg,
    1958), Vol. 3, p. 748, as quoted in Gosztony, p. 383; Borkowski, pp. 136–7.
25 O'Donnell, pp. 213–17.
26 Trevor-Roper [LDH], p. 243; O'Donnell, pp. 217–18.
27 Trevor-Roper [LDH], p. 243; O'Donnell, pp. 221–7.
28 Trevor-Roper [LDH], pp. 243–4; O'Donnell, pp. 227–9.
29 Trevor-Roper [LDH], p. 244; O'Donnell, p. 222; Tieke, p. 390 –
    Krukenberg says that in order to avoid chaos, he had not intended issuing
    his orders for the breakout before 2200 hours.
30 O'Donnell, pp. 229–32.
31 Their deaths were confirmed when the bodies were found nearby in a
    shallow grave in 1972. Positive forensic identification finally put paid to the
    Bormann survival myths that had persisted until this time.
32 Trevor-Roper [LDH], p. 245; O'Donnell, pp. 239–50.
33 O'Donnell, pp. 249–50.
34 Trevor-Roper [LDH], p. 245; O'Donnell, pp. 232–5.
35 Trevor-Roper [LDH], p. 246; O'Donnell, pp. 235–7, 256–61.
36 Tieke, p. 237.
37 Tieke, p. 232.
38 Thorwald, p. 244; Chuikov, p. 240.
39 Chuikov, pp. 240–41; Zhukov, pp. 623–4.
40 Trevor-Roper [LDH], p. 244; Zhukov, p. 624; Chuikov, pp. 241–4;
    Thorwald, p. 243; Kuby, p. 203.

41 Weidling, p. 174; Chuikov, pp. 244–67; Kuby, p. 206; Loringhoven, pp. 180–84.

42 Willemer, p. 46; Koniev, p. 189 – giving the date of the Wannsee breakout as 30 April 1945.

43 Trevor-Roper [LDH], p. 249

44 Trevor-Roper [LDH], pp. 247–8; Schöneck, pp. 132–4

45 Koniev, pp. 190–91.

46 Komornicki, pp. 232–48.

47 GPW, p. 385; Novikov, p. 95.

48 GPW, p. 385; Ryan, p. 520. It is not possible to give any accurate figures on German casualties within Berlin's perimeters, for the city administration collapsed during the critical period. From his immediate post-war research, Colonel Pierre Rocolle gave a figure of 22,349 civilian deaths directly attributable to the battle, and suggested that military losses would have been about the same. More recently the Berlin branch of the German War Graves Commission (Landesverband Berlin –Volksbund Deutsche Kriegsgräberfürsorge e.V.) records 18,320 Wehrmacht, 33,420 Berlin-registered civilians and 2,010 refugees buried in what became the Western Sectors of the city alone, but these figures relate to the whole of the war and include members of the Volkssturm as civilians. Throughout the Soviet Zone and Sector of Berlin, except in rare instances, the 'Fascist Wehrmacht' dead were accorded no honourable burial, being merely tumbled uncounted into mass graves or buried in the trenches they had defended.

Bibliography

The editions listed below are those to which I have referred in my research. Alternative editions are given in parentheses.

Altner, Helmut: *Totentanz Berlin: Tagebuchblätter eines Achtzehnjahriger,* Bollwerrk Verlag, Offenbach-am-Main, 1947.

Bezymenski, Lev: *The Death of Adolf Hitler,* Harcourt, Brace & World, New York, 1968.

Bieller, Seweryn: *Stalin and his Generals,* Pegasus, New York, 1969.

Blond, Georges: *Death of Hitler's Germany,* Macmillan, New York, 1954.

Boldt, Gerhard: *Die letzten Tage der Reichskanzlei,* Rohwoldt Verlag, Hamburg, 1947.

Borkowski, Dieter: *Wer weiss, ob wir uns wiedersehen – Erinnerungen an eine Berliner Jugend,* Fischer Taschenbuch Verlag, Frankfurt-am-Main, 1980.

Bullock, Alan: *Hitler: a Study in Tyranny,* Penguin Books, London, revised 1962. (Oldhams, London, 1952)

Burkert, Hans-Norbert, Klaus Matussek & Doris Obschernitzki: *Zerstört Besiegt Befreit – Der Kampf um Berlin bis zur Kapitulation 1945* (Stätten der Geschichte Berlins, Bd. 7), Edition Hentrich im Verlag Fröhlich & Kaufmann, Berlin, 1985.

Burn, Jeffrey: *The Waffen-SS,* Osprey, London, 1982.

Chaney, Otto P: *Zhukov,* University of Oklahoma Press, 1971.

Chuikov, Vasilii I: *The End of the Third Reich,* Progress Publishers, Moscow, revised 1978.

Clark, Alan: *Barbarossa – The Russo-German Conflict 1941–45,* Hutchinson, London, 1965.

David, Paul: *Am Königsplatz: die letzten Tage der Schweizerischen Gesandtschaft in Berlin,* Thomas Verlag, Zurich, 1948.

Dönitz, Karl: *Memories – Ten Years and Twenty Days,* Weidenfeld & Nicolson, London, 1959.

Dragunsky, David: *A Soldier's Life,* Progress Publishers, Moscow, 1977.

Eisenhower, Dwight D: *Crusade in Europe,* Heinemann, London, 1949.

Erickson, Prof. John: *The Road to Berlin,* Weidenfeld & Nicolson, London, 1983.

Fest, Joachim C: *Hitler,* Harcourt Brace Jovanovich, New York, 1973. (Weidenfeld & Nicholson, London, 1974)

Flower, Desmond & James Reeve: *The Taste of Courage,* Harper, New York, 1960.

Gellermann, Günter W: *Die Armee Wenck – Hitlers letzte Hoffnung,* Bernard & Graefe, Koblenz, 1983.

Gorltiz, Walter: *The Memoirs of Field Marshal Keitel*, William Kimber, London, 1965.

Gosztony, Peter: *Der Kampf um Berlin in Augenzeugenberichten*, Deutscher Taschenbuch Verlag, Düsseldorf, 1970.

Great Patriotic War of the Soviet Union, The, Progress Publishers, Moscow, 1974.

Höcker, Karla: *Die letzten und die ersten Tage: Berliner Aufzeichnungen 1945*, Verlag Bruno Hessling, Berlin, 1966.

Houston, Donald E: *Hell on Wheels – the 2nd Armored Division*, Presidio Press, California, 1977.

Irving, David: *Hitler's War*, Hodder & Stoughton, London, 1977.

Keegan, John: *Waffen SS: The Asphalt Soldiers*, Pan/Ballentine, London, 1972. (Purnell, London, 1971)

Klimov, Gregory: *Berliner Kreml*, Verlag Rote Weissbücher, Cologne & Berlin, 1952.

Klimov, Gregory: *The Terror Machine*, Faber & Faber, London, 1953.

Koch, H.W: *The Hitler Youth*, Stein & Day, New York, 1976.

Koller, Karl: *Der letzte Monat*, Bechtle Verlag, Munich, 1985.

Komronicki, Stanislaw: *Polnische Soldaten stürmten Berlin*, Polish Military History Institute, Ministry of Defence, Warsaw (undated).

Koniev, Marshal I.S: *Year of Victory*, Progress Publishers, Moscow, 1969.

Kuby, Erich: *The Russians and Berlin 1945*, Hill & Wang, New York, 1964.

Loringhoven, Bernd Freytag von: *In the Bunker with Hitler*, Weidenfeld & Nicolson, London, 2006.

Mabire, Jean: *Berlin in Todeskampf (Mourir à Berlin)*, Verlag K.W. Schütz KG, Preussich Oldendorf, 1977.

Mabire, Jean: *La Division Nordland*, Librairie Arthème Fayard, Paris, 1982.

Mackintosch, Malcolm: *Juggernaut*, Secker & Warburg, 1967.

Menvell, Roger & Heinrich Fraenkel: *Heinrich Himmler*, Heinemann, London, 1965.

Montgomery-Hyde, H: *Stalin – The History of a Dictator*, Rupert Hart-Davis, London, 1971.

Nicolaevsky, Boris L: *Power and the Soviet Elite*, Praeger Publications, New York, 1964.

O'Donnell, James P: *The Berlin Bunker*, J.M. Dent, London, 1979.

Plievier, Theodor: *Berlin*, Panther Books, London, 1976. (Hammond & Co., London, 1956)

Pykathov, B.V.K., K.S. Below & S.S. Frolov: *History of 3rd Shock Army*, Ministry of Defence, Moscow, 1976.

Quarrie, B: *Hitler's Samurai*, Patrick Stephens, Cambridge, 1984.

Reimann, Viktor: *Goebbels*, Doubleday, New York, 1976.

Rocolle, Col Pierre: *Götterdämmerung – La Prise de Berlin*, Indo-China, 1954.

Ryan, Cornelius: *The Last Battle*, Simon & Schuster, New York, 1966. (Collins, London, 1973)

Salisbury, Harrison E: *Marshal Zhukov's Greatest Battles*, Macdonald, London, 1969.

Schramm, Percy Ernst: *Kriegstagebuch des OKW 1940–1945*, Vol. IV, Bernard & Graefe Verlag für Wehrwissen, Frankfurt-am-Main, 1961.

Seaton, Albert: *The Russo-German War 1941–45*, Prager Publications, New York, 1971. (Arthur Baker, London, 1971)

Seaton, Albert: *Stalin as a Warlord*, Batsford, London, 1974.

Shtemnko, S.M: *The Last Six Months*, Doubleday, New York, 1977.

Shtemnko, S.M: *The Soviet General Staff at War,* Progress Publishers, Moscow, 1970.

Speer, Albert: *Inside the Third Reich,* Sphere Books, London, 1975. (Weidenfeld & Nicolson, London, 1970)

Strawson, John: *The Battle for Berlin,* Batsford, London, 1974.

Strik-Strikfeld, Wilfried: *Against Stalin and Hitler,* Macmillan, London, 1970.

Subakov, W: *Die letzte Sturm,* APN Verlag, Moscow, 1975.

Tessin, Georg: *Verbände und Truppen der deutschen Wehrmacht und Waffen-SS im zweiten Weltkrieg 1939–1945,* Biblio Verband, Osnabrück, 1977.

Thorwald, Jürgen: *Das Ende an der Elbe,* Steingrüben Verlag, Stuttgart, 1950.

Tieke, Wilhelm: *Das Ende zwischen Oder und Elbe – Der Kampf um Berlin 1945,* Motorbuch Verlag, Stuttgart, 1981.

Toland, John: *Adolf Hitler,* Doubleday, New York, 1976. (Futura, London, 1978)

Toland, John: *The Last Hundred Days,* Arthur Barker, London, 1965.

Tolstoy, Nikolai: *Stalin's Secret War,* Jonathan Cape, London, 1981.

Trevor-Roper, Prof H.R: *Hitler's War Directives 1931–45,* Sidgewick & Jackson, London, 1964.

Trevor-Roper, Prof H.R: *The Last Days of Hitler,* Macmillan, London, revised 1972.

Tully, Andrew: *Berlin: Story of a Battle,* Simon & Schuster, New York, 1963.

Vorbeyev, F.D., I.V. Propotkin & A.N. Shimansky: *The Last Storm,* 2nd edition, Ministry of Defence, Moscow, 1975.

Wagener, Ray: *The Soviet Air Forces in World War II,* Doubleday, New York, 1973.

Wagner, Gerd: *Die 9. Fallschirmjägerdivision im Kampf um Pommern,* Mark Brandenburg und Berlin, Cologne, 1985.

Werth, Alexander: *Russia at War 1941–1945,* E.P. Dutton, New York, 1964.

Willemer, William: *The German Defense of Berlin,* HQ USAREUR, 1953.

Zhukov, Georgii Konstantinovitch: *The Memoirs of Marshal Zhukov,* Jonathan Cape, London, 1971.

Ziemke, Earl F: *Battle of Berlin – End of the Third Reich,* Purnel, London, 1968.

Zippel, Martin: *Untersuchungen zur Militärgeschichte der Reichshauptstadt Berlin von 1871–1945,* Berlin, 1982.

Sundry articles from Soviet, East and West German magazines, including in particular:

Busse, Theodor: 'Die letzte Schlact der 9. Armee', *Wehrwissenschaftliche Rundschau,* 1954

Chernyayev, V: 'Some Features of Military Art in the Berlin Operation', *Soviet Military History Journal,* April 1955.

Domank, A: '1st Guards Artillery Division beats off Counterattacks of the Enemy attempting to break out of Encirclement during the Berlin Operation', *Soviet Military History Journal,* March 1978.

Novikov, A.A: 'The Air Forces in the Berlin Operation', *Soviet Military Journal,* May 1975.

Sergeyev, S: 'Battle of the 150th Rifle Division for a Fortified Stronghold', *Soviet Military History Journal,* June 1977.

Skorodumov, N: 'Manoeuvres of 12th Guards Tank Corps in the Berlin Operation', *Soviet Military History Journal,* March 1978.

Weidling, Helmuth: 'Der Todeskampf der faschistischen Clique in Berlin aus der Erinnerung des Generals Weidling', *Wehrwissenschaftliche Rundschau,* 1962.

Wenck, Walter: 'Berlin war nicht mehr zu retten', *Stern,* April 1965.

FURTHER READING

Der Kampf um Berlin 1945, the German translation of the original text, which remained in print for 15 years, attracted so much feedback that, coupled with further research, the author was able to expand on the subject with the production of *Zhukov at the Oder* (Praeger, 1996), *Race for the Reichstag* (Frank Cass, 1999) and *Slaughter at Halbe* (Sutton, 2004) on the breakthrough battle, Berlin, and the fate of the 9th Army respectively, and also produce collections of individuals' accounts in *With Our Backs to Berlin* (Sutton, 2001) and *Death Was Our Companion* (Sutton, 2003). For highly illustrated accounts, see also the author's *Berlin Then and Now* (After the Battle, 1992) and *The Third Reich Then and Now* (After the Battle, 2005).

List of Illustrations

MAPS

Maps

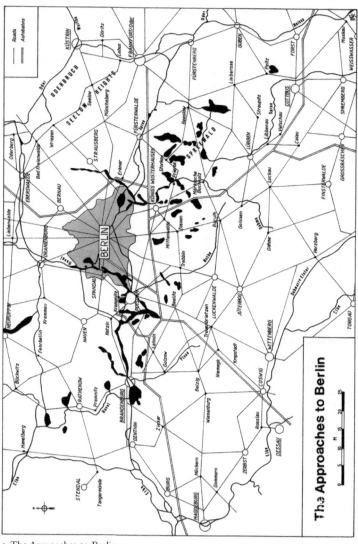

1 The Approaches to Berlin

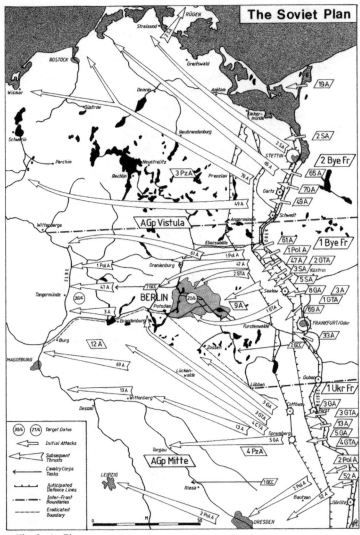

2 The Soviet Plan

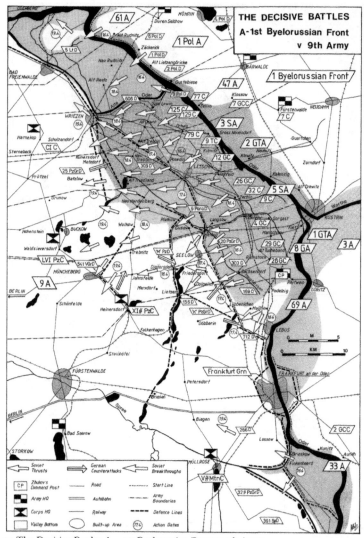

3a The Decisive Battles: A – 1st Byelorussian Front v 9th Army

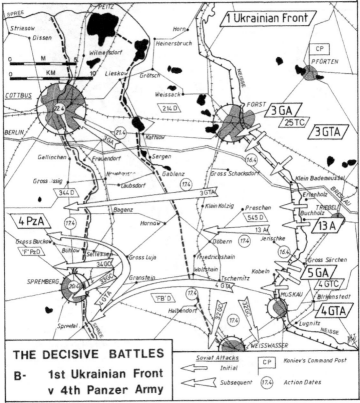

3b The Decisive Battles: B – 1st Ukrainian Front v 4th Panzer Army

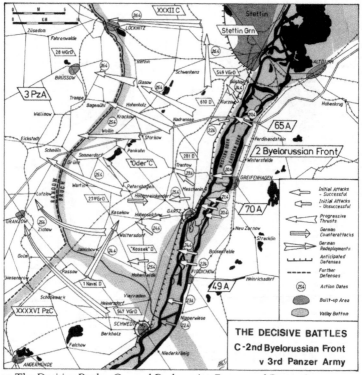

3c The Decisive Battles: C – 2nd Byelorussian Front v 3rd Panzer Army

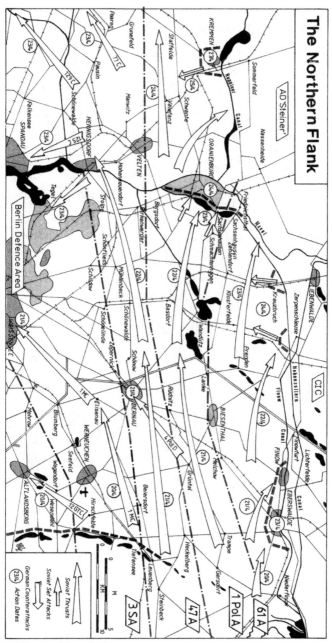

4 The Northern Flank

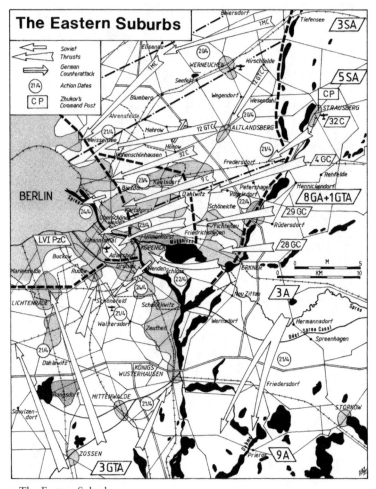

5 The Eastern Suburbs

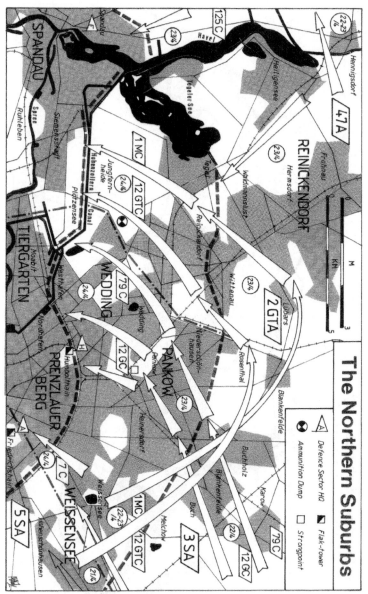

6 The Northern Suburbs

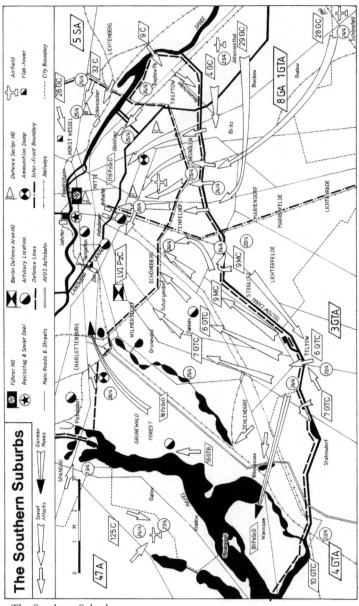

7 The Southern Suburbs

8 The Encirclement Completed

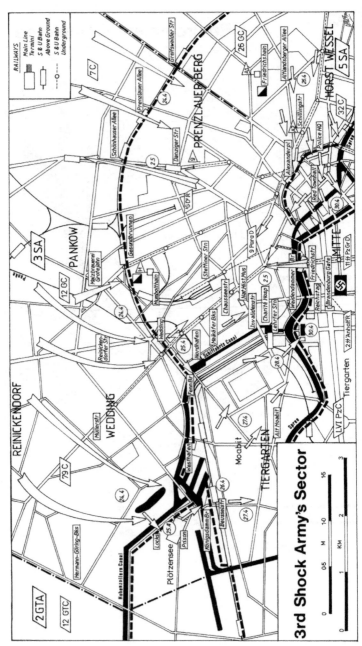

9 3rd Shock Army's Sector

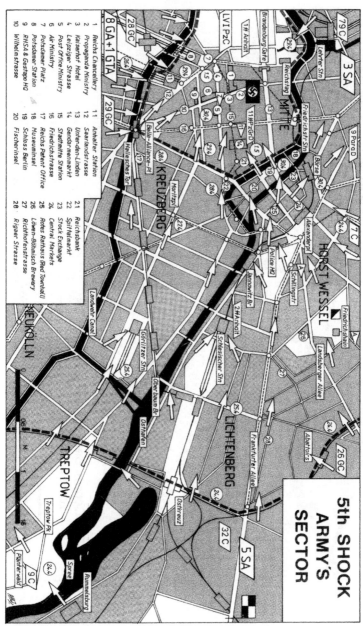

Key:

1 Reichs Chancellery
2 Propaganda Ministry
3 Kaiserhof Hotel
4 Leipziger Strasse
5 Post Office Ministry
6 Air Ministry
7 Potsdamer Platz
8 Potsdamer Station
9 RHSA & Gestapo HQ
10 Wilhelmstrasse
11 Saarlandstrasse
12 Unter-den-Linden
13 Gendarmenmarkt
14 Stadtmitte Station
15 Friedrichstrasse
16 Reichs Patent Office
17 Museuminsel
18 Schloss Berlin
19 Fischerinsel
20 Rigaer Strasse
21 Reichsbank
22 Spittelmarkt
23 Stock Exchange
24 Central Markets
25 Rotes Rathaus (Red Townhall)
26 Löwen-Böhmisch Brewery
27 Richthofenstrasse
28 Rigaer Strasse

5th SHOCK ARMY'S SECTOR

10 5th Shock Army's Sector

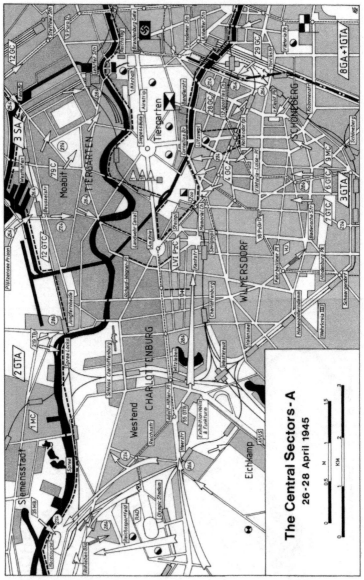

11 The Central Sectors – A

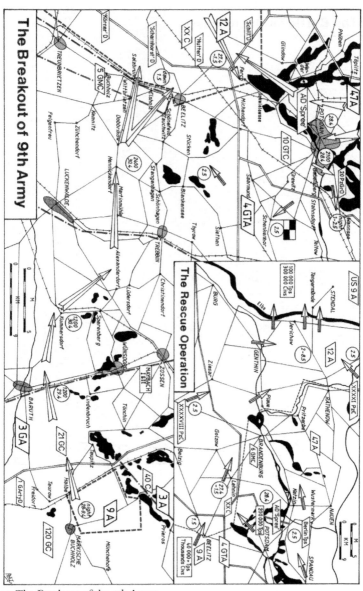

12 The Breakout of the 9th Army

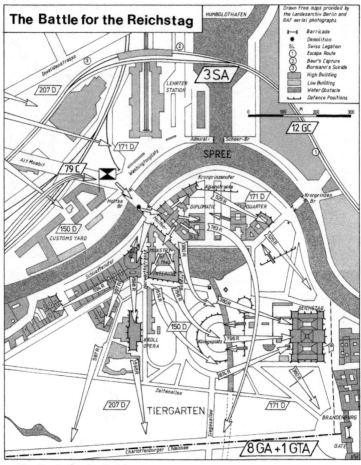

13 The Battle for the Reichstag

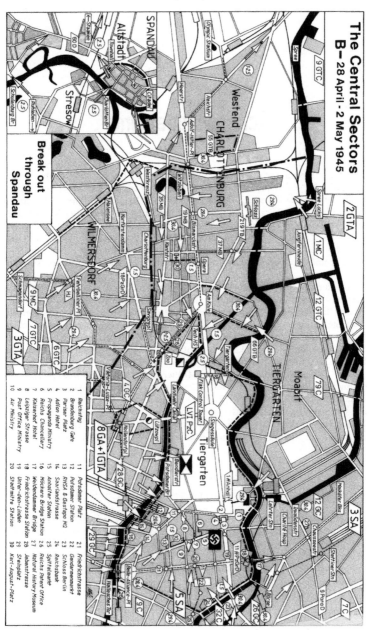

14 The Central Sectors – B

Acknowledgements

This book would not have been possible without the active encouragement and assistance of many people, among them Tom Bonas, Michael Craster, Prof. Christopher Donnelly, David Dunkelly, the late David Forrer, Dr Jürgen Freymuth, Prof. Dr Werner Knopp (late of the Stiftung Preussischer Kulturbestiz in Berlin), Otto Spitz of the Berlin Verlag, and Oberstleutnant Dr Rohde of the Militärgeschichtliches Forschungsamt in Freiburg. I am especially grateful to my good friends Peter Georgi, who did so much to promote my efforts, and the late Dorothée Freifrau von Hammerstein-Equord for all her invaluable assistance over the years.

For much of the material on which the maps are based, I am indebted to the friendly co-operation of the staffs of the Institüt für Geodäsie, Abteilung V of the Senator für Bau- und Wohnungswesen, the Landesbildstelle (since incorporated with the Landesarchiv), Firma Röhl, and the former Soviet Army Museum at Karlshorst (now the Deutsch-Russisches Museum), all of Berlin, as well as the Air Photo Library of the University of Keele, the Royal Air Force Museum, Hendon, and the Imperial War Museum in London.

I am also grateful to Colonel (retired) Pierre Rocolle for his kind permission to include translations of French eyewitness statements taken from his *Götterdämmerung – La Prise de Berlin*; to Helmut Altner for permission to quote the Oranienburg Hitler Youth's story from his *Totentanz Berlin* (*Berlin Dance of Death*), and to the Chief of the Military History Office, HQ USAREUR, for permission to include quotations from William Willemer's *The German Defense of Berlin*.

ACKNOWLEDGEMENTS TO THE 2007 EDITION

The request from Tempus Publishing to produce a revised version of my first book came within days of learning from the Ullstein Verlag that they were about to withdraw the German version of that same book from the market after a run of 15 years in various editions. The success of the German edition was due to the general consensus of opinion that it gave a fair and unbiased account of this episode in German history.

A.H. Le T
Lymington, 2006

Index

(Map references are given in *italic*)

Military Index

Also by Tony Le Tissier

9780750997997

9780750998055

The History Press

The destination for history
www.thehistorypress.co.uk

9780750998482

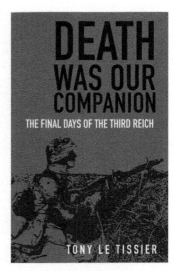

9780750998499

The destination for history
www.thehistorypress.co.uk

FAREWELL TO SPANDAU

TONY LE TISSIER

9780750998475

The destination for history
www.thehistorypress.co.uk